Key Words
A Journal of Cultural Materialism

Queerwords: Sexuality and the Politics of Culture

13
(2015)

edited by
David Alderson
Catherine Clay
Tony Crowley
Emily Cuming
Simon Dentith
Kristin Ewins
Ben Harker
Angela Kershaw
Stan Smith

i.m.
Simon Dentith, 22 March 1952–23 November 2014

Key Words: A Journal of Cultural Materialism

Editors: David Alderson (University of Manchester), Catherine Clay (Nottingham Trent University), Tony Crowley (University of Leeds), Emily Cuming (University of Leeds), Kristin Ewins (Örebro University), Ben Harker (University of Manchester), Angela Kershaw (University of Birmingham), Stan Smith (Nottingham Trent University).

Editorial Advisory Board: John Brannigan (University College Dublin), Peter Brooker (University of Nottingham), John Connor (Colgate University, NY), Terry Eagleton (National University of Ireland Galway and Lancaster University), John Higgins (University of Cape Town), Andreas Huyssen (Columbia University, New York), Peter Marks (University of Sydney), Sean Matthews (University of Nottingham), Jim McGuigan (Loughborough University), Andrew Milner (Monash University), Meaghan Morris (Lingnan University), Morag Shiach (Queen Mary, University of London), Dai Smith (Swansea University), Nick Stevenson (University of Nottingham), John Storey (University of Sunderland), Will Straw (McGill University), Jenny Bourne Taylor (University of Sussex), John Tomlinson (Nottingham Trent University), Jeff Wallace (Cardiff Metropolitan University), Imelda Whelehan (University of Tasmania), Vicki Whittaker (Publishing Advisor).

Contributions for prospective inclusion in *Key Words* should comply with the style notes printed on pp. 172–4 of this issue, and should be sent in electronic form to Catherine Clay, School of Arts and Humanities, Nottingham Trent University, at catherine.clay@ntu.ac.uk.

Books and other items for review should be sent to Angela Kershaw, Department of French Studies, College of Arts and Law, University of Birmingham, Birmingham B15 2TT, UK.

Key Words is a publication of The Raymond Williams Society (website: **www.raymondwilliams.co.uk**).

Contributions copyright © The Raymond Williams Society 2015.

All rights reserved.

Cover design by Andrew Dawson.

Printed by Russell Press, Nottingham.
Distributed by Central Books Ltd, London.

ISSN 1369-9725
ISBN 978-0-9929916-1-6

Contents

Editors' Preface	5
Obituary: Professor Simon Dentith	8
Introduction: Queerwords: Sexuality and the Politics of Culture David Alderson	11
Queers and Class: Toward a Cultural Politics of Friendship Lisa Henderson	17
Is the Queen Dead? Effeminacy, Homosociality and the Post-Homophobic Queer Stephen Maddison	39
Ever Fallen In Love (With Someone You Shouldn't Have?): Punk, Politics and Same-Sex Passion David Wilkinson	57
Queer Romances with Fascism David Alderson	77
People of the Black Mountains and the Politics of Theory John Connor	94
Uses of Shelley in Working-Class Culture: Approximations and Substitutions Jen Morgan	117
Back in the CCCS: Portraits of Alumni from the Centre for Contemporary Cultural Studies by Mahasiddhi (aka Roy Peters), University of Birmingham Claire MacLeod Peters	138
Keywords Tony Crowley	141
Recoveries Elinor Taylor and Stephen Rogers	144

Contents

Reviews 149

Notes on Contributors 166

Raymond Williams Foundation (RWF) 169

Open-Access Policy 171

Style Notes for Contributors 172

Editors' Preface

The larger part of the current issue, guest-edited by David Alderson, examines the relationship between queer theory/politics and the Left in the context of prevailing neoliberal conditions in the West which have weakened working-class solidarity and opposition to a capitalist culture. Preparing this issue for press following the Conservative Party's unexpected majority win in Britain's recent General Election, the assertion, in David Wilkinson's article, that 'it would be not simply irresponsible but also fatal for queers and countercultural forces to abandon the notion of a future which might also be won by a reconfigured left' carries a renewed sense of urgency. If the 'sexual revolution' of the 1960s has been divested of its radical potential by mass-market commodification and incorporation into the mainstream, the contemporary politics of queer radicalism – these articles suggest – still preserve the possibility of social change. To complement this search for a 'renewed affinity in hard times [...] rooted [...] in queer and class difference and shared cultural will' (Linda Henderson, this issue), we publish two further articles which take up Raymond Williams's commitment in both his critical and fictional work to building 'resources for a journey of hope' (*Towards 2000*, 1983). Questions relating to the experience of defeat and the condition of surviving are at the heart of John Connor's new and eloquent reading of Williams's historical novel trilogy *People of the Black Mountains*; Jen Morgan's article, on the transmission and reception of Shelley's poetry within Owenite socialism and Chartism, evidences the kind of detailed historical work currently being conducted in the field of periodicals/print culture research that can help us to understand the complexity of political and cultural change at precise moments in our collective history.

    Morgan's article was the winning entry in the third Raymond Williams Society Postgraduate Essay Competition, which we have renamed the Simon Dentith Memorial Prize in honour of our sorely missed colleague, Simon Dentith (1952–2014), who died in November last year. Simon joined the editorial board of *Key Words* in 2010 and during these past five years we have benefited enormously from his passionate intellectual and practical commitment to all aspects of the work of both the journal and the Raymond Williams Society. As well as playing a central role in the journal's commissioning and review processes, Simon provided instrumental advice in the development of our open-access policy (published in this issue), served as a competition judge for the RWS postgraduate essay prize and up until his death was working on a gazetteer of the *Black Mountains* fictions for the RWS website at the same time as completing his last book, *Nineteenth-Century British Literature Then and Now: Reading with Hindsight* (2014), reviewed in the present issue. It was entirely in character that he kept up his work for the journal and the Society until the very end, which is why we have retained his name in the list of editors for the present issue. We publish an obituary article in this issue, which we dedicate to his memory.

Two other members of the editorial board depart with the present issue, Elizabeth Allen and Sarah Davison, and we would like to record our thanks for their valuable contribution to *Key Words* during their time with us. We are joined by Emily Cuming, Research Fellow in the School of English at the University of Leeds, and David Alderson, Senior Lecturer in English Literature at the University of Manchester and guest editor of the current issue. Emily has already made a dynamic contribution to the visibility of *Key Words* through the creation of a Facebook page which will provide regular updates on forthcoming issues of the journal, along with links to RWS information and related activities and articles. Members are encouraged to boost our social media presence by signing up to the *Key Words* Facebook page, which can be found at the following address: www.facebook.com/keywordsjournal. We have also recently revamped the RWS website: www.raymondwilliams.co.uk.

The growing profile of research grounded in the tradition of cultural materialism is also reflected in the *Raymond Williams Now* conference in May this year. Organised by the Greater Manchester-based Radical Studies Network and supported by, among others, the Raymond Williams Society and the Raymond Williams Foundation, this was the first substantial conference devoted to Raymond Williams's work and legacy for some time, bringing in new generations of scholars and activists. Subjects covered linguistics, drama, philosophy, the visual arts, literature, social formations and intellectual history. The much praised keynote by Tony Crowley, on linguistics as constitutive of Williams's project, considered modern keywords such as 'chav' and the instrumentalising discourse of today's university management. Another high point of the conference was the talk and film of the performance art piece 'Performing Keywords' by the artist Ruth Beale, a project devised in a workshop with members of Turner Contemporary's Studio Group. Its contributors explored through performance the links between salient terms from Williams's *Keywords*. The day was attended by nearly eighty people, who took seriously the hope that the conference would explore the relevance of Williams now, both as an intellectual stimulus to current academic research and as a resource to confront some of the grimmer aspects of our own political and cultural situation. We hope to publish selected worked-up papers from this conference in future issues of *Key Words*.

The 2014 Annual Raymond Williams Society Lecture was given by Kate Lacey, Professor of Media History and Theory at the University of Sussex, on the topic of 'Listening: A Keyword Overlooked', impressively tracing the history of listening through the more collective nature of early radio to today's

Editors' Preface

often individualistic, selective, pod-style mode of listening. The venue afforded spectacular views across the Brighton seafront. This year's Annual Lecture will be given by Susan Watkins, editor of *New Left Review*, at Ruskin College, Oxford, on 21 November 2015 at 3pm. Please direct any queries to Kristin Ewins at kristin.ewins@oru.se.

Forthcoming numbers of *Key Words* include a special issue on Politics, Socialism and Language (2016) edited by Tony Crowley, one of the journal's permanent editors and author of the regular 'Keywords' feature (the history of the word 'radical' is traced in his contribution to the current issue), while in 2017 readers can look forward to a special issue on Raymond Williams and Performance Studies. We continue to welcome unsolicited submissions from both established and up-and-coming scholars, as well as ideas for our 'Recoveries' feature, which in this issue contains reassessments of two novels combining queer and working-class perspectives on late nineteenth- and early twentieth-century culture: *Jill* (1884) by the Welsh lesbian writer Amy Dillwyn, and *Saturday Night at the Greyhound* by John Hampson, first published by the Hogarth Press in 1931.

Obituary: Professor Simon Dentith

In a long and eventful career as a literary scholar and educator, Professor Simon Dentith's work was characterised by a passionate advocacy for the discipline to which he contributed distinguished research. Simon was educated at The John Fisher School, Purley, between 1959 and 1969. He studied English at Churchill College, Cambridge, graduating with First Class Honours in June 1973. After a brief period as a schoolteacher, he undertook postgraduate study at the University of Leicester, and in 1981 was awarded his doctorate for a thesis on *Ideology and the Novel in the 1850s*.

While at Leicester, he was part of a vibrant and learned circle that met to debate Althusser, Macherey, Structuralism, Feminism, Marxism and other matters urgent to this particularly theorising moment in English Studies. Its most lasting marks upon his intellectual formation can be found in his committed William Morris-influenced socialism, his championing of Raymond Williams's work and legacy and his writings on the theorist of dialogic and carnivalesque literature, Mikhail Bakhtin. He will also be long remembered for his stubborn and passionate debating of cases and causes, a debating that frequently dissolved differences in recognition of shared presuppositions, understandings and aspirations. He did not argue for victory, but for the vitality and fellowship of intellectual exchange.

From his first academic appointment at the University of Liverpool in 1980, Simon established his reputation as an engaged academic and a loyal colleague. His sustained publication record is impressive, including the volumes *George Eliot* (1986), *A Rhetoric of the Real* (1990), *Bakhtinian Thought* (1995), *Parody* (2000) and *Epic and Empire in Nineteenth-Century Britain* (2006). Simon's contribution to Victorian Studies is widely recognised and his latest book, *Nineteenth-Century British Literature Then and Now: Reading with Hindsight*, published early in the year of his death, has already been well received and, among other plaudits, been described as 'a major landmark in serious, fresh thinking about the massive issue of how to read literature in time'.

Simon was also an invaluable supporter in the early days of the British Association for Victorian Studies. Though BAVS now has an established presence in the lives of Victorian researchers, it was founded as recently as 2000, Simon being among the key scholars involved in making this happen. His support of democratic education and the research community of which he was such a valued member is also remembered in his ardent work for the Raymond Williams Society, teaching at residential adult education courses and as an editor of its journal, *Key Words*. He was, likewise, a great supporter of the English Subject Centre, where he worked closely with Ben Knights and

Obituary: Professor Simon Dentith

Nicole King to explore and promote the values and extend the influence of the discipline. When the English Subject Centre closed in 2011 he was chairperson of its Advisory Board and one of its greatest champions. At the final Board meeting, he bid farewell to his colleagues with the warmth and passion that were his trademarks.

During the first three months of 1995, Simon was a Visiting Professor at the University of Hawaii, Manoa. He had moved from Liverpool in 1994 to a Readership at Cheltenham and Gloucester College of Higher Education. There he worked with Professor Peter Widdowson, appointed in the same year, to establish the flourishing research culture that was a prerequisite of the institution's subsequent elevation to being the University of Gloucestershire in 2001. The following year he was promoted to a Professorship. During this period, Simon's contribution to this culture included the supervision of research students, many of whom remain profoundly grateful for his extensive and committed support. His professional and personal values remained steadfast, and he is remembered for his advocacy of returns to first principles in curriculum formation and the defence of library holdings in the humanities.

When Simon moved to the University of Reading in 2007 he agreed to take on the role of Head of Department, which he duly did in August 2008. It was a period of great change, which involved the Department's incorporation, during the three and a half years of Simon's tenure, into first one and then another School structure, including a short-lived merger with the Department of English Linguistics. Throughout all these changes Simon guided those above and around him with diplomatic tact, skill and vision, being particularly concerned for the welfare of colleagues undergoing personal difficulties, which he did without reference to his own.

Simon will also be remembered from his time at Reading as an ardent sustainer of the values in literature, criticism and the humanities, as well as a gifted teacher, a great raconteur and an administrator righteous in defence of core cultural standards both in and outside of the academy. In 2011 he organised a conference on *The Good of Criticism*, which explored a language to articulate the value and purpose of researching and teaching literature at university and which gave him an opportunity to speak alongside long-cherished peers such as Dinah Birch and Isobel Armstrong. As the son of the distinguished character actor Edward Dentith, of whose filmography he was evidently proud, Simon showed himself thoroughly attached to the performative and intonational aspects of speech and writing, one ambition left unfulfilled being the introduction of a module that based the teaching of poetry on its recitation out loud. He was a vital presence in the world, ready to challenge and to contribute, a person both fierce and tender, who cared about ideas and people with equal force, only too aware of how neither can thrive without a nurturing of the other. Many were the days made more cheerful, more illuminating and illuminated because Simon had given intellectual stimulus, practical advice and personal support.

Simon Dentith was born on Saturday 22 March 1952. He died in his sleep and without pain in the early hours of Sunday 23 November 2014. He leaves his wife, Kath, and their two children, Imogen and Jack, to whom profound condolences are offered.

Peter Robinson
Head of the Department of English Literature
University of Reading

Introduction
Queerwords: Sexuality and the Politics of Culture
David Alderson

The majority of articles that comprise this issue of *Key Words* focus on sexuality, culture and political economy, drawing broadly on the tradition of cultural materialism. Each insists that the relations between these dimensions of human existence are far from straightforward for reasons that have to do with their complex evolution since the sixties, when the sexual liberation movements emerged. While it is undoubtedly the case that the intervening years have witnessed a quite extraordinary liberalisation of societies in various parts of the world with respect to sexuality, they can only reductively be treated as a period of straightforward progress. Rather, they have witnessed reconfigurations of power that have accompanied, and even facilitated, that liberalisation. It is no doubt for this reason that each of the articles is concerned more or less explicitly with questions of history and narrative as a means of grasping these reconfigurations and evaluating the potential for continuing dissident challenge.

Recalling the arguments of the counterculture perhaps helps us understand just how much has changed. Bourgeois society, it was thought, repressed sexuality through its commitment to the gendered roles of the heterosexual family, which was in turn thought essential to the functioning of capitalism because of its reproduction and privatised socialisation of the labour force. In challenging that institution, therefore, the most avant-garde among lesbian and gay movements considered themselves to be taking their rightful place among the revolutionary movements of the Left, even though sections of that Left often forcefully insisted that homosexuality was a bourgeois – or was it aristocratic? – perversion. The expectation among sections of the Old Left was that, under socialism, homosexuality would disappear, just as other superstructural 'problems' would spontaneously resolve themselves.

Both countercultural and Old Left emphases now seem remote, though one frequently hears echoes of them. Both focus on a bourgeois existence to be repudiated, and emerge out of a tendency to treat such repudiation as the subjective, cultural proxy for opposing capitalism. At times – and not least during the counterculture – this emphasis has tended to displace opposition to the system as such. Part of the problem results from the conviction that we can distinguish bourgeois characteristics specifically from the more general determinations of existence by capitalism, which consist in the commodification and reification of labour and its products, and the further reifications of private and public realms, of which the individual (and potential 'pervert') and the family (the 'proper' fulfilment of her or his desire) in their distinctions from society are *both* mainstays. The Left is all too often guilty of fetishising terms in ways that are in practice divisive.[1] In my view, there is every reason why it should value both the individual and the (diversely configured, non-nuclear) family, whereas individualism and familialism are equally obstacles to social solidarity that are freighted with merely moralistic distinctions whose implications are always reactionary.

Queer thought[2] at its best has taught us to be more nuanced in speaking of capitalism and everyone's relations to it, and also fully to acknowledge the Marxist insight that is frequently repressed: that capitalism has been progressive, as well as exploitative and inegalitarian. In his classic essay, John d'Emilio argues that capitalism facilitated the emergence of queer subcultures as early as the late nineteenth century as a consequence of the emergence of 'free labour' and urbanisation.[3] More recently, Kevin Floyd has convincingly argued that the discourse of sexuality is a form of reification, both material and theoretical, but that reification may have progressive consequences. He cites the lesbian and gay movement as an instance of this, though he also qualifies that claim through an acceptance and development of the critique of 'homonormativity' articulated by Lisa Duggan.[4] For Duggan, the lesbian and gay movement has in recent years come to be dominated by an agenda 'that does not contest dominant heteronormative assumptions and institutions, but upholds and sustains them, while promising the possibility of a demobilized gay constituency and a privatised, depoliticised gay culture anchored in domesticity and consumption'.[5] Effectively, she argues, it has been bourgeoisified, though the implications of this are more far reaching in the US than in Europe, where social welfare provision is (even now) more substantial.

Let us take one recent instance of this bourgeoisification. Tim Cook, the CEO of Apple, recently came out as gay, and was welcomed as a contemporary role model who illustrated that sexual identity was no necessary hindrance to success (though he did come out *after* getting the job). Moreover, in what is clearly a corporate publicity drive centred on him, and calculated to appeal to Apple's 'cool' customers through its appropriation of sixties 'icons' and movements, he has further bolstered his progressive credentials by speaking publicly of his upbringing in Alabama, when his heroes were Martin Luther King and Robert F. Kennedy, rather than George Wallace[6] (whose notoriety was recently re-established for younger generations by the film, *Selma* (DuVernay, 2014)). Meanwhile, and in spite of repeated claims to be improving the situation, Apple continues to outsource the exploitation of thousands of Chinese production workers to Foxconn. Cook also recently spoke at a Senate sub-committee in defence of his company's tax avoidance arrangements.

David Alderson

In a show of where real power lies nowadays, he demanded that corporate tax in the US be lowered if Apple is to repatriate its funds.[7] Celebrating the potential for individuals to succeed in defiance of any particular mode of social discrimination often means overlooking the systemic relations on which that personal success is dependent.

The relevant context here is succinctly summarised in Lisa Henderson's article, because she highlights the process that has separated us from the conditions in which the counterculture emerged: 'thirty years of "gay" and "queer" life [...] have taken form amid socially and politically crippling economic conditions and a national culture of hyper-accumulation'. She is speaking of the US, though conditions are not so different elsewhere. Her phrasing strikes me as important in all sorts of ways, and effectively summarises the preoccupations of the other articles in this issue. 'Taken form' conveys a sense of economic determination that does not preclude social and cultural agency, and alerts us not merely to the social and institutional structures that have been consolidated during this period, but also to 'individual' dispositions and even corporeal modes of being. Judith Butler once spoke of the body, not as a given but rather as a process of materialisation.[8] While some of us may be inclined to resist the tendency to reification inherent in persistent talk of 'the body', even in such apparently dynamic accounts, the argument Butler develops principally in relationship to gender may nonetheless be extended to cover various forms of social determination and elaboration that are frequently mutually reinforcing. Henderson turns to Bourdieu to emphasise habitus and distinction as crucial terms in this respect.

Though people like Tim Cook may be symbolically dominant, they are hardly representative. Indeed, the very success they embody is predicated on atypicality; the culture of aspiration we hear so much about these days requires that the majority will be losers. It is not in the power of individuals to correct this. But, while Henderson fully acknowledges the objective impact of neoliberalism and its cultural effects with exemplary clarity, her aim is specifically to avoid counselling subjective despair by moving beyond the negativity of anti-bourgeois rhetoric to promote a disposition towards friendship and solidarity such as is often, even routinely, practised, but rarely acknowledged as such.

This ethic runs strikingly counter to the dominant emphasis on wealthy role models, and Henderson cites an eclectic range of instances in which the disposition she seeks to cultivate has led to alliances that might have appeared implausible but for the determination to pursue them. Her argument encourages us to identify our own examples. Recently, for instance, I have been struck by the presence of queer activists of diverse backgrounds on protests opposing Israel's continuing war on the Palestinians, though they have been derided by pro-Zionist commentators who highlight the commodified liberalism of Tel Aviv and the presence of lesbians and gay men in the Israeli military.[9]

Queer solidarity such as this is also highlighted by Steven Maddison in a somewhat different theoretical context that is nonetheless focused on social and corporeal form as these are bound to sensibility. He examines neoliberalism's implication in the reconfiguration of male homosociality through the loosening of resistance, in various senses, to same-sex passion. The all too familiar contemporary reassertion of a presumptively authentic laddish – or, in the US, jock-ish – masculinity easily enough accompanies overtly narcissistic conduct. 'Gym culture' is perhaps its apotheosis, and these days frequently entails the dissolution of any crudely conceived homophobia. Performative theories of gender hardly seem subversive in the context Maddison describes, since subjective performance – being successful, getting the job done and achieving one's goals, including sexual ones – is effectively a neoliberal injunction. In the face of all this, Maddison asserts the continuing, even renewed, dissident potential of effeminacy as a subcultural tradition in an article that draws extensively, and in solidaristic fashion, on the recent renewal of feminist critiques of women's objectification.

The category of subculture connects Maddison's article with David Wilkinson's. Both draw on the work of Alan Sinfield, and it is especially important here to acknowledge the scale and importance of that contribution, since it represents the most sustained explicitly cultural materialist project within the field of critical and theoretical work on sexuality. Distinct in emphasis from queer theory, though in dialogue with it, his writing also represents an alternative to more recent, orthodox Marxisms that have found little place for a politics of sexuality specifically.[10] For Sinfield, subcultural elaboration takes place across various institutional milieux that condition its potential. In arguing for the value of subculture, he nonetheless refuses any romanticisation of it as the source of authentic rebellion.[11] Queer radicals often contest contemporary lesbian and gay pragmatism by reminding us that Stonewall was a riot. True enough, but it was first of all a bar. There is no position outside of the system, even if our situation within it may dispose us to one or other ways of perceiving, and possibly challenging, it. The Left should seek to influence subcultures, even if its project aspires to more general transformation; but it should also learn from them.

The terms I have invoked here, counterculture and subculture, therefore designate distinct phenomena, but there is frequent overlap between them, as in the particular formation with which Wilkinson is concerned in his meticulously revisionist article on punk and its continuing appeal. By contrast with those who find in punk's uncompromising modes of negation a model for contemporary 'anti-social' protest, Wilkinson relates its forms and impulses to class fractional dissidence at a time of socio-economic disintegration and reconfiguration in a way that explains its only apparently transcendent status. The problem with the category of the radical, as Tony Crowley's account of it as a keyword indicates, is that it is – or has become – indeterminate. Punk was diverse and multi-accentual; its hostility to bourgeois life often brought into focus genuinely repressive features of everyday life, but it could also target social solidarity indiscriminately and in principle. As Wilkinson demonstrates in a nuanced evaluation that avoids mere dismissal as much as uncritical celebration, same-sex passion was advocated and stigmatised, facilitated and structured in complex ways governed by these tendencies.

My own article both expands on a point highlighted by Wilkinson and also takes up the theme of romanticism by focusing on one subcultural development out of punk: the figure of the skinhead. Neo-Nazi thug, but also object of homoerotic desire, and even queer identification, he is the focus of two recent works, the Danish film *Brotherhood* (Donato, 2009), and Max Schaefer's novel *Children of the Sun* (2010). My approach to these illustrates another point of Sinfield's, that critical reflection, even theory, is practised within subcultural production; it is not just that which the critic brings to bear on the objects of her scrutiny. These works prompt me to consider an ambiguity in fascist ideology and accounts of it: did it represent the apotheosis of bourgeois respectability and conformity or an attempt to transcend those domesticating confines? The answer is that both tendencies were present, of course, and in tension, and the consequences of this have played out in complex ways in the transformed social conditions of postwar Europe, not least in relation to the self-consciously, if distinctively, erotic figure of the skinhead.

Williams highlighted the dynamic qualities of the dominant, and the ways in which it is forced to assimilate what it can of the oppositional forces that challenge it, while suppressing others.[12] This tendency has been especially characteristic of a neoliberalism consistently euphemised as 'modernisation', which casts all resistance to it – including the socialist – as conservative. Ever since Marcuse's pioneering critique of repressive desublimation,[13] it has been understood that greater sexual freedom is hardly at odds with capital accumulation, but frequently provides one mode of furthering it. Indeed, sexuality's role in this respect is surely only surpassed by the intense sentimentalisation of the family promoted by advertising and Hollywood. These are the complex conditions that govern these articles' often acutely critical discussions of enduring subcultural, countercultural and solidaristic forms of opposition, emphasising the need for creative interventions that are nonetheless wary of romanticism of various kinds.

University of Manchester

Introduction

Notes

1. The point is made in a different context by Neil Lazarus in 'The Fetish of "the West" in Postcolonial Theory', in *Marxism, Modernity, and Postcolonial Studies*, ed. Crystal Bartolovich and Neil Lazarus (Cambridge: Cambridge University Press, 2002), 43–64.
2. I use this phrase here in the casual sense, because I don't see why we should all accept the colonisation of that term, and of our thinking, by some version of poststructuralism. I therefore make a distinction between this casual use of 'queer', and the sense clearly designated by 'queer theory', with which one may or may not have disagreements.
3. John d'Emilio, 'Capitalism and Gay Identity', in *Making Trouble: Essays on Gay History, Politics and the University* (New York: Routledge, 1992), 3–16.
4. Kevin Floyd, *The Reification of Desire: Toward a Queer Marxism* (Minneapolis: University of Minnesota Press, 2009). I summarise Floyd's general case here. For the critique of homonormativity specifically, see 195–228.
5. Lisa Duggan, *The Twilight of Equality: Neoliberalism, Cultural Politics, and the Attack on Democracy* (Boston: Beacon Press, 2003), 50.
6. 'Steve Jobs' Vision for Apple Realised, as iPhones Reveal Injustice, Says Tim Cook', *The Guardian*, 17 May 2015, http://www.theguardian.com/technology/2015/may/17/tim-cook-apple-commencement-george-washington-university-iphone (accessed 17 May 2015).
7. 'Apple Chief Calls on Government to Slash US Corporate Tax', *The Guardian*, 21 May 2013, http://www.theguardian.com/technology/2013/may/21/apple-wants-single-digit-corporate-tax (accessed 21 May 2015).
8. Judith Butler, *Bodies that Matter: On the Discursive Limits of 'Sex'* (New York: Routledge, 1993), 4–12. I prefer Toril Moi's account of the body as a situation, which draws on the work of de Beauvoir and Merleau-Ponty (*What Is A Woman? And Other Essays* (Oxford: Oxford University Press, 1999), esp. 57–83).
9. For UK activism of this sort, see http://www.nopinkwashing.org.uk (accessed 15 March 2015).
10. Donald Morton dismisses cultural materialism as revisionism and opportunism ('Pataphysics of the Closet: Queer Theory as the Art of Imaginary Solutions for Unimaginary Problems', *Transformation 2: Marxism, Queer Theory, Gender* (2001): 56). Effectively, so does Rosemary Hennessy, who discusses Williams but ignores Sinfield's contribution entirely, and goes on to speak with telling indiscrimination of 'the cultural materialisms of Michel Foucault, Ernesto Laclau and Chantal Mouffe, Slavoj Zizek, Judith Butler, and others' (*Profit and Pleasure: Sexual Identities in Late Capitalism* (New York: Routledge, 2000), 80). In *After Queer Theory: The Limits of Sexual Politics* (London: Pluto, 2014), James Penney's Lacanian Marxist argument treats queer theory as exhaustive of the theoretical possibilities opened up by an apparently exhausted politics of sexuality. Floyd's *Reification of Desire*, by contrast, attempts a *rapprochement* with queer theory, but doesn't acknowledge a model that in many ways anticipates his own argument.
11. For Sinfield's most important theorisations of subculture, see especially *Literature, Politics, and Culture in Postwar Britain*, 3rd edition (London: Continuum, 2004), 341–50, and *Gay and After* (London: Serpent's Tail, 1998), though most of Sinfield's later work is informed by his sense of himself as a subcultural organic intellectual.
12. Raymond Williams, 'Base and Superstructure in Marxist Cultural Theory', *New Left Review* I, no. 82 (1973): 8–12.
13. Herbert Marcuse, *One-Dimensional Man* (London: Routledge, 2002), 59–86. For a recent defence of the term, see Finn Bowring, 'Repressive Desublimation and Consumer Culture: Re-evaluating Herbert Marcuse', *new formations* 75 (2012): 8–24.

Queers and Class:
Toward a Cultural Politics of Friendship[1]
Lisa Henderson

Abstract: 'My art', said filmmaker Miranda July, 'is like my car, the way I get to the next place'. What if cultural critics adopted a similar disposition, using cultural forms to get to the next place? In this article I approach queer culture with July's sense of need and discovery, to explore criticism and theorisation as constructive and reparative gestures. The topic of my analysis is the relationship between queerness and class, and the endpoint is a proposal for a cultural politics of friendship. To get there, I articulate queerness and class in a variety of ways, asking how queerness, in the US especially (but not only), came to be seen as antagonistic to class struggle despite a shared intellectual and political agenda at an earlier time. I go on to consider key cultural moments in the *class project* of contemporary queerness, then close with the tactic of 'reading for friendship', considering queer friendships at the root of published biography and documentary and fiction film. How might the historical practice of queer friendship anchor a renewed cultural politics? The point is not to dematerialise class and other social differences, but to recognise the materiality of culture and affect in political development, a project that Raymond Williams, among others, made with grace and force. Like Miranda July's art, Williams's theorising is our car, how we get to the next place.

*

This article tells a story in three parts about class, culture, gayness and queerness: the first part is a capsule history of the separation of sexual difference and social class in the contemporary project of liberation; the second is an account of why culture is important in this story and how it can be used in a renewed project of affinity between queerness and class identification; and the third is a closing meditation on friendship as a form of queer attachment, a form with a history of class mixing and, hopefully, a future of flourishing solidarities.

By friendship, I do not mean niceness, or unalloyed goodness, or resolution, but an ecumenical form of social relating in a world of gender, racial and especially class difference, a world structured in the economic and cultural co-production of distinction, hierarchy and the unjust distribution of many forms of value – money, wealth, autonomy, security, voice, influence. The concept of distinction I take from Bourdieu,[2] and the idea of friendship from Raymond Williams,[3] whose writerly generosity about people and our capacities, usually against the grain of histories of domination, introduces a gentle morality or even spiritual quality[4] to an otherwise secular critique. Williams was not a queer theorist, but in combination with those, like Eve Kosofsky Sedgwick, who were, his writing contributes a palpable shift in an affectively welcome direction.

'Queerness' I use as a social descriptor for the broad spectrum of people whose gendered lives – whose bodies, identities and expression – are not captured by the historic male/female binarism or the presumption of heterosexual attraction. Sometimes queer difference is consciously anti-heteronormative, openly challenging this sex-gender system. 'Gayness' can mean those things, too, though it tends to be shorthand for homosexuality or same-sex attraction. So does 'lesbianism', though its long articulation to feminism also expresses a historical challenge to patriarchal gender configurations (if not to gender identity expression).

In distinguishing 'gay' and 'queer', I see the first term as coming to signify a politics of respectability in the US that troubled the prospect of alliance with a politics of class. The second term, 'queer', is potentially better aligned – if not integrated – with the value of class solidarity. These are expressive practices I explore in the comments to come.

The Political Opposition of Sexual Difference and Class

I write in 2015 as a 57-year-old whose personal queer life started in 1986, at the age of 28. (Some may see my queer life having ended with my marriage to a heterosexual man, but I see it differently.)[5] My environmentally queer life started years earlier, with graduate school and my evolving intellectual relationship and friendship with Larry Gross, my graduate supervisor at the University of Pennsylvania. Gross has been an openly gay scholar, teacher and activist since a period when there were few, and he is a Red Diaper baby, his father Bertram Gross having been a prominent critic of the US social and political system. My interactions with Gross and his political context were part of my sensitisation to the spirit of collectivity. My coming of age in Quebec in the late 1970s amid broad and deep government support for public higher education and national health care, my everyday training in protest (at school and elsewhere) in support of those resources and my family's privileges and misfortunes also contributed to this process. Later, I was sensitised by academic training to the idea that different struggles for justice and well-being go together – the activist side of what has since been theorised in black feminism as intersectionality.[6] Gross's activism and example were rooted in his identification as gay, but his politics were also rooted in his critique of a world structured in accumulation, inequity and empire, in which so many forms of social difference and dissent are punished by shame, deprivation and extraction at the cost of security and well-being. Gross's critique took shape before the language of intersectionality was common, but it expressed the theory and politics of overdetermination – the multiply-articulated condition of any social group – a theory central to left analysis since its development by Louis Althusser in the early 1960s.[7]

In the time of my queer formation – the 1980s – queerness was a sexual possibility but also the promise of new forms of belonging, a chance for social attachments that might otherwise have been impossible. Something about the alloy of erotic energy, social shame, new interiorities, the open smudging of private and public sexual culture, shifts in psychic expectation at once gradual and dramatic and the limits of family acceptance would impel us to social creativity. We would find affection and strength in new places, inhabit the world across old divisions, be slow to judge and curious about modes of living beyond our own.

Since that time, North America has witnessed an improvement in fortune for many lesbian and gay-identified people, with the cultivation of openly gay professional circuits in electoral politics, law, corporate life, the academy, non-profits, government, consumer markets and cultural production. The numbers remain modest but the accrued changes in institutional enfranchisement are striking. Such changes, however, were not linear. They occurred amid uneven politics and parallel practices of street activism, civil disobedience and subterranean manoeuvring, forms of activity often though inconsistently identified as 'queer'.

In the US, as elsewhere, the period includes the transformative losses of the AIDS crisis, an epoch that resembled wartime in its claim on young lives and that is far from over, though the epidemic has shifted ground.[8] Even people who once lived enfranchised (if closeted) lives found themselves ill and cut off by families, medical insurers and the federal government. With others they acted up, and a community health care movement took shape amid medical and policy inattention and the absence of a standard of care – a movement echoed in more recent arguments in the United States for a national health system. Ronald Reagan's second presidential term, beginning in 1984, became ground for vocal, organised protest against the hypocrisies of family values in the federal government and among its religious conservative provocateurs.

It was also during this period that *queer* artists responded collectively to the renewed witch-hunting of the culture wars, in particular to conservative demonising of the homoerotic and sacrilegious visual art of Robert Mapplethorpe and Andres Serrano and the queer performance art of Holly Hughes, Karen Finley, Tim Miller and John Fleck – the 'NEA Four'. These attacks were part of a broader attempt to dismantle the US National Endowment for the Arts, tarring it and related cultural institutions as 'deranged', 'elitist' and unfit for public support. It was a protracted renewal of aggression against an old ghost in conservative political rhetoric: the twisted, aristocratic queer, once a bohemian figure, now a privileged and criminally entitled gay professional drowning in excess and illegitimate claims of social oppression. The Right's ghost, however, would share a troubled ether with the straight Left's promotion of class over culture and disdain for gay sex,[9] and with grassroots *queer* disenchantment with 'mainstream' gay struggle. It was a complicated, often bitter, cocktail of cultural and political registers.

In the early 1990s, US activists from Queer Nation to college campuses challenged the status-based terms of representation and inclusion, seeking a multiracial, multi-ethnic, multi-abled, multigender, multigeneration and multiclass home to queer dissenters, setting aside the rhetorical legacy of nationalism in favour of an imagined community of protest. They wanted refuge from both hostile regulation and the newly professional milieu of gay activists who cultivated centrist power. Closeted gay power in government, entertainment and corporate life resurfaced as a grotesque form of opportunism amid the death and urgency of AIDS and HIV, and outing became queer activist strategy, exposing the open secret of homosexuality in high places.[10] Thus a mixed universe of newly-acquired power, backlash and grassroots counter-politics became the ground for a *queer* assertion of class disenchantment with *gay* life, a politics etched across historic divisions between Left and queer radicalism and between queer dissent and gay professional culture. In private life, 'queer' and 'gay' could be interchanged and bandied about with pleasure. In public politics, however, by 1990 the terms roughly signified differences in status and political practice. Gays (especially men) were gaining admission to the precincts of power as well-turned-out players; queers preserved the historical margins of sexual culture and sought a mixed agenda where race, gender and sexual difference converged. High-status gays expressed the promise of post-war liberalism, in the United States a pluralist, anti-authoritarian social world of education and reason. Ironically it was this same liberal ideal that, by the late-1970s, rendered working-class people the embodiment of resentment, authoritarian righteousness and, by extension, homophobia, a stereotype that would further separate gay progress and class solidarity.[11]

As a witness to this period and a person formed in its rhythms, places and losses, I wrote *Love and Money*[12] to rethink the class legacy of gay vs queer, to return queer cultural studies to Left critique and to cultivate interdependence between queer radicalism and Left political economy in the practice of cultural politics. My approach was not to wish away harm or to set aside antipathy among arguments and the people who make them, but to take for granted the need for solidarity and soft landings and thus animate what Sedgwick[13] famously called a reparative mode of reading and a counterpart mode of imagining the future. For Sedgwick, reparative criticism signified a departure from a 'paranoid' disposition and critical practice habitually prepared to see the worst and to get there first. Because there can be no bad surprises, Sedgwick argued, no textual or worldly violence a critic did not see coming, there can be no surprises at all.[14] Culture, in this paranoid view, is the place of reproduction and foreclosure, not of liberation, new formation or possibility.

As a critic trained and experienced in the paranoid tradition, but also as an ethnographer committed to the study of everyday life, I had grown weary of finding the worst – the regressive cycle of reproduction in favour of dominance – and teaching others to find it too. I sought instead a critical practice that could reconstruct the world around us in equal proportion to its deconstructions. 'My art', said filmmaker and writer Miranda July, 'is like my car, how I get to the next place'.[15] With July, I wanted to look to culture and cultural theory to think about where to go and how to get there. There is guiding resonance among July's insight as artist, Sedgwick's commitment to repair and Williams's dedication to a cultural politics of non-dominance.

Reimagining, however, is not easy to justify when we live in what Princeton economist Larry Bartels[16] called the new gilded age. Bartels's analysis, which has since been affirmed and promoted by French economist Thomas Piketty,[17] criticises the current period (starting in the mid-1970s) as one of wealth disparity that would make nineteenth-century robber barons blush, dominated by some of the most regressive social and tax policy (primarily Republican but also Democrat-authored) the United States has ever seen. Thirty years of 'gay' and 'queer' life, in other words, have taken form amid socially and politically crippling economic conditions and a national culture of hyper-accumulation.[18] Some, like I, have survived and ascended, and other gay or queer people who've always had what they need got to go public with diminished risk. Those who didn't and who could not or would not conform – sexual dissidents, sex workers, undocumented people, gender nonconforming people, uninsured people, poor queers of all kinds – have continued to be punished by deprivation, extraction and death.[19] Like so many forms of cultural distinction, moreover, some versions of gayness (professional, wealthy, white, usually male, increasingly familial) are available to firms and governments to cultivate prestige living and urban development under the banner of Richard Florida's 'creative class' analysis and the dogged pursuit of cultural elites as the foundation for urban renewal. In Florida's analysis and its policy counterparts, cultural eclecticism is a form of capital that 'knowledge sector' elites want and can get in the right kinds of cities. As taste arbiters and the embodiments of a fashionable variety of cultural difference, the right gay people and their cultural establishments (restaurants, boutiques, high-profile festivals and other events) are a population to be served in the project of urban recruitment and development, and to be served *to* non-gay others whose worlds are flattered by high-end mixing.[20]

But rather than concluding that nothing can be done short of a revolutionary reversal of fortune forever out of reach (a nostalgic stance entrenched if not consciously promoted by the paranoid habit), this horizon makes it all the more essential to seek, instead, renewed affinity in hard times, a feeling of possibility rooted less in identity *per se* (though there are worse gestures) than in a form of recognition rooted simultaneously in queer and class difference and shared cultural will. In this project of recognition and action, culture has a particular role to play.

Queer Class Culture: From Trouble to Optimism

Culture has a role to play. I am likely to make that claim as cultural critic and fieldworker. But I *am* a cultural critic in part through an orientation to the world rooted in culture as a source of thriving. We do not live on music alone, and that has made it easy to reduce culture to the 'merely cultural'.[21] I do not seek to reverse the chauvinism of the 'merely cultural' and replace it with claims about salvation. I ask a plainer and more partial question about what culture might do for solidarity – particularly queer/class solidarity – and how. Offering reparative readings and counterpart action, I ask how we might represent the move from the compulsive (re)discovery of cultural trouble to the articulation of cultural sustenance, not to ignore trouble but to cultivate a less exclusive and a more practically optimistic cultural politics, rewiring our dispositions toward a recognition of possibility in the present. In other words, I first consider what is troubling about how queerness/gayness and social class have been portrayed so as to affirm mainstream class stereotypes (the familiar or paranoid move) and next, how to shift to a reparative practice and the kind of political difference that would make.[22]

Trouble. There are many places to look for queer-class trouble in popular culture, whether or not its class coordinates are named (they usually aren't). Consider, for example, ideologies of class in commercial versions of queerness, especially in television and film. Commercial cultural production has been the site of what many observers have called the 'new queer visibility', a shorthand that refers to the relative burgeoning of queer characters in broadcast and premium cable television in the late 1990s and early 2000s, for example *Ellen* (1994–98)*,* then *Will and Grace* (1998–2006), *Queer as Folk* (2000–2005) and *The L Word* (2004–2009) in the US. In television's new queer visibility, the interaction between queerness and class has an economic logic, embedding enough fragmented class recognition – bits and pieces of class typification here and there – to appeal to a range of consumers and still flatter those managers and professionals at the crest of advertising trade value, and to sweeten content with just a *soupçon* of queer edge, enough to draw newer, hipper, younger audiences in the hyperdiversified landscape of popular forms. Within this logic, queerness delivers cultural expansion, a new commercial horizon broadened beyond old typifications of queer marginality but well shy of heterosexual disarmament. In the case of television, it was a horizon fitted to the 'postnetwork' era,[23] a competitive context in which smaller, more-defined 'niche' audiences acquire industrial value (as they did in Richard Florida's urban development campaign), cable outlets compete as targeted brands with each other and with traditional broadcast networks, and industrial distinction relies on a combination of old formats (situation comedy, nighttime soap opera, family melodrama) and new themes and characters, queers among them. In this new environment, an audience of 'socially liberal, urban-minded professionals'[24] comes with a high price tag for advertisers and is thus especially desirable for networks, outlets, cable operators, portals and production companies. Many producers and executives, gay and straight, are themselves a part of that audience, brokering elite class fantasies, queer trade value and industrial ratings as they shuttle back and forth between the specialised domain of cultural production and more diffuse forms of meaning-making in everyday life. In Sherry Ortner's[25] terms, the *class project* of queer visibility takes shape through their creative, technical, and managerial labour. Ortner's hitching of 'project' to class is apt, reminding us that class is as much something we do (and do again) as it is something we, or others, have. 'Class project' resonates with Bourdieu's practice theory, Williams's foundational concept of cultural materialism and Butler's recognition of the performativity of gender;[26] like gender, class is something we do.

The familiar critique of class in the new queer visibility, one I have largely supported, is that it promotes a version of homosexuality – gayness – populated by rich, white, healthy men detached from sex, lovers and queer political communities. Will Truman of *Will and Grace* comes to mind. Will is a white, wealthy, healthy lawyer, his best friend is a straight woman, and his one queer friend, Jack, is an appealing and campy mooch. There is thus truth in the familiar critique, but it is partial, and its partialities are worth rethinking. In US commercial popular culture, the class spectrum is compressed. The ruling class and routine (not criminal) poverty are largely absent, and the image of wealth is way out of proportion to the world as we know it. The under-representation of lower-middle-class citizens and communities meets an overabundance of superrich celebrities and corporate up-and-comers (e.g., the British and

US casts of *The Apprentice*), and even modest living is more luxurious and better-heeled on television than in strapped neighbourhoods and working households. That doesn't mean, however, that amid this class compression the engines of distinction are still. As is true in everyday life, they are steady, neither thunderous nor silent but a coarse drone sustained by comportment (how characters act), family attachment (who their primary relationships are with) and legitimate modes of acquisition (how they get what they have) as the class markers of queer worth. Naming these markers is a different kind of analysis than describing class types among queer characters, since such markers are variably applied to a range of characters across the familiar categories of blue-collar, middle-class and rich, shifting queer characters' relative class value in the world of narratives, genres and moral outcomes.

The class markers of queer worth organise not only the concentrated narratives of popular culture but the diffuse and contradictory partial narratives of everyday living. Commercial culture's most visible class and queer fantasies are thus not a world apart, but a part of our world, elements of a continuous cultural stream in which ideologies of class and queer worth rooted in managed bodies, family attachments and legitimately acquired things are as likely to surface off television as on. My conclusion, then, is not that adequate representation in commercial culture will promote adequate representation in social life, or that as critics we ought to expect that popular media will deconstruct popular fantasy. Instead, I suggest that there is a continuity of affective attachment inside the media and out, in a universe where people *really do* enjoy, endure and equally suffer the terms of existing class projects, including the class project of queer visibility.

Optimism? That conclusion is draining, however, if it means that critics and images have nowhere to go and nothing to do, save to live with the limits class dominance imposes. What, alternately, might class solidarity in queerness look and feel like? If cultural forms and everyday life are more connected than the fear of 'media influence' communicates, it is also true that attachments to other kinds of narratives and characters matter. But what other kinds? I would like to make the case for a critic's attachment to the disposition of friendship and for critical attention to friendships of different kinds among queer stories and characters. The gesture is not purely topical – a study of 'friendship images' (which would include *Will and Grace*). It is also a matter of tilting towards friendship in the name of recognising a past and imagining a future of queer friendship across class lines, of queer-class solidarities. There is no essentially queer claim to make on friendship, though to ask about it as critics is both to turn to abundant histories of class recognition and mixing in the queer practice of friendship and to imagine the queer future through that historical lens – a project aligned with Williams's commitment to a class politics of non-domination.

Though 'friend' does not appear in Williams's *Key Words*, his critique of the dominative mode from the Left and the Right of the political spectrum is instructive. People, Williams observed, know when they're being dominated, a disposition that thwarts collective projects whose value to all might otherwise seem obvious. At the height of the Cold War, he wrote:

> We live in almost overwhelming danger, at a peak of our apparent control. We react to the danger by attempting to take control, yet still we have to unlearn, as the price of survival, the inherent dominative mode. The struggle for democracy is the pattern of this revaluation, yet much that passes as democratic is allied, in spirit, with the practice of its open enemies. It is as if, in fear or vision, we are now all determined to lay our hands on life and force it into our own image, and it is then no good to dispute on the merits of rival images […] We project our old images into the future, and take hold of ourselves and others to force energy towards that substantiation. We do this as conservatives, trying to prolong old forms; we do this as socialists, trying to prescribe the new man. A large part of contemporary resistance to certain kinds of change, which are obviously useful in themselves, amounts to an inarticulate distrust of this effort at domination.[27]

Williams is critical of both bourgeois privilege and state socialism as reactive modes of domination. His critique shares a tenor and an invitation to ideological opening with Sedgwick's[28] reparative mode of criticism and J.K. Gibson-Graham's[29] 'weak' theorising of the economy. Strong theory, Gibson-Graham argues, has 'an embracing reach and a reduced, clarified field of meaning'[30] in which outcomes are mostly known before practical conditions are explored, a field in which 'social experiments are already co-opted and thus doomed to fail or to reinforce dominance' or in which 'the world economy will be transformed by an international revolutionary movement rather than through the disorganised proliferation of local projects'.[31] 'Weak' theory, in contrast,

> can be undertaken with a reparative motive that welcomes surprise, entertains hope, makes connection, tolerates coexistence and offers care for the new. As the impulse to judge or discredit other theoretical agendas arises, one can practice making room for others, imagining a terrain on which the success of one project need not come at the expense of another. Producing such spaciousness is particularly useful for a project

of rethinking economy, where the problem is the scarcity rather than the inconsistency of economic concepts.[32]

Producing spaciousness and avoiding conceptual foreclosure have been invaluable to me for rethinking culture – as Gibson-Graham rethinks the economy – on new ground, for finding a new mood and a new theoretical point of entry, and thus for rethinking queer class cultural politics. If culture is where society *tends to* its formation, where it cultivates its future in the most creative and 'unplannable' ways,[33] and if democratic culture is a 'struggle for the recognition of equality of being',[34] then a democratic queer cultural politics stands to gain considerable breadth and return considerable value from the openness and practice of weak theory. From this perspective, friendship, as a form of relating both tenacious and loose, can realign our understanding of the interdependency of queerness and class.

There are revolutionary friendships, but there is also a more open and familiar form of queer friendship *as a way of life* born of 'estrangement in common',[35] suggested in, among other places, gay men and lesbians' account of the role of friendship in their lives in the 1980s.[36] It is a form that Roach, among others, proposes was refined mightily in communities of care among strangers during the early period of the North American and UK AIDS crisis (1981–96). Classed, and raced, narratives of queer friendship are places to seek new critical attachments to friendship as a way of life and to the non-dominative mode Williams, in his own reparative way, advocated.

Friendship

> I know my music can help bring people together, and that's what is important. I think that jazz is the thing that has contributed the most to the idea that one day the word 'friendship' may really mean something in the United States.[37]

In the preface to the second edition of his beautiful and prodigious biography of Thelonious Monk, historian Robin D.G. Kelley acknowledges how much new material and insight came to him after the first edition was published. Readers from all over the world sent their memories, snippets and documents, sometimes gently challenging and other times adding detail to Kelley's scholarship, always with a sense of warmth and good faith rooted in their shared love of Monk and in appreciation for Kelley's labour of love as historian – his long project of telling Monk's story, sustaining and opening a life for old Monk listeners and new. 'Suddenly', writes Kelley, 'I was swept into a vast, intimate network of "friends" that crossed national borders, oceans, color, and language barriers, all connected through songs like "Well, You Needn't", "Brilliant Corners", and "Criss Cross". Monk, indeed, brought us together; as he predicted, his music has become the connective tissue for an ever-expanding, global friendship.'[38]

Kelley's fond acknowledgement of new networks enabled by writing about Monk reminded me of the scholarly acknowledgements that precede virtually every book of cultural critique I've read, though unlike in Kelley's work on Monk, such acknowledgements usually precede accounts of a world gone awry. As critics, we narrate social trouble (as paranoid critics, we see it coming *before it even happens*), but it appears we do so in a world of supportive readers, students, teachers, lovers, family members and, indeed, friends. Why, I have often wondered, is the framework of our scholarship so different from that of the worlds in which we say we make it? Are we the only beneficiaries of a solidary life, so much so that we make it our habit, born of accountability and guilt, to tell the stories of a domineering world full of corrupt actors and unintended consequences? 'Thank you to my kind friends and others', we seem to say, 'who have enabled me to narrate a world devoid of kindness'. This is not, thankfully, Kelley's approach to writing a biography of Thelonious Monk, where a historian's rigour is matched by open affection and multifaceted care for his subject.

Like the monographs they precede, 'Acknowledgements' are a genre, not a species of truth (we can all envision our anti-acknowledgements – satisfying dismissals of the small-minded people who got in our way). But our commitment to one genre – acknowledgement – in describing our proximate world, and to another – trouble – in describing a wider one, is a split that overdrives our critical work if it means we cannot locate the conditions of thriving in harsh or oppressive circumstances.

Thelonious Monk survived a hard life in every sense, through a network of musicians, composers, family members, lovers and patrons, an internal compulsion to live in music and an unusual – really unusual – set of external gifts and capacities as player, composer, band leader and band member. Kelley's readers responded, I expect, to the equally composed story of Monk's life as one of glorious contribution when, at points, Monk mightn't even have survived. Such an account could be described as romantic, but it isn't necessarily; it is the condition of so many people and so many groups.

Monk's story is not queer, but Kelley's biography and his recognition of the 'global friendship' produced by expression – in music and writing about the musician – are instructive. One of my interests in Kelley's work, in addition to my own love of Monk's music, is what it contributes to a quasi-method I call 'reading for friendship'. It is an approach that might equally be applied to queer biography and history, and queer cultural production in the present. It lies in understanding how queer people outside the limited conditions of enfranchisement survive a homophobic world of class and racial hierarchy, drawing an account of those practices into a cultural critique devoted to sustenance and solidarity.

Friendship is a term familiar but undersung in cultural theory and social analysis. It is a form of relating no less determined by habitus[39] or the deep tastes and dispositions of class fractions; no less psychically complicated than family attachments and romance; no less painful than those other forms when it ends badly, nor less nostalgic when it fades. But it is potentially a different, more flexible good than other normative attachments. It is easier to come and go within, more responsive to circumstance, devoted and familiar, but perhaps less burdened by obligation, classical ideas of sameness and fit[40] or the deadening weight of *relationship work*. This last category Laura Kipnis[41] described as the adult obligation to always be fixing and improving one's primary romantic relationships, with lots of regularly-scheduled talk and, as often as not, therapeutic interventions in book or clinical form (Kipnis called it 'domesticity's gulag'). I work on relationships, but as a model for other social forms, friendship and its mixture of looseness and capacity can lighten things up. Amid political heaviness, this is an affective and social virtue, which is why *Love and Money* concludes with friendship's optimism in thinking about future class solidarities in queer life.

To open a new project of reading for friendship, here I take examples from Martin Duberman's biography *Hold Tight Gently: Michael Callen, Essex Hemphill, and the Battlefield of AIDS*,[42] especially about black American poet Essex Hemphill (1957–95); Jim Hubbard and Sarah Schulman's documentary video *United in Anger: A History of ACT-UP*, about the Aids Coalition to Unleash Power and the early AIDS crisis in the United States (a documentary rooted in their monumental project of recording, transcribing and accessibly archiving over 175 long-form, oral history interviews with those involved);[43] and *Pride*, a recent fiction film (UK, 2014) directed by Stephen Warchus and based on the lived story of solidarity between London lesbians and gays and striking coal miners in Wales' Dulais Valley. *Pride* is set in the mid-1980s, at the height of Margaret Thatcher's mine closures and her attack on the National Union of Mineworkers, among other labour organisations.

I read historian Martin Duberman's *Hold Tight Gently* with the heightened attention of someone who, briefly and modestly, called Essex Hemphill a friend. (I never met Michael Callen or saw him perform.) In 1993, Hemphill spoke at the Pennsylvania State University at my invitation, and thereafter we stayed in touch, occasionally exchanging notes and meeting for lunch in Philadelphia until the summer of 1995, at which point he was physically no longer able.

Hemphill died from complications related to AIDS on 5 November 1995 at the age of 38. I spoke with him on the telephone that autumn – briefly, as it was not easy for him – but I was not part of the close group who provided care, sometimes, as Duberman describes it, against the grain of Hemphill's desire for solitude.

In *Hold Tight Gently*, Duberman delivers a gift – an urgent biography, as urgent as Kelley's about Monk, comparing the lives, creativity, illness and deaths of two leading lights among US gay men in the 1980s and '90s, one – Callen – a white singer and songwriter, and another – Hemphill – a black poet, author and spoken-word performer. Callen and Hemphill never met – partly incidental but also an expression of racial segregation in gay circles, even young gay art circles of the period in New York, Washington, DC, and Philadelphia.

To read Duberman's account is to recognise disparities of access to medical, financial, social and even activist support among white and black gay men in the period, access which, predictably, privileged white men. It is also to recognise how deeply friendships structured both Hemphill's and Callen's lives. In queer art, like queer biography, friendships are everything – people's day-to-day relationships amid strain or disengagement from families of origin, the creative partnerships that command intimacy and surrender to criticism, the displays of faith and solidarity amid stress, loss and even a friend's withdrawal.

Hemphill's longest friendships and creative relationships were with poet and performer Wayson Jones and filmmaker and poet Michelle Parkerson. Hemphill met Jones in 1975, as teenage roommates at the University of Maryland, where they were assigned together, in a room designed for one, as the only African-Americans on their dormitory floor.[44] He met Parkerson in 1980 when they performed together at the Ascension Poetry Reading Series at Howard University's Founders Library.[45] Both Jones and Parkerson served among Hemphill's pallbearers in 1995, at a family funeral which, like so many other family ceremonies at the time for white and black gay men who had died of AIDS, made no mention of their homosexuality. 'We must always bury our dead twice', wrote black lesbian author and activist Barbara Smith in her 1998 tribute to James Baldwin, following a moving funeral that celebrated Baldwin's blackness so deeply and yet made no mention of his homosexuality, despite his candour in his own lifetime.[46]

Hemphill was a brilliant, demanding poet and critic, generative, not always simple to work or to live with. His friendships sometimes bore the brunt of his personal intensity and of the body and soul-taxing symptoms of HIV, but equally they rose on his clarity about the form and importance of love. At lunch in a West Philadelphia café in the summer of 1994, Hemphill told me he felt like the last surviving member of a high school class, having outlived most of the young contributors to *In the Life: A Black, Gay Anthology*[47] and

Brother to Brother: New Writings by Black, Gay Men,[48] both daring and beautiful collections in which he'd had a major part as author or editor. Essex survived his compatriot *In the Life* editor Joseph Beam, who died in 1988 and for whom Essex took over as editor of *Brother to Brother* in the late 1980s. A couple of years earlier, he had written to assure Joe that love would come, and to affirm his love as Joe's friend, his brother. Essex had recently separated from a lover and missed 'the domestic repetition of beauty that is found in caring for and being cared for by a lover'.[49] But, Duberman writes, Essex didn't want to dwell on his own complaints. He wanted simply to tell Joe

> quite frankly I love you, for the man you are, which is why I believe our friendship will be forever […] A friendship tied to concerns that when galvanised will [help] us all […] Please stay well in spirit, and believe love will come to you and make you stronger, but be strong, now, while it seems love is not near. And please know, we're brothers.[50]

Duberman's story about Hemphill is not all solidarity and light, though friendship is the medium of Hemphill's adult universe – of its highs and its lows but more importantly of the very fact of it, of his earthly presence. Not all his relations were friendly, but that doesn't challenge the condition of friendship as his social foundation. Friendship is equally the medium of Duberman's work; virtually all of his living sources for Callen's and Hemphill's stories were their friends, sometimes also their lovers then friends again.[51] Without friends, I would argue, there is no queer biography, any more than there was or is queer living with AIDS.

The class character of Hemphill's friendships is legible, if not through the direct language of class, which is rarely quoted in Duberman's work, though Duberman himself remains a Left author devoted to class questions in queer history. Hemphill and Jones were college students together, neither from well-to-do families though both able to make it to college through early histories of academic achievement and through scholarships, and to live, later, endowed with cultural capital as artists if not with economic security. Supported by both literary and speaking agents, Hemphill commanded a decent fee as campus speaker (and as his host on one campus, I can attest to his generosity and his expectation that he would contribute a great deal as campus guest). Still, as is true for so many artists, including those with some visibility and visionary weight in their own time and since, it was an uncertain existence normalised by bohemian habitus and community support. As Duberman's account makes clear, however, each of Hemphill's marked artistic performances in the 1980s and '90s, often with Jones and Parkerson, was hard-earned – occasions eked out of non-profit art networks and organisations in Philadelphia and

Lisa Henderson

Washington, DC. Together they made thrilling, watershed moments in black, queer, expressive life, moments that did not pay the rent. Nor did those performances guarantee the next such moment, or warm reception during the period from white gay and black heterosexual communities, boundaries that friends like Hemphill, Jones and Parkerson navigated together.[52]

Reading for friendship is one form of reading for thriving in raced and classed queer life. There is nothing essentially queer about thriving or friendship, though structural histories of exclusion and dependency heighten the role of queer friendship and group solidarity, as Duberman's work illustrates. Other examples, no less harrowing, are easy to find; indeed they become impossible to avoid once you start looking. In *United in Anger: A History of ACT UP*[53] filmmaker Jim Hubbard and co-producer Sarah Schulman tell the story of AIDS activism from the perspective of 'people in the trenches fighting the epidemic', fighting with hand-wrought research, sustained provocations to pharmaceutical and policy development, civil disobedience, media intervention, art, community health care and lots and lots of meetings. Members of ACT UP described themselves as a 'diverse, non-partisan group of individuals united in anger to end the AIDS crisis', and indeed *United in Anger* draws from oral history interviews with ACT UP New York members of many colours, genders, ages, and stations. Some interviewed in the film (e.g., surviving activists Ron Goldberg and Maxine Wolfe) comment on the reversal of privilege and entitlement that AIDS produced for so many professional, white men more or less accustomed to having what they needed (men whose image and audience had structured television's 'new queer visibility'). Where once they had housing, now they faced eviction; where once they had employment, now they faced discrimination; where once they had medical insurance, now they faced uninsurability; where once they could expect expert medical care, now they were medically reviled or isolated by haughty inexpertise; where once they could count on family support, now so many families turned their backs. The withdrawal of privilege radicalised many people with AIDS (PWAs) in the AIDS activist movement: 'nothing', says Goldberg in the film, 'gets people riled up like entitlement being taken away'. But from that energy had to be wrought a programme of multi-issue organising – recognising, for example, the intersection of HIV and long-standing racial and class discrimination in housing, employment and medical access for African-American, Latino and poor white people with AIDS (the discrimination that confronted Hemphill) and thus recognising the need to act up on multiple fronts.

United in Anger also tells the story of conscious affinity as the basis for safety and effectiveness in activist sub-groups (a strategy borrowed from civil rights activism), and of organising across populations and self-interest, for example young men with AIDS committing their remaining years to fighting for the recognition and differential care of women with AIDS. Surviving activist Jim Eigo comments on affinity groups – themed assemblages of people with a particular claim in the AIDS movement who would lay down their bodies together in dangerous public encounters with detractors and antagonists, usually security forces and the police:

> Affinity groups, if they worked, when they worked, for their lifetime could be almost like these close-knit communities. But if an affinity group did something that put your bodies on the line, risked arrest and sometimes actually did arrest – I'll speak at least for myself – my fear level was always very high and I don't know if I could have done it without a group of people which I felt close to, I'd seen in similar situations, lots liked, trusted, and several of them loved, some of them I was as close to as any people I have been in my life.

Later in the film, Maxine Wolfe, a feminist and activist veteran of many social movements, speaks to the commitment of men in ACT UP working on a four-year campaign to recognise women of all colours with AIDS, whose symptoms did not resemble those of male PWAs and who were thus excluded from AIDS trials and treatment programmes authorised by the official definition of the disease from the Centers for Disease Control (CDC).

> People came together to work on that that *everybody* said would not work together, and that's what was amazing about it. My affinity group had twenty-four people in it, and only seven of us were women, okay? And several of the men had HIV, and several of them are dead at this point, okay? They spent four years working on a campaign about changing the CDC definition for women, and for poor people, and for drug users, and that is something that no one ever talks about in ACT UP. You know it's gay white men, gay white men, gay white men, you know selfish gay white men, and that was not […] You know, we got tremendous support in ACT UP for that work.[54]

Wolfe's comment does not deny fractiousness, self-interest or confusion in ACT UP, but recognises critical occasions of integration and solidarity – occasions to return to in producing historical accounts and activist futures (using, perhaps *United in Anger* and its free programmes for community and activist development).[55]

Finally, it is easy to read for friendship across sexuality and social class in the recent independent release *Pride*, a deliriously encouraging feature film based on a solidarity group in London called Lesbians and Gays Support the Miners (LGSM), who, led by Mark Ashton, a gay, socialist activist from Northern Ireland, began collecting money for striking miners at parades and in front of London's long- and still-standing Marchmont Street bookstore Gay's the Word. At the outset, LGSM didn't have a particular group of miners in mind, though one member, himself Welsh, proposed finding a union chapter in the Dulais Valley of South Wales. Asked in *Pride* by news reporters why gays would support the miners amid Thatcherite economic retrenchment in the United Kingdom (with an incredulity that assumed British miners were as likely as their stereotypical US blue collar workers to manifest authoritarian contempt for homosexuality), Ashton responded in two ways. Like gays and lesbians, he said, miners had long endured aggression and demonisation from the public and the police, so they had that experience in common. Besides, they performed dangerous and difficult jobs – mining coal – that made it possible for others to live, work and dance, jobs, that is, that Ashton himself didn't want to do.

Below, Ashton speaks to an interviewer for a community video documentary released in 1986, titled *All Out! Dancing in Dulais*.[56] This is not his character in *Pride* speaking (played by Ben Schnetzer) but Ashton himself, in the video that became the inspiration for the feature and much of its dialogue, released 28 years later.

> *Mark Ashton*: The group started off in July, after Gay Pride, so that one community could give solidarity to the other, right? When you think about it is quite illogical to actually say 'well, I'm gay, and I'm into defending the gay community, but I don't care about anything else'. It's ludicrous. It's important that if you're defending communities, that you're also defending all communities, not just one, and that's one of the reasons, really the main reason that I'm involved.
> *Interviewer* (unidentified): Yeah, but a lot of people would say, you know, if you're collecting, 'why should we support the miners, the miners don't support us'. What do you tell people who say that to you?
> *Ashton*: Well, what do you mean when you say the miners don't support us? The miners dig coal, which creates fuel, which actually makes electricity. People … I mean, would you go down a mine and work? I wouldn't like to go down a mine and work. One of the reasons I support miners is because they go down and do it. I wouldn't do it.

(And later)

> *Ashton*: It's not just about defending the miners, it's about defending the right to organise. It's about defence organisations, which unions are. We've

got a gay community, we need a good gay defence organisation. That's what CHE [Campaign for Homosexuality Equality, established in 1964] should be. The miners and workers need defence organisations, and that's what unions are. And what this strike's about is smashing those defence organisations, and smashing their unions. And I'm not going to stand up for that, 'cause you start that and there's no stopping it.

It is easy to watch *Pride* and, from the paranoid position of bleakness as truth, dismiss its feel-good energy, its recreation of the 'Pits and Perverts' benefit ball with Bronski Beat at the Electric Ballroom in Camden, its tender-hearted recognition between members of a deeply familial but economically shaken community in Wales and a threadbare, bohemian group of lesbians and gays in London, many of whose members had (and would) endure family rejection.

Such a response, however, would say as much about the respondent as the circumstances that *Pride* depicts and the feelings it offers. The solidarities in the feature film are paired with community squabbles, and they are also underwritten by truths from the historical record which are portrayed in the film and mustn't be set aside by critics. These were not feel-good times: police oppression of striking miners was violent and well-documented; the strikers lost and returned to work defeated and depleted; events in the film took place in 1984, just as AIDS and HIV were beginning to be recognised as an illness moving among and eventually killing gay men (Ashton himself died in 1987, one year after *All Out! Dancing in Dulais* was released); at the London Pride parade of 1985, busloads of miners arrived to support LGSM and gay politics at large; later that year, it was a bloc vote from the National Union of Mineworkers that finally put gay rights on the agenda of Britain's Labour Party.

And there were, of course, gay miners and gay members of mining communities, including in South Wales (something *Pride* recognises), and gay activists who came from mining and other working class contexts, like Ashton. There are also comparable American records of gay/labour coalitions in the 1970s and '80s, for example, those undertaken by San Francisco activist and city supervisor candidate Harvey Milk. In 1977, Milk joined forces with the Teamsters Union to get Coors beer out of gay bars in San Francisco's Castro district, in support of striking Coors workers.[57] Coors was anti-union and, in its family-owned corporate policy, openly anti-homosexual. Milk and the Teamsters' gay/labour coalition was formed in solidarity against a common antagonist, Coors, in terms reminiscent of Ashton's analysis of gay and lesbian support of Welsh miners. There are also gay teamsters, and lots of beer-drinking queers.

Lisa Henderson

Conclusion: Taking Care of Our Blessings

In 'An Old Queen's Tale', downtown New York City performance artist Penny Arcade's recent love letter to Christopher Street, Arcade writes:

> When I speak to young queers who want to know the differences between today and back then I say quietly, 'Show me one twenty-seven-year-old queer guy who is going to take in a homeless seventeen-year-old girl. Back then we knew we had to take care of each other [...] It was humane and inclusive [...] Everyone recognised their people intuitively.[58]

Queer history is full of community friendship and protection across the lines of gender, class and race. Friendship is sustenance in queer life; it reorganises class and queer boundaries (even where, on other occasions, it entrenches them), it mixes class within queer communities and it offers imperfect solidarities in states of crisis. To borrow a term from Essex Hemphill, it is a blessing, one to be cared for equally by friends, critics and activists against the grain of professional ascent and its social, economic and political exclusions.

Sometimes, the intersection of queerness and class in my examples is explicit; at other times it must be drawn out by reading the situation even where the word 'class' does not appear. That is not opportunistic, but an analytic gesture that corresponds to a familiar form of social competency. We know when we are crossing class lines as well as we know the traversal of gender and race. To do so from the prospect of friendship rather than the presumption of sameness or difference reorganises feeling, not towards 'feeling good' but 'feeling solidary'. It offers critics and other actors a chance to re-articulate their critical practice away from the diminishing position of paranoia.

Those who read Essex Hemphill or were fortunate to have heard and seen him perform know that he closed his performances, essays and even correspondences with the phrase 'take care of your blessings'. This handful of examples of queer friendship amid stress are not infrastructures, but they speak to the prospect of repair, a move toward an intentional and analytic form of care for the social blessing and cultural-political resource of solidarity. The recognition and practice of these gestures are not the state, the wage, the union or the apparatus, and thus they are not the means of redistribution as we familiarly imagine them. But reading them releases affects and energies to be returned to and accrued against the tide of political depression. They express a social form of queerness which has a rich archive in North America, the United Kingdom and elsewhere, and that it is never too late to rekindle against the class and race protectionism that has come to define gay enfranchisement.

University of Massachusetts, Amherst

Notes

1 Passages in the early part of this article first appeared in my book *Love and Money: Queers, Class, and Cultural Production* (New York: New York University Press, 2013). Thanks to David Alderson and Liliana Herakova for their editorial generosity and care.
2 Pierre Bourdieu, *Distinction: A Social Critique of the Judgment of Taste* (Cambridge, MA: Harvard University Press, 1984), esp. Ch. 1, 'The Aristocracy of Culture', 1–96.
3 Raymond Williams, *Culture and Society, 1780–1950* (New York: Columbia University Press, 1958), 295–358.
4 Alan O'Connor, *Raymond Williams* (New York: Rowman and Littlefield, 2006), 5.
5 Lisa Henderson, 'Communication, Sexuality, Defamiliarisation', *International Journal of Communication* 7 (2013): 2468–81.
6 Kimberlé Crenshaw, 'Mapping the Margins: Intersectionality, Identity Politics, and Violence Against Women of Colour', *Stanford Law Review* 43, no. 6 (1991): 1241–99
7 Louis Althusser, 'Contradiction and Overdetermination', in *For Marx*, trans. Ben Brewster (London: Verso, 2005 [1969]), 87–128.
8 Martin Duberman, *Hold Tight Gently: Michael Callen, Essex Hemphill, and the Battlefield of AIDS* (New York and London: The New Press, 2014), 1–3.
9 Martin Duberman, 'The Divided Left: Identity Politics versus Class', in *Left Out: The Politics of Exclusion: Essays 1964–2002* (Cambridge, MA: South End Press, 2002), 451–68, esp. 464–7.
10 Larry Gross, *Contested Closets: The Politics and Ethics of Outing* (Minneapolis: University of Minnesota Press, 1993), esp. 1–14.
11 See Daniel Wickberg, 'Homophobia: On the Cultural History of an Idea', *Critical Inquiry* 27, no. 1 (2000): 42–57. Wickberg unbraids the development of a post-war liberal critique of the 'authoritarian personality' – intolerant, irrational, fearful, traditional – and the use of that figure to understand 'homophobia', coined in the early 1970s. Studies of the time used authoritarian personality inventories to demonstrate that those with 'high homophobia scores [are] more likely to (a) live in the South and Midwest, (b) have less education, and (c) have strict religious beliefs', all also considered sources of working-class retrenchment in contrast to liberalism's self-image (55).
12 Henderson, *Love and Money*.
13 Eve Kosofsky Sedgwick, 'Paranoid Reading and Reparative Reading, or, You're So Paranoid, You Probably Think This Essay is About You', in *Touching Feeling: Affect, Pedagogy, Performativity* (Durham, NC: Duke University Press, 2003), 123–53.
14 Sedgwick, 'Paranoid Reading', 130–1.
15 Julia Bryan-Wilson, 'Some Kind of Grace: An Interview with Miranda July', *Camera Obscura* 55, no. 19:1 (2004): 196.
16 Larry M. Bartels, *Unequal Democracy: The Political Economy of the New Gilded Age* (Princeton: Princeton University Press, 2008), 24.
17 Thomas Piketty, *Capital in the Twenty-First Century* (Cambridge, MA: Belknap Press, 2014).
18 See Escoffier on the emergence of a 'hyper-commodification homo-economy' in the late 1990s. Jeffrey Escoffier, 'The Political Economy of the Closet: Notes toward an Economic History of Gay and Lesbian Life Before Stonewall', in *Homo Economics: Capitalism, Community, and Lesbian and Gay Life*, ed. Amy Gluckman and Betsy Reed (New York, Routledge, 1997), 123–34, esp. 124.
19 On the particular punishments visited upon transgender people in employment, immigration, police brutality, incarceration, medical care and housing, see Dean Spade, *Normal Life: Administrative Violence, Critical Trans Politics and the Limits of Law* (Cambridge,

20 MA: South End Press, 2011), esp. 'Introduction: Rights, Movements, and Critical Trans Politics' (19–48) and 'Trans Law and Politics on a Neoliberal Landscape' (49–78).
20 Richard Florida, *The Rise of the Creative Class: And How It's Transforming Work, Leisure, Community, and Everyday Life* (New York: Basic Books, 2003).
21 Judith Butler, 'Merely Cultural', *Social Text* 52/53, no. 15 (1997): 265–77, esp. 265.
22 In addition to marking the class overtones of 'gay' versus 'queer', hereafter I use queer more generally as an omnibus term to signify sexual and gender nonconformity in popular culture.
23 Amanda Lotz, 'Textual (Im)possibilities in the US Post-network Era: Negotiating Production and Promotion Processes on Lifetime's *Any Day Now*', *Critical Studies in Media Communication* 21, no. 1 (2004): 23.
24 Ronald Becker, 'Prime Time Television in the Gay 90s: Network Television, Quality Audiences, and Gay Politics', *The Velvet Light Trap* 42 (1998), 36–47, quoted in Lotz, 'Textual (Im)possibilities', 38.
25 Sherry Ortner, *New Jersey Dreaming: Capital, Culture and the Class of '58* (Durham, NC: Duke University Press, 2003), 13.
26 Judith Butler, *Gender Trouble* (New York: Routledge, 1990), 194–203.
27 Williams, *Culture and Society*, 336.
28 Sedgwick, 'Paranoid Reading', 128–9, 150.
29 J.K. Gibson-Graham, *A Postcapitalist Politics* (Minneapolis: University of Minnesota Press, 2006), 7–9.
30 Gibson-Graham, *A Postcapitalist Politics*, 4.
31 Gibson-Graham, *A Postcapitalist Politics*, 8.
32 Gibson-Graham, *A Postcapitalist Politics*, 8.
33 Williams, *Culture and Society*, 336.
34 Williams, *Culture and Society*, 337.
35 Tom Roach, *Friendship as a Way of Life: Foucault, AIDS, and the Politics of Shared Estrangement* (Albany: SUNY Press, 2012), 2.
36 Kath Weston, *Families We Choose: Lesbians, Gays, Kinship* (New York: Columbia University Press, 1991), esp. Ch. 5, 103–36.
37 Thelonious Monk quoted in Robin D.G. Kelley, *Thelonious Monk: An American Original* (New York: Free Press, 2010), xv.
38 Kelley, *Thelonious Monk*, xv.
39 Bourdieu, *Distinction*, 101.
40 In the tradition of Aristotle and then Shakespeare, friendship was, first, an expression of likeness, of the self in another. See Laurie Shannon, 'The Early Modern Politics of Likeness: Sovereign Reader-Subjects and Listening Kings', in *Sovereign Amity: Figures of Friendship in Shakespearean Contexts* (Chicago: University of Chicago Press, 2001), 17–53.
41 Laura Kipnis, *Against Love: A Polemic* (New York: Pantheon, 2003), 52.
42 Duberman, *Hold Tight Gently*.
43 Actuporalhistory.org.
44 Duberman, *Hold Tight Gently*, 27.
45 Duberman, *Hold Tight Gently*, 30.
46 Barbara Smith, 'We Must Always Bury Our Dead Twice: A Tribute to James Baldwin', in *The Truth That Never Hurts: Writings on Race, Gender, and Freedom* (New Brunswick, NJ: Rutgers University Press, 1998), 75–80.
47 Joseph Beam, ed., *In the Life: A Black Gay Anthology* (New York: Alyson Books, 1986).
48 Essex Hemphill, ed., *Brother to Brother: New Writings by Black Gay Men* (New York: Alyson Books, 1991).
49 Duberman, *Hold Tight Gently*, 107.

50   Duberman, *Hold Tight Gently*, 108.
51   Duberman, *Hold Tight Gently*, 306.
52   Jones continued as composer and performer, then moved to painting and visual art, where he sustains a career. Parkerson has had several academic appointments as an award-winning filmmaker and film teacher, most recently (and enduringly) at her *alma mater* Temple University in Philadelphia. She lectures widely and is currently principal in Eye of the Storm Productions in Washington, DC, a production company she founded. Both Parkerson and Jones survived as working artists, with regard and hopefully with greater security as their careers evolved. On Jones, see his website, http://waysonjones.com/home.html (accessed 28 April 2015). On Parkerson, see the programme and biography from Scribe Video Centre (Philadelphia) 'Eye of the Storm: The Films of Michelle Parkerson', http://www.scribe.org/about/eyestormfilmsmichelleparkerson (accessed 28 April 2015).
53   Jim Hubbard, dir., *United in Anger: A History of ACT UP* (New York, 2012), DVD.
54   For a distinctive collection of essays by lesbians and gay men writing about their lives together (including, sometimes, across class and race) see Joan Nestle and John Preston (eds), *Sister and Brother: Lesbians and Gay Men Write about Their Lives Together* (Toronto: Harper Collins Canada: 1995).
55   '*United in Anger* Activist Guide', http://www.unitedinanger.com/activist-guide/ (accessed 20 August 2014).
56   *All Out: Dancing in Dulais* is embedded in full in Kate Kellaway, 'When Miners and Gay Activists United: The Real Story of the Film *Pride*', *The Guardian* (US Edition), 31 August 2014, http://www.theguardian.com/film/2014/aug/31/pride-film-gay-activists-miners-strike-interview (accessed 27 April 2015).
57   Michael Roberts, 'A Brewing Disagreement', *Westword*, 27 June 2002, http://www.westword.com/news/a-brewing-disagreement-5070883 (accessed 18 March 2015).
58   Penny Arcade, 'An Old Queen's Tale', *Lambda Literary Review*, 11 June 2012, http://www.lambdaliterary.org/features/06/11/penny-arcade-an-old-queens-tale/ (accessed 18 March 2015).

Is the Queen Dead? Effeminacy, Homosociality and the Post-Homophobic Queer

Stephen Maddison

Abstract: Gay effeminacy has historically been associated with deferential class identifications, pathologising medical discourses, lingering intimations of self-loathing and restrictively safe and desexed images of our acceptability. It has also, crucially, been associated with an extraordinary range of dissident opportunities.

What of effeminacy today? Does the effeminate queen remain a central part of gay cultures that increasingly seem defined by assimilation and homonormativity?

In this context some academic studies have suggested that traditional cultures of homosocial masculinity, structured by phobic anxieties about male same-sex intimacy, are in decline, and that in their place we're witnessing the emergence of 'softer' and more 'inclusive' masculinities.

This article attempts to consider the implications of these apparently new forms of masculinity, by considering the modes of power being 'softened' and 'diversified' here, and for what kinds of men (and women). Are we witnessing a radical breakthrough in the range of permissible forms of intimacy and self-expression available to men? And if so, has the effeminate queen finally been rendered historically and culturally obsolete? Are softer masculinities symptomatic of renegotiations in the sphere of gender power or are they a function of changes in the nature of work and the responsibilities of affective and immaterial labour?

*

Alan Sinfield has suggested that 'effeminacy has over manliness the advantage of being a central gay cultural tradition which we may proudly assert'.[1] If gay effeminacy has been historically complex, potentially tying us to deferential class identifications, to pathologising medical discourses, to lingering intimations of self-loathing and to restrictively safe and desexed images of our acceptability, it is also the case, as Sinfield acknowledges, that effeminacy has afforded an extraordinary range of dissident opportunities to gay cultures.

Gay culture has historically manifested the abundant fault lines in the prevailing accounts of sexuality and gender inherited from medical, political and social commentary, from the birth of sexology onwards. In the late 1980s, Joseph Bristow suggested that 'gay men are out to show that we are not "pansies", "poofs", "faggots", "queers" – all those feminizing and, implicitly, misogynistic insults first heard at school and which remain with us for the rest of our lives'.[2] In 1983 Richard Dyer noted that the effeminate queen and the butch dyke have been associated with 'failing' to be 'real women or men' and 'are thus often seen as tragic, pathetic, wretched, despicable, comic or ridiculous figures'.[3] Yet elsewhere Dyer has noted that as a young gay man attempting to forge an identity he was positively drawn to culture and the arts because of its associations with sensitivity and femininity: 'being queer was not being a man'.[4] Earlier still, in 1976, Dyer had suggested that 'camping about is not butch [...] camp is a way of being human, witty and vital [...] without conforming to the drabness and rigidity of the hetero male role'.[5] Again, however, he registers the ambiguity of effeminacy, noting that 'one of the sadder features of the gay movement is the down so many activists have on queens and camp – on the only heritage we've got'.[6] Eric Anderson has suggested that 'camp culture [...] served to show heterosexuals that we [...] were not afraid of them'.[7] Controversy surrounding the Austrian winner of the 2014 Eurovision Song Contest, Conchita Wurst, would indicate that camp culture remains challenging. Wurst's win became an international political event, simultaneously hailed as a 'victory [...] for tolerance and respect'[8] and as a 'freak show'[9] that signalled 'the end of Europe'.[10] Wurst, aka Tom Neuwirth, has been described as an 'emphatically [...] gay male performer rather than being trans' whose 'look is perhaps Eurovision's most genderqueer yet [...] a drag queen with a beard [...] this is not the comedy butch bloke in a frock look but something altogether more striking (and apparently hard for many people to compute)'.[11]

These accounts of the tribulations of effeminacy indicate some of the ways in which contemporary gay identities have struggled to reconcile same-sex passion with gender roles, identifications and structures.[12] They indicate the vexed history of a concept that has been seen as emblematically oppressive and self-hating, and indicative of gay men's troubled relationship with women and feminism. Effeminacy is politically significant and life-affirming as a resistance to gender expectations – a bulwark against drab gender conformity, yet self-hating and misogynistic. Effeminacy is historically and culturally vital ('the only heritage we've got') yet inherently a symbol of failure. But what of effeminacy today? If effeminacy has historically posed a series of political and cultural dilemmas for gay men, does it continue to do so? Does the effeminate queen remain a central or significant part of gay culture?

In this article I aim to situate effeminacy culturally and historically in order to attempt to locate some of its political effects. I will be drawing on two key works in queer theory in order to do this: firstly, Alan Sinfield's *The Wilde Century* and, secondly, Eve Kosofsky Sedgwick's *Between Men*. Sinfield's work allows us to isolate the cultural moment in which the ideas of effeminacy and male same-sex desire became conflated, and Sedgwick's allows us to understand the leverage exerted by this conflation upon the field of masculinity. Insights drawn from both will then be used to critique work by Anderson on new patterns of 'inclusive' masculinity which apparently evidence an emerging post-homophobic environment; I suggest that such environments merely work to underwrite the ubiquity of masculinity as both a site of desire and of aspirational identification for gay culture. Finally, I aim to consider the idea of effeminacy in the context of neoliberal capital and the enterprise culture in order to consider whether gender dissent, 'refusing to be a man', can offer gay culture a way out of the impasse of identity politics and a way of imagining resistance to neoliberal biopolitics, which despite offering affluent gays consumer entitlements, continues to underwrite structural inequality. If the contemporary historical conjuncture is characterised by both an increasing public tolerance of diversity and a decline in the social and welfare obligations of the state,[13] the legal equality of gays in advanced neoliberal democracies can almost be taken for granted. Whilst some gay liberation ideology was characterised by social radicalism, the current privileges afforded to gays are largely a function of consumer freedoms and the competitive individualisation propagated by neoliberal ideology.[14] In this context, Lois McNay has suggested that 'individual autonomy becomes not the opposite of, or limit to, neoliberal governance, rather it lies at the heart of its disciplinary control'.[15]

Effeminacy and *The Wilde Century*

Sinfield's *The Wilde Century* offers a key contribution to the literature on the question of effeminacy. Published in 1994, at the high water mark of optimism of the emerging discipline of queer theory, and drawing on a legacy of radical literary work in cultural materialism, Sinfield's highly influential account benefits from both a long historical view and a sense of urgency informed by the flowering confidence of lesbian and gay intellectual work in a post-AIDS environment. Sinfield traces the history of the association of effeminacy with male same-sex passion, his starting point being the acknowledgement of a series of serious discontinuities between accounts of same-sex intimacy and accounts of effeminacy that lead him to suggest that it was only through the trials of Oscar Wilde in 1895 that a clear association between the two became instated. Even up to the point of Wilde's literary and cultural notoriety, the equation of effeminacy with same-sex passion was not fixed: Sinfield suggests that 'effeminacy was still flexible, with the potential to refute homosexuality, as well as to imply it'.[16] It was in the midst of a set of moral panics about manliness and sexual propriety that the Wilde trials took place, and 'as a consequence, the entire, vaguely disconcerting nexus of effeminacy, leisured idleness, immorality, luxury, insouciance, decadence and aestheticism, which Wilde was perceived as instantiating, was transformed into a brilliantly precise image'.[17] This intelligibility of the queer subject, sexualised and recognisable in appearance and manner, operates as a 'Wilde-shaped silence'; famously, Maurice in E.M. Forster's novel fears becoming 'an unspeakable of the Oscar Wilde sort'.[18]

What are the key problems associated with the effeminate homosexual as he emerges from the Early Modern period onwards, through Mollies and leisured dandies, finally to become emblematically identifiable in the figure of Wilde? Firstly, from the point of view of that effeminate homosexual himself, Sinfield suggests that 'the effeminate model of queerness', as manifested in the late twentieth-century archetype of Quentin Crisp, 'was precisely self-defeating'.[19] Tracking an inversionist notion of same-sex desire, the effeminate homosexual, bearing the soul of a woman trapped in his man's (if not manly) body, desires a 'real' man, but a 'real' man doesn't go with other men, and thus reciprocal homosexual desire is impossible. The legacy of inversionist accounts continues to constitute patterns not only of desire in contemporary gay culture but of identification too. We might see the fixation of gay porn and gay sexual cultures (erotic fiction, Tumblr, personal ads, magazines, calendars, fashion and fetish wear, and so on) with a highly masculinised, putatively heterosexual figure, as at best a hegemonic and ubiquitous aspirational ideal and at worst a hysterically overdetermined counter-identification with contemporary genderqueer notions and historical third sex accounts of queer male identity.

Secondly, the concept of the effeminate homosexual rests on a medical model of homosexuality which, according to Sinfield, sets up a 'cross-sex grid' that designates masculine and feminine traits attached to men and women respectively, locking in place expectations associated with sexual activity and passivity and social and cultural agency.[20] Sinfield is clearly right in problematising the naturalising effect of such binary structures, yet his critique is itself weakened by a residual investment in the homo/hetero binary: 'feminine and masculine are cultural constructs, obviously with the primary function of sustaining the current pattern of heterosexual relations'.[21] How far would we agree that this *is* the primary function of femininity and masculinity? Do gender roles police sexuality and a specific form of heterosexuality, as Sinfield seems to be suggesting here, or does sexuality police gender in order to protect men's interests? Gender may signify through highly overdetermined, eroticised and commodified performances and aesthetic codes, but what it signifies is a structurally unequal distribution of social, cultural and political power. The issue in considering gay gender dissent is the extent to which our practices of gender reinforce or trouble this distribution of power. If we collapse notions of gay identity and culture back into desire and sexuality without a political engagement with gender, we obscure the extent to which those desires potentially underwrite the signifying practices and structural conditions not only of homophobia but of a patriarchy that has become stronger, not weaker, in the era of neoliberal ideology and the metrosexual. I will return to this problematic in relation to the question of homosociality presently.

Thirdly, there is the legacy of biologism in relation to what Sinfield refers to as the question of 'who we are'.[22] Sinfield suggests that 'our terms – "gay", "lesbian", "lesbian and gay" […] are markers of political allegiance, far more than ways of having or thinking about sex'.[23] Anxieties about macho and effeminate formations articulate the difficulty 'we' gay men have in finding conducive modes of identity in hostile conditions, and reactions to this difficulty tend to seesaw between poles of Sinfield's cross-sex grid. In this context, 'dumping effeminacy because it has been stigmatised hardly seems heroic' and indeed, 'macho-man has a good deal in common with the effeminate, Wildean tradition – not surprisingly, since he is premised on a comparable acceptance of the masculine/feminine binary structure'.[24] Sinfield suggests that 'effeminacy, is founded in misogyny […] The function of effeminacy as a concept, is to police sexual categories, keeping them pure. The effects of such policing extend vastly beyond lesbians and gay men'.[25] However, this rehearses a problem that the schematic offered in *The Wilde Century* can't resolve; the cross-sex grid is indeed restrictive and oppressive in a range of ways, but its ideological and material force is not primarily concerned with inscribing multitudinous queer identities as deviant, pathological or socially unacceptable. As we shall see below, Sedgwick has suggested that homophobia is merely a secondary effect of the larger project of maintaining an 'exchange-of-women framework'.[26] The 'terrorist potential' of 'blackmailability' arising from subjecting all men to a homosexual 'panic' arises from their inability to determine whether their bonds with other men are homosexual.[27] In this context, 'dumping effeminacy' not only lacks heroism but actually colludes with, and reinforces, gender inequality and the homophobia it inscribes. If we are to find a dissident negotiation of gender, then we need to address ourselves to the effects of the policing of sexual categories Sinfield alludes to above, a project which is beyond the scope of *The Wilde Century*.

As a rejoinder to the difficulties associated with negotiating the Wildean model, Sinfield asserts the importance of gay subculture, and offers a critique of the idea of working for mainstream acceptance: 'this is self-oppressed […] the centre takes what it wants, and under pressure will abuse and abandon the subcultures it has plundered'.[28] What is the political objective here? And how is it to be assessed? The move to abandon a desire to be tolerable is surely right, but to what extent does the claim for a dissident subculture resolve the problem of effeminacy, macho-man and the cross-sex grid? Sinfield suggests that 'lesbians and gay men have long been perceived as disturbing conventional categories – masculine souls in feminine bodies and so on – and it hasn't got us very far',[29] but far where? Far along which road, and to what end? *The Wilde Century* concludes with a series of contemporary case studies, designed to celebrate gay culture and avoid demonising its varieties and to posit a subcultural dissidence based in flexibility and cunning, with the objective of improving the life chances and experiences of lesbian and gay people – examples given include overcoming experiences of shameful fantasy and obscure frustration, not being prosecuted for soliciting, having your child taken away, and so on.[30] These case studies aim to animate historical and conceptual theorising for a subcultural audience, and such a move characterises Sinfield's self-consciousness about the politics of being a queer intellectual: he is working to clarify not only what is at stake in cultural theorising for marginal subcultures, but why public intellectuals have a responsibility to the subcultures of which they are a product. But this important project notwithstanding, even at the time Sinfield was writing it was becoming clear that far from inhibiting the social progress of certain kinds of gay men, lesbians and queers, the prevailing ideologies of neoliberal capital were enabling their advancement and consolidating their economic and social privileges. Many of the specific political goals Sinfield offers in *The Wilde Century* have since been achieved, largely in the name of promoting neoliberal competitive individualism.[31]

In this context, what does being gay or lesbian mean, politically? And once we've achieved a degree of protection from having our lifestyles and choices punished and discriminated against, do we need to be gay or lesbian any more? This is an argument pursued by James Penney in his recent book *After Queer Theory*. He argues that the rise of identity politics, which he suggests reached its apogee in the 1990s when Sinfield published *The Wilde Century*, has been exploited by ideologies of liberal democracy and multinational capital that have offered fragmented identity groups important concessions, thereby forcing us 'to abandon ambitious agendas for social change as the price paid for the defence of hard-fought victories on the terrain of race, gender and sexuality'.[32] Again, I will return to this below.

From Homosociality to 'Inclusive' Masculinity?

Sedgwick's concept of male homosocial relations has been highly influential. In her account, homosocial bonds describe relations between men, be they intimate, combative, competitive or collegial, through which the authority and centrality of men's interests are secured. In the homosocial network, women are exchanged as tokens of social desire between men, and homosexuality is constantly conjured as a visible and threatening proximity to the interior plausibility of masculinity. Sedgwick suggests that male homosocial bonds maintain a functional relationship with homosexuality that acts as a policing mechanism: 'the result has been a structural residue of terrorist potential, of *blackmailability*, of Western maleness through the leverage of homophobia'.[33] Sedgwick's formation of homosociality has been influential because it addressed many problems that have haunted homosexual identity categories. Here, any residual understanding of homophobia as caused by latent or repressed homosexuality was debunked: all male relations, according to Sedgwick, are circumscribed by homoeroticism, by virtue of the instability of being a 'man's man'; this doesn't mean that all men are latently homosexual, but that masculinity is predicated on an identification not only with the materiality of male power but the symbols and aesthetics of that power. In the homosocial model, masculinity is governed not by fear of male intimacy, but by fear of feminisation; effeminacy is not a property of queers, but a fear organising masculinity itself and transposed on to queers. Homophobia is fear of being a feminised man, of inadequately demonstrating actual and potential exchange of women and of being unable to display the social and economic privileges attendant on such exchange.

For the present project, the key challenge of applying Sedgwick's mapping of homosocial structures to the contemporary question of effeminacy is the status of homophobia. For Sedgwick, homophobia exerts 'definitional leverage over the whole range of male bonds that shape the social constitution' and is a '*necessary* consequence of such patriarchal institutions as heterosexual marriage'.[34] But gayness isn't as foreign or feared as it was in 1985, at least not in the overdeveloped North. As Finn Bowring has pointed out, the 2010 British Social Attitudes survey showed a 'radical thawing in people's conservative attitudes to same-sex relationships'.[35] And this view is supported by a number of smaller studies of traditionally homosocial environments, such as team sports and schools, where once we would have expected to find virulent homophobia but instead may now discern patterns of a 'softer' masculinity. Mark McCormack has suggested that 'homophobia maintains markedly less significance in twenty-first century Britain and America than it used to'.[36]

McCormack undertook an ethnographic study of three state secondary schools in the south of England and documents evidence of heterosexual students 'espousing pro-gay attitudes, being inclusive of gay students, condemning homophobia, and having close friendships with gay students'.[37] Furthermore, he asserts that 'there is a total absence of evidence suggesting that homophobia is present or esteemed'.[38] McCormack concludes that 'the stigma now attached to homophobia indicates that the concept of gay equality has become dominant [...] even if this has yet to be fully realised'.[39]

For any of us with school experiences radically less tolerant and inclusive than those described in McCormack's study, his work is not only politically welcome but emotionally reparative. But despite his optimism, we should be wary of overstating the case for a post-homophobic environment; whilst it is clear that things are improving for LGBT people in a range of contexts, the studies that show these improvements derive from precise social circumstances. In the US a report published in 2010 and based on the FBI's national hate crime statistics found that LGBT people were 'far more likely than any other minority group in the United States to be victimised by violent hate crime'.[40] And in the context of the cultural environment in the UK, the Archbishop of Canterbury remains opposed to gay marriage, despite its legalisation, because he believes the Church of England's potential support for it would have a 'catastrophic' effect on Christians in South Sudan, Pakistan and Nigeria.[41] Here, an assumption of the social tolerability of homophobia underwrites a call on gay people to put aside their interests and subscribe to hegemonic racist 'truths' in the name of a 'civilising' Christian mission. That his statements met with such little opprobrium in the mainstream press indicates the residual authority of mutually reinforcing ideologies of colonialism and homophobia in UK culture, to say nothing of a powerful and troubling anti-secularism that is increasingly offsetting liberal advances made by queers. In 2013 Stonewall published research that showed that one in six lesbian, gay and bisexual people had experienced a homophobic hate crime or incident in the previous three years.[42]

McCormack's work is predicated on a framework of so-called 'inclusive masculinity' proposed by Anderson in his studies of team sports and fraternities in the US and UK. 'Inclusive' masculinity, according to Anderson, describes conditions in which we might find Connell's notion of 'hegemonic' masculinity subject to flux, under pressure from a decline in 'homohysteria' and a rise in the stigma associated with overt displays of homophobia.[43] In such circumstances, 'multiple forms of equally esteemed inclusive masculinities exist, even if heterosexism persists'.[44] But the conditions under consideration here are ones in which white middle-class young college men are experiencing a high degree of entitlement and little threat: far from demonstrating a liberalisation of the possibilities of being a man, these college jocks tolerate variations as long as they reinforce the power and desirability of masculinity.

An acknowledgement of the reactionary nature of 'inclusive' masculinity haunts Anderson's theorising of it: 'while decreased sexism is a characteristic of an inclusive culture of masculinities, it does not guarantee social parity for women' but 'there should at least be *some* social benefit for women'.[45] Such feeble optimism points to a failure to connect the idea of inclusive masculinity to a structure of homosociality, and Anderson indicates this failure in his conclusion, where he suggests that 'inclusivity and the ability to homosocially bond is simply the byproduct of decreasing homohysteria'.[46] A moment of incoherence reveals the investment in a conventional organisation of gender roles in which masculinity is privileged: 'while inclusive masculinities are not built around any of the traditional variables of masculinity, it may remain vital to have one trait that might help keep men's dominant social status – maleness'.[47]

Conceptual slippages and incoherences aside, Anderson's central contention is perfectly intelligible and unambiguous: 'inclusive' masculinity arises from decreasing levels of 'homohysteria' and represents a shift in the gender system that allows 'heterosexual men to both engage in behaviours and permit them to occupy arenas that were previously associated with homosexuality without threat to their heterosexual masculinity'.[48] For Anderson, scholars who hold on to the idea that homophobic violence points to a persistence of homophobic culture are guilty of 'poor sociology', whilst men being 'permitted to carry one-strapped bags' or photos of heterosexual male students kissing one another on Facebook point to a 'rapidly changing culture' of inclusive masculinity.[49] Here, the evidence Anderson documents of decreasing patterns of homophobia in male sporting environments, whether we accept his overarching thesis of declining 'homohysteria' and rising 'inclusive' masculinity or not, points, in his own terms, to a lessening of the restrictions placed upon men and an expansion of their cultural, sexual and social opportunities. Meanwhile, patriarchy '*should*'[50] retreat in such contexts; but why would it? Anderson's post-homophobic, inclusively masculine, heterosexual young men kiss one another, wear one-strap bags and vilify gays, lesbians and other queers less because their masculinity is beyond reproach, and not because it has been deconstructed. The implication of Anderson's work is simply that homosexuality no longer challenges heterosexual masculinity, and has instead been assimilated by it, in terms that chime with Henning Bech's suggestion of the 'disappearance' of homosexuality.[51] To be clear: Anderson is describing a culture of masculinity in which, contrary to his claims for it, Sedgwick's structure of homosociality remains fundamentally intact in its valorisation of bonds between men in the interests of securing an 'exchange-of-women framework'. What has changed is the extent of homosexual panic that terrorises these bonds as the range of permissible expressions of masculinity has expanded.

A key problem of Anderson's work is the implicit valorisation of masculinity, and one that rests upon a fetishistic investment in the erotic potential of homosocial environments from the perspective of an outsider-observer gay male voyeur. This desiring gaze upon the spectacle of masculinity is so naturalised in gay male culture that we could note it as almost being constitutive of that culture. The ubiquity of this desiring gaze attests to the continuing influence of inversionist models of homosexuality, and of what Sinfield describes as the 'cross-sex grid'. What has changed is the extent to which that desiring gaze can now be understood as being consistent with the masculine identification of the gazer, rather than confirming him as pathologically third sex. In another article presenting his research in all-male team environments, Anderson notes that such environments are governed by a logic in which 'one same-sex sexual experience is equated with a homosexual orientation in masculine peer culture, ruling out the possibility of men engaging in recreational same-sex sex without being homosexualised by their behavior'.[52] Here, as elsewhere, the trope of apparently heterosexual men engaging in same-sex genital acts haunts Anderson's discursive framework as it haunts gay porn. Anderson notes that one research subject allows a flamboyantly camp member of the male cheer leading squad to drink a shot off his torso, and then admits to a history of same-sex intimacy in the 'good cause' scenario: 'If I have to kiss another guy in order to fuck a chick, then yeah it's worth it. It's a good cause.'[53] Here, not only is a post-homophobic and inclusive masculinity attractive to heterosexual men because of the range of masculine behaviours it allows, but because it facilitates a wider range of contexts for getting your sexual needs met ('We let Aaron give the three of us a blow job'; 'Hey, getten some is getten some').[54] For all the prurient value such scenarios offer Anderson's text, such encounters nevertheless retain a 'conventional gender hierarchy'.[55] The dominant partner here retains the privileges and status accorded to men in homosociality who exchange women (or in this case, feminised men) and is not subject to homophobic injunction.

Anderson's work points to a pattern of declining homophobia in certain all-male environments, where that decline is signified both by a willingness to be more physically intimate with other men (including genital contact in the 'good cause' scenario, or being serviced by gay men) and by a rising intolerance for explicitly anti-gay behaviour and sentiment. The question is, do such changes signal a restructuring of homosocial networks and the power such networks underwrite? And who prospers from such changes? In Sedgwick's formation, homophobia is simply a by-product of the ways in which homosocial patriarchy exchanges women. What we see in Anderson's notion of an inclusive masculinity is a potential lessening of the restrictions placed on gay men in all-male sporting environments to be closeted or fearful (as long as they are themselves sporting, 'professional' and masculine); we also see that such men may be condescendingly afforded opportunities to service the sexual needs of heterosexual men. These seem like slight advances in the context of a virulently masculine culture predicated on the sexual exchange and marginalisation of women (and effeminate, passive or willing gay men).

Beyond Metrosexual Homosociality? Effeminacy and Gender Dissent

David Alderson suggests that the conduct and appearance of masculinity is increasingly circumscribed by 'metrosexual' values, the defining characteristic of which is 'a narcissism fed by consumerism'.[56] Here the reconfiguration of masculinities – whether they are becoming 'softer', more 'inclusive', more 'sexualised' or 'metrosexual' – opens up the possibilities available to heterosexual men and expands the range of their entitlements, at least in the context of self-presentation, aesthetics and the organisation of same-sex intimacy. There may be new, commodified standards for displaying homosocial masculinity, an awareness of clothing, grooming and domestic fashions and an ability and willingness to spend money on them, but we must question the extent to which such opportunities and standards, like those offered by an 'inclusive' masculinity to sporting jocks, have much effect in terms of reconfiguring the power relations inscribed through homosocial structures. An enlargement of the privileged category of masculinity and a lessening of the legislative force of homophobia upon the homosocial continuum may have offered gay men and other queers advantages, and as such we might celebrate them. But a number of pressing questions remain. The opportunity to acquire the privileges associated with homosocial masculinity represents a structural concession offered to some gay men that arises from a reconfiguration of masculinity, and of subjectivity more widely, and not principally because of social pressure exerted by queers. These changes are part of a wider neoliberal project to secure conditions of competition in every sphere. In *The Birth of Biopolitics* Foucault describes neoliberal governmentality as 'a formal game between inequalities', designed to propagate the equality of inequality, where competition and the enterprise form become generalised as the primary mode not only of social institutions and interaction, but of individuality itself.[57]

Thus, whilst this lessening of homophobic effects in the homosocial continuum may feel liberatory, or be identified as social progress, such advances potentially mark the redundancy of gay identities: if heterosexual masculinity accepts us, and looks like us, and is willing to cultivate intimate relations with itself and us, what does 'gay' mean? Moreover, if we are to preserve a meaningful engagement with the realm of politics *as gay men and queers*, shouldn't we be working to make sense of the extent to which the 'advances' we might be experiencing are actually predicated on our relative local advantages in conditions that more broadly work to maximise economic and social inequalities? Where does the apparent decline of homophobia leave effeminate gay men and other men disenfranchised by their relative economic or social poverty, ethnic heritage or racial identification, or who may lack access to metropolitan cultural resources and who may therefore experience difficulty in acquiring the contemporary trappings of metrosexual man? And more importantly, as I've been noting throughout, whilst this reconfiguration of the homosocial continuum seems to offer opportunities and privileges to (suitably privileged and aspirational) gay men, the position of women is much less clear. As Laura Harvey and Rosalind Gill have suggested, postfeminist culture has offered women entitlements, but it has also given rise to new modes of heterosexual femininity. These modes of femininity stress the importance of 'sexual entrepreneurialism', where beauty, sexual performance and desirability to men are 'tightly policed' and require labour, skills and economic privilege.[58] Furthermore, neoliberalism depends upon, and reproduces, a social and economic repression of women that Lisa Duggan has suggested is upheld by what she describes as a class of 'homonormative' gay men.[59] This is a mode of gay politics, and a powerful and influential one, that reinforces and underscores an intensely patriarchal and masculinist set of values, where erotic celebration of masculinity and economic and political celebration of masculinity are mutually reinforcing. Here, the lessening of the force of homophobia in homosociality facilitates not a reconfiguration of masculinity but a reconfiguration of homosexuality, such that it not only upholds the desirability of masculinity but upholds a suppression of the economic and political interests of women. Susan Stryker articulates a similar problematic in her critique of the liberal politics of 'LGBTQ' in which the 'T' can get bundled up, assimilated, by the wider rainbow coalition of queers. She says: 'trans thus conceived of does not trouble the basis of the other categories – indeed, it becomes a containment mechanism for "gender trouble" of various sorts that works in tandem with assimilative gender-normative tendencies within the sexual identities'.[60] Thus, mainstream gay and lesbian politics may accept trans in liberal terms that effectively outsource those connotations of homosexuality previously associated with gender dissent or gender dysphoria to transgendered 'others'.

Conclusion: Effeminacy as Gender Dissent?

If the Wilde trials installed, as Sinfield suggests, a particular equation of same-sex passion with effeminacy, it is important for us to be clear that this cultural break was not simply about an emergent intelligibility of the queer male, his recognisability. A man of the Oscar Wilde sort was unspeakable because he was politically threatening. Effeminacy as a mark of queerness was not just about aesthetics and flamboyance, but about gender dissent. If, as Sinfield suggests, the trials resolved a nexus of ideological unease about masculinity, class, culture and sex into a 'brilliantly precise image',[61] the force of this image lay in its formation of a dissident subject position that gave rise to 'the Wilde century'. Edward Carpenter was pessimistic about this: 'the Wilde trial had done its work [...] and silence must henceforth reign on sex-subjects'.[62] But Sinfield takes a more nuanced view from the vantage point of history: Wilde 'afforded a simple stereotype as a peg for behavior and feelings that were otherwise incoherent or unspeakable' and 'it became much harder to maintain that same-sex practices might be an obvious way to intensify manly bonding'.[63] Certainly, once identifiable and particular, the effeminate queer could be located and punished but more importantly, after the Wilde trials same-sex passion and effeminacy became mutually politicising: manly bonding could no longer be lubricated by a bit of 'how's yer father' without it implying a threat to homosocial masculinity, and swishing about with dyed hair and make up no longer just meant that you were cultured or artistic but rather that you were intolerable and challenging. Sinfield suggests that Quentin Crisp was 'ashamed',[64] but elsewhere I've suggested that for Crisp and his peers effeminate homosexuality 'was not about engaging in sexual transactions [...] but about resistance of straightness, dullness, suburban mediocrity, masculinity and normality'. Such resistance necessitated becoming fabulous, not getting fucked.[65] Boy George notes that on watching *The Naked Civil Servant* on TV, he identified with Crisp and in that identification rejected the taunts of heterosexual classmates at school ('I didn't want to be part of their boring little world');[66] this response articulates the dissident opportunity afforded by the effeminate homosexual as he emerged through Wilde, and later through Crisp. To linger on the self-loathing rhetoric of a figure like Crisp is not only to miss the point in terms of his deployment of camp affectation, but to misrecognise the force of his effeminate challenge to the masculine homosocial continuum.

A reconfiguration of homosociality, and a partial lessening of the force of homophobia, has made homosexuality less threatening to masculinity (and especially if the gay man is willing to lick shots off jocks' torsos), and has given rise to a politically and economically significant class of homonormative gay men, especially in the US, whose influence works to promote the terms through which homosocial masculinity underwrites the competitive individualism of neoliberal capital. Given the extent to which the emergence of 'recreational' sexual subjectivities, like that of the homosexual, are in part dependent on the history of capital,[67] the dialectical relationship between sexuality and economic formations shouldn't surprise us; what is surprising, and disappointing, is the extent to which LGBT culture has so uncritically allowed itself to become co-opted to dominant neoliberal trends. As Michael Warner so eloquently suggested back in 1993: 'post-Stonewall urban gay men reek of the commodity. We give off the smell of capitalism in rut.'[68]

Where does this leave the question of the effeminate homosexual? Homosocial masculinity has been exploited by neoliberal ideologies that foreground competition and emphasise the social value of a domestic nuclearity that is atomised and works to offset conditions in which the state has become increasingly 'weightless' in terms of its social welfare obligations and, at the same time, increasingly 'weighty' in terms of its political authority. Duggan points out how such conditions put increasing pressure on women, whilst Angela McRobbie forcefully reminds us of the importance of gender difference to neoliberal forms of both labour and governmentality, and upbraids a generation of *operaismo* writers for their failure to account for gender in their critique of capital and for their enthusiasm about the creative affectivity of the multitude.[69] I'm conscious of potentially over-reaching here, but surely it is not outlandish to connect up a legacy of political ideas about effeminacy as a refusal of masculinity with a critique of neoliberal ideology that depends upon a continuing and increasing repression of women and feminism, in part facilitated by an 'inclusive' and less homophobic homosocial masculinity? Penney suggests that:

> The current state of rights-based queer political activism, including that aspect of it that acknowledges the limitations of the liberalist rights framework, is so deeply mired in the exploitative logic of capital that the optimal radical strategy is actually to declare the whole category of sexual orientation irremediably bourgeois.[70]

But the histories of gay cultural dissent, of effeminate and other articulations, are not reducible to a 'liberalist rights framework'. If queer theory, and the politics it apparently underwrites, has reached the impasse Penney describes – an impasse of identity politics and its failure to gain a purchase on the deprivations of the enterprise culture – but we remain invested, despite Penney's somewhat lofty dismissal, in the importance of identifying ourselves culturally, socially and politically as gay men (and other queers), then effeminacy may offer one way of organising our identities as gender dissent where that dissent not only refuses the heteronormativity and masculinity of homosocial assimilation but its neoliberal and entrepreneurial privileges too.

In as much as we might agree that there are some limited contexts in which homophobia is declining, this represents an expansion of the range of permissible ways of being a man on the homosocial continuum. In such a context, the opportunity for a gay man to lick a shot off the torso of a willing heterosexual man, or even have (unreciprocal) sex with him in the 'good cause' scenario, is politically (if not sexually) meaningless. What would be considerably more meaningful, however, is a gay male culture less preoccupied with the value of masculinity, and one willing to apprehend its growing privileges not as liberal breakthroughs but as precariously contingent upon political and economic conditions that do not serve our interests. One direction such an apprehension could take, drawing on a rich cultural legacy of the tribulations of effeminacy, is gender dissent: refusing to be an entrepreneurial, neoliberal or homonormative queer. Mattilda Bernstein Sycamore represents a potential archetype of a dissenting effeminate queer for neoliberal times. An activist and writer, he draws on the rich legacy of camp iconography in gay culture to articulate a politics that is socialist, pro-feminist, anti-capitalist and anti-imperialist. Sycamore was a founder member of Gay Shame, an activist group that opposed the commercialism of US gay culture using parodic tactics and 'revolting' drag performances. His blog, 'Nobody Passes, Darling', combines autobiographical reflections on life as a young gay man, with political commentary on subjects such as the fixation of the gay scene with masculinity, US patriotism in the context of Israeli air strikes against Gaza in 2014 and lack of state funding for the arts. A particularly noteworthy recent entry, 'Ashamed to Play', argues that despite official corporate endorsement of LGBT athletes by Google, YouTube and others during Pride week, gay athletes should be ashamed to play in the 2014 World Cup that has seen massive investment go into building sporting venues that have caused mass displacement and structural inequality, and where opposition has been savagely repressed. Sycamore suggests that '[y]et again, an allegedly pro-gay agenda is deployed as a covert advertising gimmick for multinational corporate whitewashing'.[71] Elsewhere he has suggested that 'as […] gay sexual culture morphs into "straight-acting dudes hangin' out", we wonder if we can still envision possibilities for a flaming faggotry that challenges the assimilationist norms of a corporate-cozy lifestyle'.[72] At its most striking, post-Stonewall effeminacy has manifested a stylised yielding of masculine privilege that has offered gay men the opportunity to undermine the 'terrorist' potential in homosocial structures. But those structures have changed, and gay men have become more tolerable and privileged, and their stylisation of gender dissent has become more masculine, in metrosexual terms. We therefore need new terms for imagining dissent that reconnects effeminate legacies to the urgent politics of the moment. Otherwise, why bother being gay?

University of East London

Notes

1. Alan Sinfield, *The Wilde Century: Effeminacy, Oscar Wilde and the Queer Moment* (London: Cassell, 1994), 196.
2. Joseph Bristow, 'Homophobia/Misogyny: Sexual Fears, Sexual Definitions', in *Coming on Strong: Gay Politics and Culture*, ed. Simon Shepherd and Mick Wallis (London: Unwin Hyman, 1989), 62.
3. Richard Dyer, *The Matter of Images: Essays on Representations* (London: Routledge, 1993), 37.
4. Derek Cohen and Richard Dyer, 'The Politics of Gay Culture', in *Homosexuality: Power and Politics*, ed. Gay Left Collective (London: Allison & Busby, 1980), 178–9.
5. Richard Dyer, 'It's Being So Camp As Keeps Us Going', reprinted in *Camp: Queer Aesthetics and the Performing Subject: A Reader*, ed. Fabio Cleto (Edinburgh: Edinburgh University Press, 1999), 110–1.
6. Dyer, 'It's Being So Camp', 111.
7. Eric Anderson, *Inclusive Masculinity: The Changing Nature of Masculinities* (New York: Routledge, 2009), 87.
8. President Heinz Fischer of Austria, quoted in Caroline Davies, 'Conchita Wurst pledges to promote tolerance after jubilant welcome home', *The Guardian*, 11 May 2014, http://www.theguardian.com/tv-and-radio/2014/may/11/conchita-wurst-pledges-to-promote-tolerance (accessed 8 June 2015).
9. Veteran UK broadcaster Terry Wogan, quoted in Aaron Day, 'Terry Wogan says Conchita Wurst made Eurovision a freak show', *Pink News*, 3 November 2014, http://www.pinknews.co.uk/2014/11/03/terry-wogan-says-conchita-wurst-made-eurovision-a-freak-show (accessed 3 July 2015).
10. Russian politician Vladimir Zhirinovsky, quoted in Caroline Davies, 'Conchita Wurst pledges to promote tolerance'.
11. Thomas Calvocoressi, 'Can a bearded Austrian drag queen give Putin the bird?', *New Statesman*, 28 April 2014, http://www.newstatesman.com/culture/2014/04/can-bearded-austrian-drag-queen-give-putin-bird (accessed 8 June 2015).
12. Stephen Maddison, *Fags, Hags and Queer Sisters: Gender Dissent and Heterosocial Bonding in Gay Culture* (London: Palgrave and New York: St Martin's Press, 2000); David Halperin, *How to be Gay* (Cambridge, MA: Harvard University Press, 2012).
13. Finn Bowring, 'Repressive Desublimation and Consumer Culture: Re-Evaluating Herbert Marcuse' *new formations* 75 (2012): 8–24.
14. Jeremy Gilbert, 'Signifying Nothing: "Culture", "Discourse" and the Sociality of Affect', *Culture Machine* 6 (2004).
15. Lois McNay, 'Self as Enterprise: Dilemmas of Control and Resistance in Foucault's *The Birth of Biopolitics*', *Theory, Culture and Society* 26, no. 6 (2009): 62.
16. Sinfield, *The Wilde Century*, 93.
17. Sinfield, *The Wilde Century*, 118.
18. E.M. Forster, *Maurice* (Harmondsworth: Penguin, 1972), 136.
19. Sinfield, *The Wilde Century*, 139.
20. Sinfield, *The Wilde Century*, 162–6.
21. Sinfield, *The Wilde Century*, 169.
22. Sinfield, *The Wilde Century*, 177.
23. Sinfield, *The Wilde Century*, 180.
24. Sinfield, *The Wilde Century*, 195–6.
25. Sinfield, *The Wilde Century*, 26.
26. Eve Kosofsky Sedgwick, *Between Men Between Men: English Literature and Male Homosocial Desire* (New York: Columbia University Press, 1985), 86.

27　Sedgwick, *Between Men*, 88–9.
28　Sinfield, *The Wilde Century*, 198.
29　Sinfield, *The Wilde Century*, 200.
30　Sinfield, *The Wilde Century*, 207.
31　Gilbert, 'Signifying Nothing'.
32　James Penney, *After Queer Theory: The Limits of Sexual Politics* (London: Pluto, 2014), 51.
33　Sedgwick, *Between Men*, 89, emphasis in original.
34　Sedgwick, *Between Men*, 89, emphasis in original.
35　Bowring, 'Repressive Desublimation'.
36　Mark McCormack, *The Declining Significance of Homophobia: How Teenage Boys are Redefining Masculinity and Heterosexuality* (Oxford: Oxford University Press, 2012), 57.
37　McCormack, *The Declining Significance of Homophobia*, 123.
38　McCormack, *The Declining Significance of Homophobia*, 123.
39　McCormack, *The Declining Significance of Homophobia*, 136.
40　Mark Potok, 'Anti-Gay Hate Crimes: Doing the Math', *Intelligence Report* 140 (2010).
41　*Huffington Post*, 'Archbishop of Canterbury Justin Welby Suggests African Christians Will Be Killed if Church Accepts Gay Marriage', http://www.huffingtonpost.com/2014/04/04/archbishop-of-canterbury-gay-marriage_n_5091301.html (accessed 10 June 2014).
42　Stonewall, *Homophobic Hate Crime: The Gay British Crime Survey* (2013), https://www.stonewall.org.uk/documents/hate_crime.pdf (accessed June 2014).
43　Anderson, *Inclusive Masculinity*, 93–7.
44　Anderson, *Inclusive Masculinity*, 97.
45　Anderson, *Inclusive Masculinity*, 98, emphasis in original.
46　Anderson, *Inclusive Masculinity*, 158.
47　Anderson, *Inclusive Masculinity*, 159.
48　Anderson, *Inclusive Masculinity*, 159.
49　Anderson, *Inclusive Masculinity*, 160.
50　Anderson, *Inclusive Masculinity*, 158, emphasis in original.
51　Henning Bech, *When Men Meet: Homosexuality and Modernity* (Chicago: University of Chicago Press, 1997).
52　Eric Anderson, '"Being Masculine is not About who you Sleep with…:" Heterosexual Athletes Contesting Masculinity and the One-time Rule of Homosexuality', *Sex Roles* 6, no. 1 (2007): 105.
53　Anderson, 'Being Masculine is not About who you Sleep with', 109.
54　Anderson, 'Being Masculine is not About who you Sleep with', 115.
55　Alan Sinfield, *Gay and After: Gender, Culture and Consumption* (London: Serpent's Tail, 1998), 55.
56　David Alderson, 'Acting Straight: Reality TV, Gender Self-Consciousness and Forms of Capital', forthcoming; see also Mark Simpson, 'Here Come the Mirror Men: Why the Future is Metrosexual', http://www.marksimpson.com/here-come-the-mirror-men/ (accessed June 2014).
57　Michel Foucault, *The Birth of Biopolitics: Lectures at the Collège de France* (Basingstoke: Palgrave, 2008), 120.
58　Laura Harvey and Rosalind Gill, 'Spicing It Up: Sexual Entrepreneurs and *The Sex Inspectors*', in *New Femininities: Postfeminism, Neoliberalism and Subjectivity*, ed. Rosalind Gill and Christina Scharff (London: Palgrave, 2011), 2.
59　Lisa Duggan, *The Twilight of Equality: Neoliberalism, Cultural Politics, and the Attack on Democracy* (Boston: Beacon Press, 2003), 50.
60　Susan Stryker, 'Transgender History, Homonormativity and Disciplinarity', *Radical History Review* 100 (2008), 148.

61 Sinfield, *The Wilde Century*, 118.
62 Quoted in Sinfield, *The Wilde Century*, 124.
63 Sinfield, *The Wilde Century*, 125.
64 Sinfield, *The Wilde Century*, 171.
65 Stephen Maddison, 'Small Towns, Boys and Ivory Towers: A Naked Academic', in *Temporalities: Autobiography in a Postmodern Age*, ed. Jan Campbell and Janet Harbord (Manchester: Manchester University Press, 2002), 157.
66 Boy George, *Take It Like a Man: The Autobiography of Boy George* (London: Sigdwick & Jackson, 1995), 52.
67 John D'Emilio, 'Capitalism and Gay Identity', reprinted in *The Lesbian and Gay Studies Reader*, ed. Henry Abelove et al. (New York: Routledge 1993); Michel Foucault, *The History of Sexuality*, vol. 1 (Harmondsworth: Penguin, 1978).
68 Michael Warner, 'Introduction', in *Fear of a Queer Planet: Queer Politics and Social Theory*, ed. Michael Warner (Minneapolis: University of Minnesota Press, 1993), xxxi.
69 Angela McRobbie, 'Reflections on Feminism, Immaterial Labour and the Post-Fordist Regime', *new formations* 70 (2010): 60, 69.
70 Penney, *After Queer Theory*, 48.
71 Mattilda Bernstein Sycamore, http://nobodypasses.blogspot.co.uk/2014/06/ashamed-to-play.html (accessed 10 July 2014).
72 Mattilda Bernstein Sycamore, *Why Are Faggots So Afraid Of Faggots?: Flaming Challenges to Masculinity, Objectification, and the Desire to Conform* (Oakland: AK Press, 2012), 1.

Ever Fallen In Love (With Someone You Shouldn't Have?): Punk, Politics and Same-Sex Passion
David Wilkinson

Abstract: This article critically examines existing queer theoretical takes on punk and same-sex passion, highlighting the politically troubling implications of retrospectively romanticising punk's transgressions. Drawing on a range of examples including the fashion designs of Vivienne Westwood and Malcolm McLaren, the punk subcultural nucleus of the Bromley Contingent and the work of the Buzzcocks, it argues that a new approach is needed: one that provides an accurate historical portrayal of the complex and varied relations between British punk, sexual politics and identities and the conjuncture of the late 1970s. Such analysis makes possible an assessment of the ways in which these relations might inform crucial issues faced by LGBTQ people and countercultural forces in the present. What resources of hope might punk offer, and how might we learn from its missteps and dead ends, which, to be fair, are always easier to see in hindsight?

*

The 2013 festival of the LGBT arts and social justice organisation Homotopia, held in Liverpool, featured an exhibition entitled 'England's Erotic Dream/ Germ Free Adolescents'. It consisted of a selection of archival photographs of British punk in London, upon which its curator had 'focuse[d] a queer gaze'. Pleasingly described as an 'unapologetically homosexual exhibition on British punk', it made an important contribution to highlighting the under-historicised role of sexual and gender dissidence in the movement. The contextualising panels, though, were marked by various difficulties. In them, the specificity of the photographs was largely elided in favour of queer theoretical interpretations concerned with 'binaries' and 'failure', with a casual inattention to historical detail; for example, the band X-Ray Spex was said to have existed within the context of 'Thatcher's Britain', but had broken up by 1979. Punk approaches to sexuality, meanwhile, were celebrated as 'transgressive', 'deviant' and 'parodic', though not, interestingly, as liberating. Furthermore, there was no mention of the disturbing crossover of same-sex passion with the far right in certain strains of punk that were documented by the photographs on display.

I found that the exhibition set in motion a train of thought about the influence of queer theory beyond the institutional setting of academia on LGBT subculture more broadly.[1] Whilst accepting that the meanings and implications of intellectual work can change according to the context in which they are received, I want to understand what part this intellectual production in and of itself has played in giving rise to the problems of the exhibition noted above, and what alternatives might be possible to such situations.

Here, then, I consider existing queer theoretical approaches to punk in order to show that the limitations of such takes render them not simply inadequate and problematic in terms of their influence on LGBT subcultural production, but curiously similar to some of the most negative political consequences of certain ways of living and framing same-sex passion within punk itself.[2] A cultural materialist approach offers different possibilities. In particular, I am sympathetic to the strategy proposed by Alan Sinfield as one way for left intellectuals working on cultural production to 'make themselves useful' at a time when a neoliberal alliance of class interests has overturned many of the gains of the postwar settlement and severely weakened organised working class opposition. This is the suggestion that our efforts should 'work with and through [...] a subcultural constituency'.[3] In the long run, such an approach cannot be a substitute for a counter-hegemonic strategy rooted in class politics. However we negotiate that daunting terrain though, cultural and political engagement with those who are in some way marginalised by the dominant would seem to be an important and complementary task. I therefore wish to instigate a more conscious subcultural dialogue on the question of punk and same-sex passion than the example I began with, and one that avoids its pitfalls.

I aim to achieve two things: first, an accurate historical characterisation of punk approaches to same-sex passion, given the ahistoricism of queer accounts and the fact that the issue has so far only been addressed sporadically elsewhere;[4] second, a consideration of the ways in which those approaches might inform crucial issues faced by LGBTQ people and countercultural forces within the present conjuncture. What resources of hope might punk offer, and how might we learn from its missteps and dead ends, which, to be fair, are always easier to see in hindsight?

No Future: Punk and Queer Theory

Despite the decidedly queer beginnings of British punk,[5] the first wave of cultural studies scholarship on the movement[6] was fairly quiet on the question of distinctively 'punk' approaches to same-sex passion.[7] Even in the 1990s, with the concurrent rise of queer theory and a further wave of published academic work on subcultures and popular music, the work of Mark Sinker was a rare example of sustained attention to the issue.[8] Sinker's idiosyncratic and provocative reading of punk through the anti-relational turn in US queer theory was, it seems, an early example of the terms in which subsequent discussions of punk and queerness would be framed. This anti-relational or antisocial turn can be summarised as a theory of sex, especially gay sex, as 'anti-communitarian' and 'self-shattering', bound to the death drive and supposedly dissident in its connection of pleasure with 'selfishness', irresolution and 'destructive power'.[9] Its roots are in psychoanalytic and poststructuralist thought on the one hand and a particular canon of queer literary production, including figures such as Jean Genet and Marcel Proust, on the other. Key exponents include Leo Bersani and Lee Edelman. As I later conclude, there are historical reasons why there may be a resonance in the connections made between punk and anti-relational theory by writers such as J. Jack Halberstam and Tavia Nyong'o. Nevertheless, there are two main difficulties with these often strained equations between the specific moment of punk in Britain, and the very different context of a body of intellectual work first popularised within US academia from the 1990s onwards.

The first difficulty is one of method. The running together of punk with the work of writers such as Bersani and Edelman is one more example of a persistent tendency within certain formations of cultural studies that reduces the 'complex historicity' of formations and their cultural production to 'the status of mere evidence' for particular theoretical positions.[10] Nyong'o, writing for *Radical History Review*, clearly feels some pressure to justify the decision to analyse punk as being in some ways representative of anti-relational theory. Yet the passing claim that both punk and anti-relational theory 'originate' in 'the 1970s' is somewhat tenuous.[11] In the case of Halberstam's argument, even simple historical details matter little: the Sex Pistols' 'God Save The Queen' is described as their 'debut song'[12] (it was their second single, released six months after 'Anarchy in the UK' and the infamous Bill Grundy incident which catapulted both the band and the punk movement into the media spotlight). Here I am reminded of comparable historical inaccuracies in the example of the Homotopia exhibition with which I began. The second difficulty is the political consequence of such an approach: once punk is separated from rooted judgement through failure to locate it within a particular conjuncture, its politics can be celebrated as uniformly positive. Halberstam approvingly describes the Sex Pistols' 'God Save the Queen' as constituting a 'politics of no future', asserting that the song rejects 'the ideological system which […] takes meaning away from […] the queer'.[13] Nyong'o, meanwhile, shares with Halberstam the belief that punks 'and other anti-social types' share a queer 'bad attitude'.[14] Halberstam's straightforward association of punk with an oppositional queer politics is in stark contrast to some of the movement's more troubling articulations of same-sex passion. It is ironic, then, that the final chapter of *The Queer Art of Failure* is an investigation into the historical crossover of same-sex passion and Nazism in which Halberstam states that 'we have to be prepared to be unsettled by the politically problematic connections that history throws our way', yet which misses precisely such 'problematic connections' in punk.[15]

The problem here is actually more serious than an uncritical stance on punk's sexual politics. Despite their gestural radicalism, the politics of queer anti-relational theory are incompatible with any project of leftist transformation, including liberation at the level of sexuality and gender. Edelman's understanding of futurity as purely heteronormative and conservative is not only blinkered, but also leads him into the argument that queers should embrace their ideological positioning as representative of the death drive, of negativity, nonsense and limit.[16] Whilst Halberstam is rightly doubtful of Edelman's claims to stand outside politics altogether, this does not lead to a rejection of his terms. Instead, Edelman's work is folded into Halberstam's aim of 'a more explicitly political framing of the antisocial project'.[17] Leftist politics, however, are constitutively dependent on both alternative conceptions of the future and some kind of meaningful intervention in the world. Similarly, whilst it may be the case that the future of humanity is dependent upon the reproduction of the species, reproduction need not be a hegemonic expectation. Nor must it necessarily be a heteronormative pursuit, as shown by the theories and living experiments of gay and women's liberationists in the 1970s and the less utopian, sometimes incorporated but potentially prefigurative development of 'families of choice' since that moment.[18]

It's important to reflect on how such an abstracted, unsustainable political position actually manifests itself in anti-relational theory. The somewhat tame rhetorical gestures toward transgression in the tone of Edelman and Halberstam seem to be an important component: Edelman, for example, writes 'fuck the social order […] fuck Laws […] fuck the whole network of Symbolic relations',[19] begging the question of whether to bother taking his argument seriously, whilst Halberstam loosely sketches 'a truly political negativity' which would 'fail […] make a mess […] fuck shit up […] shock'.[20] These formulations recall Alan Sinfield's questioning of such an approach as far back as 1998 in his critique of Bersani's *Homos*: 'Transgression', he writes, 'is always in danger of being limited by that which it transgresses'. Sinfield characterises transgression as an 'individualist […] romantic gesture', recommending instead a project of 'shared subcultural work' to which I am sympathetic, as I indicated earlier.[21] Sinfield also makes the obvious but necessary point that an 'anti-relational' position is a myth: as social animals existing within a material environment, it is impossible that any of our actions, experiences and feelings could not in some sense be relational.[22] We could go further and identify one source of this myth in the powerful hegemonic hold of US liberal individualism within which anti-relational queer theory is usually produced.

As this point indicates, there are determining pressures on the theory and politics of queer studies, anti-relational and otherwise, which I do not have the space to explore fully here, though it seems to me that such a sustained investigation is long overdue. Halberstam's advocacy of the word 'failure' to characterise the cultural politics pursued in *The Queer Art of Failure*, however, is telling of one of the most significant of these dimly acknowledged pressures: that of the large-scale defeat of the left as political force and significant counter-hegemony since the 1970s, leading to an embattled and pessimistic discourse of 'resistance' still unbroken by the biggest economic crisis in eighty years, and the incorporation of gay and women's liberation by way of consumerist subcultural development and a heteronormative focus on gay marriage.

Nyong'o gives signs of being more conscious of such matters in his observation that 'in the early twenty-first century […] the possibility of socialist revolution appears to be off the table, to put it mildly' and that 'we' – presumably a reference to queer theorists – 'seem to succumb very easily to a disorienting left melancholy that attempts to substitute a radical critical negativity for the absence of a robust radical politics'.[23] Yet Nyong'o's insistence on a celebratory elision of punk and a particular theoretical inflection of queerness is, like Halberstam's, suggestive of Todd Gitlin's claim that much cultural studies scholarship has exaggerated the radical potential of popular culture as a compensatory move in response to the declining fortunes of the left.[24] It is this combination of 'radical critical negativity' and false optimism that seems to be partly responsible for the positive stress which the 'England's Erotic Dream' exhibition placed on transgression at the expense of liberation, and its inattention to the political problems of certain punk approaches to same-sex passion. To summarise then, such an approach is unconducive to a balanced, reasoned and historicist assessment of punk and same-sex passion. Just as Matthew Worley has argued that punk was resistant to dominant and lasting definition and ownership by political forces on the right or the left,[25] so its sexual politics were complex and varied. It is to those various approaches and their conjuncture that I now turn.

Liberation, Disillusion and 'Terrorist Chic'

As established by Jon Savage's still exemplary history of early British punk, *England's Dreaming*, the duo of Malcolm McLaren and Vivienne Westwood were, if not the originators, the undoubted catalysts for the movement in Britain. Their activities would therefore seem a good place to begin. To understand the pair's take on same-sex passion, it is necessary to situate it within their broader take on sexuality.

In the first half of the 1970s, McLaren and Westwood's Kings Road shop in Chelsea existed within the ambit of the cultural formation identified by style journalist Peter York as 'Them'. Savage notes that the 'Them' were 'too young to benefit from the full sixties explosion but old enough, by 1976, to have established themselves as London's leading artistic/bohemian circle'.[26] York characterised the sensibility of this formation as a reaction against the mass consumerist dissemination of 'Applied Art' influenced by twentieth-century modernism and of US culture into British popular culture. This process had its roots in the expansion and changing curriculum of British art schools in the 1950s and '60s.[27] An elitist breakaway formation with no patience for the 'boring mainstream trendiness' of 'James Taylor' and 'knotty pine', the 'Them' merged Pop Art's enthusiasm for pastiche, Americana and 'trash' ('Euro and arty became démodé and middlebrow') with the ironic distancing of camp. Developing a proto-postmodernist style, which York dubbed 'Art Necro', the 'Them' began to supplant their disdained predecessors as 'their quick-change revivalism […] became very big business around the turn of [the 1970s], when […] people were looking for something *silly* to take their minds off depressing things'.[28]

York's emphasis on the word 'silly' suggests the overall frivolity of 'Them'. This was a sensibility that served them well in market terms, as an anxious embrace of hedonistic escapism took hold in response to early signs of the collapse of postwar consensus. It was, however, 'apolitical'[29] and 'jaded' with regard to 'odd sex'.[30] Politics and sex were the two pressure points upon which McLaren and Westwood leaned to effect their own break, swimming with the tide of increasing polarisation as the decade progressed, economic crisis sharpened and dislocation set in. Savage notes, for example, that 'their interest in fifties clothes had nothing to do with fun or camp' and argues that 'in their different ways, Westwood and McLaren were politicised: this gave them a *moral* purpose in their approach to clothes'.[31]

But theirs was an idiosyncratic, peculiarly hybrid kind of politics, especially in relation to sexuality. McLaren and Westwood clearly had a nose for hypocrisy, recognising the mass market incorporation of the 'sexual revolution' of the 1960s, and the 'real dynamics of desire […] and repression which were being "fudged" by this "window dressing"'.[32] Their response drew from a variety of sources. One such was McLaren's bohemian habitus. This began with a strong childhood relationship with his eccentric grandmother and continued through his involvement in Soho nightlife, travels in France and a series of uncompleted art school courses in reaction against the career-focused expectations of a middle-class upbringing. From this came the long-held bohemian understanding of sexuality as an instinctive, irrational force capable of disrupting social norms once unanchored from the private sphere,[33] resurgent once more in the counterculture of the 1960s. Thus the pair's shop was renamed Sex in 1975, and its stock began to include the kind of fetish wear usually only available by mail order, with the tongue-in-cheek slogan 'rubberwear for the office'.[34] T-shirts attempted to go one further, with designs including an image from a paedophile magazine and a picture of the mask worn by a serial rapist from Cambridge who was then still unconvicted and active. Similarly, the re-use of subcultural styles of the past as one resource for expressing this understanding of sex (such as the associations of biker gear with 'sexuality, violence and death'[35]) may well have been driven less by the Pop Art pastiche of 'Them' than by the belief that 'bohemia is always yesterday', a nostalgic impulse for authenticity arising from the founding contradiction which continually re-animates the bohemian myth, that of the role of art in industrialised capitalist society.[36]

It is this contradiction, too, which produces the love-hate relationship between bohemia and the wider bourgeoisie of which it is often a class fraction.[37] McLaren and Westwood's tempestuous relationship, and their personalities, are microcosmic metaphors on this score. Each combined elements of the bourgeois – their restless entrepreneurialism and Westwood's Calvinist work ethic rooted in her petit-bourgeois background – with the bohemian – McLaren's erratic lifestyle and their shared desire to shock. In an *NME* interview after the shop was raided by police, Westwood claimed: 'I'm trying to de-mystify these silly taboos […] you don't make people think unless you upset them emotionally.'[38] For all such talk (and there was a lot of it from both of them), not to mention McLaren's past involvements with explicitly politicised manifestations of the counterculture such as the Situationist-inspired King Mob group, their conflicted stances meant that the designs they produced were often squarely within the terms of the conservative orthodoxies they provoked. Indeed, Savage shrewdly observes the parallel between Westwood's 'moral authority' and class background and the ascendency of Margaret Thatcher, opining that 'they are mirror images of the same national archetype'.[39]

McLaren and Westwood shared an understanding of sexuality as a waywardly disruptive force with significant fractions of the liberation movements that had sprung up and overlapped with the counterculture from the late 1960s; Elizabeth Wilson, a key participant in gay and women's liberation, even quotes the same entry from the diary of playwright Joe Orton to encapsulate this attitude, as Savage does in relation to the name of McLaren and Westwood's shop: 'Yes. Sex is the only way to infuriate them. Much more fucking and they'll be screaming hysterics in next to no time.'[40] The conviction that this force could be harnessed for transformative political purposes marked the point at which the pair diverged. The Gay Liberation Front in Britain, for instance, produced in its short lifetime a bewildering and still captivating range of theory and praxis which merged libertarian attitudes to sexuality with feminism, a critique of the nuclear family and a humanistic, often radical socialist collectivism.[41] Not for nothing was the movement's paper named after the Beatles' 'Come Together'. As previous mention of Sex clothing designs indicates, McLaren and Westwood had no such normative stance. On a visit to the shop in 1977, York was told by Westwood that the clothing implied 'commitment', upon which he drily commented 'commitment to *what* is less clear'.[42] Commitment to transgression could well have been the response: rather than consciously alternative or oppositional values, the designs deliberately inhabited dominant understandings of unsanctioned sexuality as perverse, sordid and violent in order to provoke a reaction. Furthermore, though the pair had broken with 'Them', a shift symbolised by a violent and confrontational early Sex Pistols gig at the loft party of artist Andrew Logan in February 1976, a residual affectlessness carried over from that formation in the particular images and styles selected in order to shock. Referring back to the performance, Nick Kent evoked the 'air of heavy-duty ennui', feeling that the Sex crowd's 'aesthetic gang warfare' was as 'sexless and desperate' as the formation it opposed.[43]

This was an approach to sexuality that was at once inchoate, not consciously ideological and highly emotively charged, presenting difficulties for analysis. The concept of 'structure of feeling', understood as a means of explaining the social determinations of that which is usually mystified as implicit, subjective and felt,[44] and grasping the development and implications of cultural trends at moments during which they have not fully taken shape,[45] is useful here. Westwood and McLaren's approach exemplified a mood that York was on to, characterising it as 'leisure nightmares' and tracing it back through the fashion world's flirtations with terrorism, sado-masochism and fascism earlier in the 1970s.[46] Interestingly, York also referred to the thesis of US academic Michael Selzer, who named this structure of feeling 'terrorist chic' and characterised it as 'a fascinated approval of violence' which 'apotheosises meaninglessness'.[47] Via a series of case studies that included punk and gay sado-masochist clubs, Selzer argued that one determining factor in the development of 'terrorist chic' was the focus within the counterculture on new experiences combined with pushing boundaries. After a time, and in a less idealistic conjuncture, such impulses had taken increasingly extreme and amoral forms in their attempts to achieve novel kinds of sensuous stimulation. Importantly, however, even these forms struggled to connect within the alienating environment of consumer society, often resulting in cynical detachment and nihilism. Selzer's judgement of the phenomenon was conservative, but his analysis had a degree of accuracy. Savage notes that the 'overt sexuality' of Sex designs 'became an abstraction of sex', referring to a 'distinctly unsettling' shirt that featured a cut-out photograph of a pair of breasts at chest height. Attributing a polemical intent to the designs, Savage views them as a comment on 'industrialised sex districts like Soho, where, by the mid-1970s, the great promises of liberation had been honed down into a series of stock postures'.[48]

It is difficult to ascertain what McLaren and Westwood viewed as the alternative to what David Alderson, adapting the work of Herbert Marcuse, has theorised as 'repressive incitement': a provocation of sexual awareness and desire which commodifies, fetishises and alienates sexuality in the pursuit of profit.[49] What is clear is that it was within the approach to sexuality that I have so far described that McLaren and Westwood situated same-sex passion. Thus designs might feature the 'fervid lesbian fantasies'[50] of Scottish writer Alexander Trocchi, whose work and activities bridged 1950s bohemia and 1960s counterculture. One of the most well-known Sex designs, meanwhile, brought together transgression, affectlessness and intimations of violence: two men in cowboy outfits, minus the trousers, face each other outside a dance hall. One is grabbing the other by the lapels and their penises are almost touching. As Savage observes, their genitals are at the same height as one cowboy's pistol in its holster. The caption reads: 'ello Joe, been anywhere lately? Nah, its all played aht Bill, gettin to (*sic*) straight.' Through its explicit depiction of two semi-naked men, the image aimed to shock. Simultaneously there is a hint of 'terrorist chic' in the forceful gesture, the elision of pistol and penis and the debt to gay pornographic artist Tom of Finland, whose illustrations featured eroticised images of Nazis. Yet the image also conveys a jaded artifice, an absence of connection, in the cowboys' weariness with the scene, the fact that they are actually Cockneys dressed up as cowboys and the small but all-important gap between cocks.

Given this positioning of same-sex passion as alienated, perverse and violent, it is unsurprising that McLaren and Westwood not only seemed to have little interest in the radically transformative aims of gay liberation, but were also prone to homophobic gestures that were calculated to shock in their contempt of even reformist demands for respect, understanding and openness. Westwood's response to her belief that Derek Jarman's punk film *Jubilee* had misrepresented the movement was to produce a rambling 'open letter' on both sides of a t-shirt. It claimed that the costumes had 'something to do with a gay (which you are) boy's love of dressing up […] ("does he have a cock between his legs or doesn't he" kinda thing)' and compared the film to 'watching a gay boy jerk off through the titillation of his masochistic tremblings. You pointed your nose in the right direction then you wanked'. McLaren plays the predatory homosexual stereotype for comic effect in the Sex Pistols film *The Great Rock 'n' Roll Swindle*, and the pair's attitudes transferred unevenly to their protégés: at a gig in Texas, John Lydon wore the cowboys t-shirt whilst Sid Vicious heckled the crowd by shouting 'you cowboys are all a bunch of fucking faggots!'[51] Jordan, the imperious and startlingly dressed shop assistant at Sex who played the character of Amyl Nitrate in *Jubilee*, was once interviewed by Julie Burchill for the *NME*. Discussing Jarman's milieu and her attitude to gay subculture, Jordan claimed to have 'hated' Jarman's film *Sebastiane*, saying 'it was full of prancing, whining queens'. A diatribe against '*Gay News* readers and all that lot' followed: 'they're so precious [...] so *weak* [...] the ones who don't need to mention it I don't dislike.'[52]

As I suggested earlier, McLaren and Westwood's approach to sexuality was closely bound to the historical conjuncture of late 1970s Britain, and would not have provoked a broader response had this not been the case. As resentful structures of feeling began to surface in response to economic crisis, amplified and given reactionary shape by a newly vociferous tabloid media,[53] so the progressive advances of the 1960s and early 1970s were homogenised and demonised by the ascendant New Right as a corrupting, destabilising 'permissiveness'. Same-sex relations were no exception: even before the downfall of Liberal Party leader Jeremy Thorpe and Mary Whitehouse's successful legal campaign against *Gay News*, the 1975 documentary *Johnny Go Home*, which implicitly associated homosexuality with paedophilia,[54] provoked a media furore that engulfed Alan Jones, a young gay shop assistant at Sex. Arrested by plain-clothes policemen for wearing the cowboys t-shirt in public, Jones was prosecuted and the arrest reported on the front page of *The Guardian*.[55] In what amounted to a dress rehearsal for the Bill Grundy incident just over a year later, McLaren and Westwood achieved the publicity they sought. As with the intensification of McLaren's manipulation of the Sex Pistols once the band became headline news, his response to Jones's arrest was accompanied by a level of self-interest which betrayed a certain cynicism regarding shock tactics: Jones claims that McLaren promised 'a really good lawyer [...] What happened? Fuck all'.[56]

Early Punk Subculture in London: The Bromley Contingent

Despite the somewhat sceptical account I have offered so far, the presence of queer imagery in McLaren and Westwood's designs was undoubtedly a central factor in the coalescence of what *Melody Maker* journalist Caroline Coon dubbed 'the Bromley Contingent' as the original nucleus of punk subculture.[57] For this collection of largely teenage sexual dissidents, mainly originating from the middle-class southeast London suburb, the nascent formation later codified as punk offered a classic metropolitan escape route, irrespective of Westwood and McLaren's questionable commitment to gay politics.

Punk also offered an emergent form of subcultural belonging for a new generation of sexual dissidents at a moment of backlash, when the initial impetus and publicity of gay liberation had declined and its countercultural links had weakened as reformist identity politics came to predominate over the radical concerns of the movement's early years. The Bromley Contingent, it should be noted, set the precedent for the frequent regional germination of punk subculture on the gay scene. In Manchester punks congregated in the Ranch, the basement of a club belonging to drag queen entertainer Frank Foo Foo Lammar, a boxer and son of an Ancoats rag-and-bone man.[58] Jayne Casey of Big in Japan recalls that 'in Liverpool you went to gay clubs like the Bear's Paw'[59] and Marc Almond, later of Soft Cell, noted the crossover during his punk years at Leeds Polytechnic.[60] Even in far-flung Norwich, gay club the Jacquard was adopted by punks.[61] Importantly, the Bromley Contingent's introduction of the Sex Pistols to the gay scene influenced the early portrayal of punk in the weekly music press, the most powerful cultural intermediary when it came to defining and representing punk.[62] A camp gossip column in the *NME* written under the pseudonym 'Velda', for example, reported John Lydon's attendance at London gay club the Sombrero and his involvement in preventing a robbery – 'such a *plucky* act, don't you think?'[63] – and featured an interview with Jordan in which she claimed obliquely of Lydon: 'He doesn't have actual girlfriends.'[64] Though the press would later collude with the masculinised, heterosexist and sometimes blatantly homophobic turn of certain punk bands,[65] such early articles may well have been influential on the fostering of subcultural connections.

There was an affinity, though, with the activities of McLaren and Westwood at various levels, including fashion. The pair had drawn inspiration for their designs from the grassroots innovations of those young people, including the Bromley Contingent, who frequented the Kings Road, pioneering new subcultural styles of their own. There were also resonances that would lead to more awkward consequences. The predominantly middle-class background of the Bromley Contingent meant that there was often a shared residual bohemianism as regards same-sex passion: Bertie Marshall, who renamed himself 'Berlin' aged 16 in 1976, opined of a homophobic assault he suffered that 'it wasn't queer bashing, it was freak bashing'.[66] Prior to punk, the Contingent had been fans of the art school glam associated with 'Them', including Roxy Music and David Bowie. Savage noted in 1980 that the model of same-sex passion that Bowie had introduced into British pop slotted into the broader images of decline in his 1970s output, which chimed with the breakup of postwar consensus: 'The puritan hangover still bit; homosexuality had to be perceived

Ever Fallen In Love (With Someone You Shouldn't Have?)

as part of some greater decadence [...] if it's all ending, anything goes.'[67] There was a shared fascination amongst the group for the film *Cabaret*, and Marshall mythologises the Contingent's early days by comparing them with Isherwood's *Goodbye to Berlin*.[68] As in McLaren and Westwood's designs, then, same-sex passion was both one component of a broader transgressive sensibility and loosely conceived within the bounds of conservative ideology. There was a comparable attraction to publicity too, bound to the same New Right dynamic: members of the Bromley Contingent appeared on the front page of the *Daily Mail* on 19 October 1976 under the headline 'These People Are the Wreckers of Civilisation' after they attended the opening of performance art group COUM Transmissions' (later to become post-punk industrial act Throbbing Gristle) 'Prostitution' exhibition at the ICA. The exhibition included framed pages taken from pornographic magazines and used tampons, and the scandal it provoked led to the Arts Council withdrawing support for COUM.[69]

The structure of feeling known as 'terrorist chic' was also present. There may well be occasional creativity with the truth in Marshall's memoir *Berlin Bromley*, evoking Elizabeth Wilson's emphasis on a kind of mythologising performance of everyday life as a central component of bohemia.[70] However, its overall depiction of Marshall's milieu and experiences seems largely believable and accurate, and is corroborated by the recollections of others. There is a gleeful element of teenage rebellion in the anecdotes recounted, such as the occasion when Susan Ballion, later Siouxsie Sioux, posed as a dominatrix and Marshall as a dog on a lead, causing havoc in a fashionable Bromley wine bar by refusing to leave until a bowl of water was provided. Yet the power relations played out here hinted at a darker undertow, as various members of the Contingent, including Marshall, became romantically involved at a young age with a lifestyle of prostitution and drug abuse. Marshall also experienced a string of exploitative relationships and encounters, the most extreme of which was a sado-masochistic threesome which led to his being raped.[71] The affectless distance present in Westwood and McLaren's clothing designs, and which separated them from what was depicted, appeared at first glance to have been dramatically closed by the Bromley Contingent. Savage claims that 'the women and men that Vivienne collected acted out their wildest fantasies [...] they became part of the Sex Pistols and gave punk its Warholian edge'.[72] But there was something unnerving about the character of these fantasies, both in the risks they entailed and the fact that, though there was nothing sexless about experiences such as Marshall's, a callous, violent and amoral affectlessness continued to permeate them. It was one that frequently spilled over into other kinds of relations too, as in Marshall's claim that, inspired by Pier Paolo Pasolini's film *Salo*, he shat in the grocery cupboard of neighbours described as 'a crip and his God-fearing Aussie nurse' who had attempted to report Marshall and his flatmate to the police for prostitution.[73]

The structure of feeling was perhaps most clearly visible at the level of cultural production in Siouxsie and the Banshees' 'Carcass'. The song depicts a protagonist who, in his desire for 'raw love', butchers his objects of desire and hangs them in 'cold storage'. Its chorus ('be a carcass [...] be limblessly in love') neatly encapsulates the transgressive violence and alienation that characterised certain of the Bromley Contingent's socio-sexual relations, including instances of same-sex passion. Meanwhile, the song's tongue-in-cheek humour – in a reference to the food company Heinz, the victim is referred to as the '58th variety' – generates an affectless distancing. Paul Morley's generally positive account of *The Scream*, the LP on which 'Carcass' featured, nevertheless worried that 'there is a twisted passion but no compassion'.[74]

Another way in which this want of compassion expressed itself was in the exclusivity of the Bromley Contingent. Siouxsie Sioux recalls that 'it was a club for misfits [...] no one was criticised for their sexual preferences'.[75] The inclusiveness of the latter statement, however, belies the earlier use of the word 'club'. Same-sex passion was often lived through this elitism. Some, like Marshall, adopted an identity that passed the test with its references to Genet, Isherwood and Warhol.[76] Others, such as Phillip Sallon, were considered to be 'screaming' and 'unbearable'.[77] It is also telling that Polari was spoken amongst the milieu. Rather than its connotations of a solidarity developed in response to oppression, it was the slang's potential for exclusion and its historical use to criticise others without them knowing[78] that appealed. A residual bohemianism was evident in both instances: in the case of Phillip Sallon, I am reminded of Pierre Bourdieu's argument that competition over cultural capital is often especially fierce amongst those avant-garde cultural producers with whom bohemia is associated.[79] As regards Polari, the opposition to populism often generated by a romantic suspicion of the mass market can be detected in Marshall's description of those who began to frequent the Soho lesbian club Louise's once punk became popular, not only as 'cattle' and 'riff-raff', but also as 'naffs'.[80]

Like McLaren and Westwood's approach to sexuality, the Bromley Contingent's framing of same-sex passion at the level of desires, identity and subcultural belonging had implications that went beyond their milieu. In the late 1970s, the fascist National Front experienced a growth in popularity through racist scapegoating for the economic and social dislocation of Britain. It was in this context that same-sex passion was being lived in transgressive, exclusive and often compassionless ways. Alan Sinfield has argued that whilst our political alignments may be at odds with the character of our sexual desires, we must nevertheless accept that such desires are determined by social forces. Contra to attempts such as those of Foucault to distance practices like sado-masochism from direct social and political resonances, it is important to recognise continuities between desires, interpersonal relations and the unequal and exploitative power relations of the dominant.[81] Thus the fact that Marshall's response to Pasolini's *Salo* was not to share in the film's understanding and critique of the links between fascism and libertinism but to shit in the cornflakes of someone he held in contempt takes on an even more worrying aspect. And so Marshall's memoir romanticises, more than any other of his encounters, his relationship with Martin, a 19-year-old 'bloke' who had been in a youth detention centre, passed through the Navy and was a member of the National Front. For Marshall, Martin was 'pure Jean Genet'.[82] This flirtatious referencing of the historical crossover of fascism and same-sex passion extended to members of the Bromley Contingent wearing swastika armbands at Louise's against the wishes of the DJ, a Jewish lesbian.[83]

Parallel and Subsequent Developments

Reassuringly, the punk scene recognised and auto-critiqued such leanings almost immediately. Jon Savage's *London's Outrage* fanzine featured cut-ups from Wilhelm Reich's *The Mass Psychology of Fascism* and worried that 'the English have always been great ones for emotional and physical S&M – now we are as weak as so many kittens, nationally, the bully-boy sex-power of Nazism/fascism is very attractive'.[84] By 1978, Rock Against Racism, set up by members of the Socialist Workers Party partly in response to Bromley Contingent hero David Bowie's 1976 claim that Britain might benefit from a fascist leader, had become one of the key infrastructural supports in the regional dissemination of punk.[85] Especially during 1978 and 1979, its influence shaped the ideological character of punk and post-punk, and RAR's concerns tended to extend beyond racism to encompass issues of gender and sexuality, reflecting the cumulative effect of the new social movements on the left. Telford's *Guttersnipe* fanzine, facilitated by local RAR activists, earnestly featured an interview with a lesbian aimed at furthering understanding amongst its largely teenage readership,[86] whilst RAR's official fanzine *Temporary Hoarding* promoted gay protest singer Tom Robinson and included fascist persecution of gay people in its nightmare scenario of a Britain ruled by the NF: 'If we're gay we're locked away […] sexual orthodoxy, patriotic ditties on the radio, mashed potato for tea.'[87]

In Manchester, punk's second city, forms of same-sex passion took on a very different character from those of London even before the increase in momentum of RAR. This was due in large part to Pete Shelley of the Buzzcocks, whose activities and cultural production showed a strong residual connection with the methods, preoccupations and institutions of gay liberation. Shelley was born in the Lancashire mining and cotton town of Leigh, where Coal Board clerk Alan Horsfall had established the North Western Committee for Homosexual Law Reform (later the Campaign for Homosexual Equality) in 1964.[88] Shelley himself had been involved with gay and women's liberation whilst studying at Bolton Institute of Technology in the mid 1970s.[89] He gave an interview with *Gay News* in 1977 and openly discussed his bisexuality in the music press.[90] Echoing the emphasis of liberation politics on pride, he wore a badge which declared 'I Like Boys' for the Buzzcocks' first *Top of the Pops* appearance the following year.[91] The early scepticism of gay liberation regarding clear-cut sexual identity, and the desire of its more radical elements to 'change the sexuality of everyone, not just homosexuals',[92] may well have played a part in Shelley's repeated emphasis that the lyrics of Buzzcocks songs were deliberately non-gender specific in an attempt to maximise their potential for empathetic response. Shelley's own fanzine, *Plaything*, was concerned with 'personal politics', one of the hallmarks of gay liberation and of the libertarian left in general. It argued that punk or 'new wave' was 'not just about music' but 'a challenge to consider everything you do, think or feel […] the way you react to the people around you. The ways that you love them, fuck them, hate them, slate them'.[93] Manchester's key post-punk fanzine *City Fun*, run from the office of the New Hormones record label set up by Buzzcocks' manager Richard Boon, featured adverts for Manchester Gay Centre and national advice line, Friend. It displayed the influence of both gay liberation's irreverent countercultural style and Shelley's witty and heartfelt interrogations of desire and romance in articles such as 'The Joys of Oppression – By Mouth or by Rectum'.[94]

Despite this distinctively Mancunian take on punk and same-sex passion, and the success of RAR and related movements such as Rock Against Sexism in claiming the movement as broadly progressive for a time, the fascist flirtations first explored by the Bromley Contingent persisted and developed more concretely in isolated pockets of the fall-out from punk. By the early 1980s a consciously fascist sub-genre of punk had crystallised that had direct links to the National Front and was led by Blackpool band Skrewdriver. It later transpired that the band's roadie Nicky Crane, a skinhead with a series of convictions for racist violence, had been leading a double life on London's gay scene and working as a doorman for a sado-masochist club.

Conclusion

As I indicated earlier, the weakness of queer theorists' treatment of punk and same-sex passion so far is not simply a question of historical amnesia. It is also to do with the way in which that historical amnesia allows for the celebratory backwards projection of a naive 'anti-relational' sexual politics of transgression and negativity onto punk. If we consider the differing components of punk as a broad movement explored here, it is the approaches of McLaren and Westwood and the Bromley Contingent that would seem to resonate closest with such a politics. The emphasis of each on transgression rather than oppositional alternatives matches the focus on negation and the rejection of futurity in the anti-relational perspective. It is not just the ideological features of the positions of McLaren and Westwood and the Bromley Contingent that might be seen, at a push, as pre-emergent instances of the anti-relational, but the broader structure of feeling which characterised them. Halberstam artificially separates out the 'affective' character of queer negativity into 'ennui' and 'ironic distancing' on the one hand and 'rage', 'spite' and 'intensity' on the other,[95] though it could be said that the 'terrorist chic' which marked the designs of Sex and the activities of the Bromley Contingent united both such tendencies in its dialectical interplay between affectlessness and the fetishising of violence.

Rather than fetishising punk in turn as an instance of queer anti-relational politics, a gratifyingly romantic move which risks unwitting political endorsement of some unsavoury historical positions, it is worth concluding by considering briefly what queer and countercultural subcultures might learn from punk in the contemporary conjuncture. Despite the ahistoricism of Nyong'o and Halberstam with regard to punk and sexuality, both acknowledge the pressures of the present on their arguments, Nyong'o in the previously quoted claim that a revolutionary left currently seems untenable and Halberstam in the location of a 'politics of negativity' in opposition to 'a US imperialist project of hope'.[96] This latter might be less myopically framed as the dominant tendency of neoliberalism in the States, Britain and most of Europe to have dealt with recent systemic crisis economically via what David Harvey presciently identified as a project of 'recapitalisation' and the further consolidation of ruling class power through the socialisation of financial sector losses in the form of brutal cuts to public expenditure.[97] Ideologically this has translated, at least for the moment, into a renewed hegemonic claim on the future by the neoliberal, socially conservative right after a brief crisis of legitimacy in the years immediately following 2008. In Britain this tendency has recently made itself felt in the ability of the UK Independence Party to appeal to both disaffected Labour and Conservative voters, performing reasonably well in local elections and frighteningly successfully in European elections.

In this context, it would be not simply irresponsible but also fatal for queers and countercultural forces to abandon the notion of a future which might also be won by a reconfigured left (such as the hopeful successes of Syriza in Greece and Podemos in Spain), or to flirt with transgressive, aggressive and alienated structures of feeling which tend to fetishise unequal power relations. This risks the consolidation of both the scapegoating appeals to bigotry currently being made by the right with ever greater intensity and a residually persistent postmodern cynicism regarding the possibility of progressive change. I am unavoidably reminded of the gay smartphone app Grindr, dominantly populated by professed 'tops' and 'bottoms' and the supposed innocence of a consumer preference for Caucasians, the sensibility topped off by a mixture of aggressive negation – 'no x, y and z' – and a listless cynicism: 'no agenda', 'not interested in […] ' and 'nothing serious' are all common phrases.

Instead, we might look not to the 'anti-relational', but to the productive, collectivist and potentially counter-hegemonic connections made between punk, queer subculture and populist political movements like RAR for inspiration regarding the fostering of comparable links in the present. The continued focus on some form of transformative sexual liberation in certain quarters of punk, inherited from an earlier countercultural utopianism, is likewise a salutary feature of the movement in an era in which notions of sexual freedom are now colonised by the market. Like Pete Shelley's Buzzcocks, I am still 'nostalgic for an age to come'.

Acknowledgement

This article is based on research undertaken as part of the Leverhulme project 'Punk, Politics and British Youth Culture', 'England's Erotic Dream', http://www.homotopia.net/festival-item/englands-erotic-dream/#.U2nx8F6WRFI (accessed 7 May 2014).

Notes

1 'Subculture' is understood as a collective though not homogenous social identification between those who have found themselves in some way at odds with the dominant culture. The ways of life and cultural production of subcultures may be oppositional, in the terminology of Raymond Williams, but this is not guaranteed – they may simply be alternative or, as Alan Sinfield puts it, 'ways of coping'. See Alan Sinfield, *Literature, Politics and Culture in Postwar Britain*, 3rd edition (London: Continuum, 2004), 175 and Raymond

Williams, 'Base and Superstructure in Marxist Cultural Theory', in *Culture and Materialism: Selected Essays* (London: Verso, 2005), 41–2.
2. The term is Sinfield's and is used to avoid the historically specific and identity-based connotations of 'gay' or 'homosexual' – see Alan Sinfield, *The Wilde Century* (London: Cassell, 1994).
3. Sinfield, *Literature, Politics and Culture*, xxxv–xxxvi.
4. Two useful accounts are Jon Savage, *England's Dreaming: Sex Pistols and Punk Rock*, 2nd edition (London: Faber and Faber, 2005) and Lucy Robinson, *Gay Men and the Left in Postwar Britain: How the Personal Got Political* (Manchester: Manchester University Press, 2007).
5. Savage, *England's Dreaming*, 183.
6. See, for example, Dick Hebdige, *Subculture: The Meaning of Style* (London: Methuen, 1979); Dave Laing, *One Chord Wonders: Power and Meaning in Punk Rock* (Milton Keynes: Open University Press, 1985); Simon Frith and Howard Horne, *Art Into Pop* (London: Methuen, 1987); and Angela McRobbie, *Feminism and Youth Culture* (London: Macmillan, 1991).
7. Though I use the profoundly multi-accentual term 'queer' as an umbrella term for various lived instances of sexual and gender dissidence, I concentrate here on same-sex passion in order to focus the argument within a limited space. There is no doubt, however, that punk entailed a far greater range of sexual and gender dissidence, as well as anxious and exaggerated re-assertions of heteronormative positions.
8. Mark Sinker, 'Concrete, So as to Self-destruct: The Etiquette of Punk, its Habits, Rules, Values and Dilemmas', in *Punk Rock: So What? The Cultural Legacy of Punk*, ed. Roger Sabin (London: Routledge, 1999), 120–40.
9. J. Jack Halberstam, 'The Anti-Social Turn In Queer Studies', *Graduate Journal of Social Science* 5, no. 2 (2008), 140.
10. John Higgins, *Raymond Williams: Literature, Marxism and Cultural Materialism* (London: Routledge, 1999), 162–5.
11. Tavia Nyong'o, 'Do You Want Queer Theory (Or Do You Want the Truth?) Intersections of Punk and Queer in the 1970s', *Radical History Review* 100 (2008), 106.
12. J. Jack Halberstam, *The Queer Art of Failure* (Durham, NC: Duke University Press, 2011), 107.
13. Halberstam, *The Queer Art of Failure*, 107.
14. Nyong'o, 'Do You Want Queer Theory', 115.
15. Halberstam, *The Queer Art of Failure*, 171.
16. Lee Edelman, *No Future: Queer Theory and the Death Drive* (Durham, NC: Duke University Press, 2004).
17. Halberstam, *The Queer Art of Failure*, 106–7.
18. Jeffrey Weeks, Brian Heaphy and Catherine Donovan, *Same Sex Intimacies: Families of Choice and Other Life Experiments* (London: Taylor and Francis, 2004).
19. Edelman, *No Future*, 29.
20. Halberstam, *The Queer Art of Failure*, 110.
21. Alan Sinfield, *Gay and After* (London: Serpent's Tail, 1998), 141–2.
22. Sinfield, *Gay and After*, 141.
23. Nyong'o, 'Do You Want Queer Theory', 116.
24. Todd Gitlin, 'The Anti-political Populism of Cultural Studies', in *Cultural Studies in Question*, ed. M. Ferguson and P. Golding (London: Sage, 1997), 27.
25. Matthew Worley, 'Shot by Both Sides: Punk, Politics and the End of Consensus', *Contemporary British History* 26, no. 3 (2012), 333–54.
26. Savage, *England's Dreaming*, 147.
27. Peter York, *Style Wars* (London: Sidgwick & Jackson, 1980), 114.
28. York, *Style Wars*, 116.

29 York, *Style Wars*, 119.
30 York, *Style Wars*, 122.
31 Savage, *England's Dreaming*, 9.
32 Savage, *England's Dreaming*.
33 Elizabeth Wilson, *Bohemians: The Glamorous Outcasts* (London: I.B.Tauris, 2000), 179.
34 http://viviennewestwood.co.uk (accessed 9 May 2014).
35 Savage, *England's Dreaming*, 52.
36 Wilson, *Bohemians*, 3, 9.
37 Wilson, *Bohemians*, 7.
38 'Seditionaries T-Shirt Raid', *NME*, 18 November 1978, 3.
39 Savage, *England's Dreaming*, 19.
40 Elizabeth Wilson, *Mirror Writing: An Autobiography* (London: Virago, 1982), 125; and Savage, *England's Dreaming*, 92.
41 See Lisa Power, *No Bath But Plenty of Bubbles: An Oral History of the Gay Liberation Front 1970–73* (London: Cassell, 1995).
42 York, *Style Wars*, 129.
43 Nick Kent, 'Malcolm McLaren', *NME*, 27 November 1976, 20–1.
44 Raymond Williams, *Marxism and Literature* (Oxford: Oxford University Press, 1977), 128–35.
45 Alan O'Connor, *Raymond Williams: Writing, Culture, Politics* (Oxford: Blackwell, 1989), 84.
46 York, *Style Wars*, 9–10.
47 Michael Selzer, *Terrorist Chic* (New York: Hawthorn, 1979), xiv.
48 Savage, *England's Dreaming*, 101–2.
49 David Alderson, 'Postmodernity, Hegemony, Sexuality', *Theoretical Studies in Literature in Art* 33, no. 1 (2013), 116.
50 Savage, *England's Dreaming*, 100.
51 Savage, *England's Dreaming*, 449.
52 Julie Burchill, 'The Kid Who Wouldn't Wear Clarke's Sandals', *NME*, 15 April 1978, 7–8.
53 Stuart Hall, 'The Great Moving Right Show', in *The Politics of Thatcherism*, ed. Stuart Hall and Martin Jacques (London: Lawrence & Wishart, 1983), 19–39.
54 Richard Phillips, 'Imagined Geographies and Sexuality Politics: The City, The Country and the Age of Consent', in *De-Centering Sexualities*, ed. Richard Phillips, David Shuttleton and Dianne Watt (London: Routledge, 2005), 102–24.
55 Savage, *England's Dreaming*, 102.
56 Savage, *England's Dreaming*.
57 Caroline Coon, *1988: The New Wave Punk Rock Explosion* (London: Omnibus, 1982).
58 'Farewell, Foo Foo', *Manchester Evening News*, 12 August 2004, http://www.manchestereveningnews.co.uk/news/greater-manchester-news/farewell-foo-foo-1156337 (accessed 19 May 2014).
59 Savage, *England's Dreaming*, 298.
60 Marc Almond, *Tainted Life: The Autobiography* (London: Pan, 2000), 67.
61 'The Jacquard', http://norwichmusic.wikia.com/wiki/The_Jacquard (accessed 19 May 2014).
62 Dave Laing, 'Anglo-American Music Journalism: Texts and Contexts', in *The Popular Music Studies Reader*, ed. Andy Bennett, Barry Shank and Jason Toynbee (London: Routledge, 2005), 333–9.
63 'Love Lines', *NME*, 22 January 1977, 12.
64 'Special Friend of J Rotten Reveals All (Shock)', *NME*, 16 April 1977, 12.

65. JJ Burnel of The Stranglers commented disdainfully of his punk peers: 'There are a lot of ponces involved, and a lot of poofters, and a lot of posers who have never dirtied their hands.' Harry Doherty, 'The Stranglers', *Melody Maker*, 17 September 1977, 38.
66. Bertie Marshall, *Berlin Bromley* (London: SAF, 2006), 71.
67. Jon Savage, 'David Bowie: The Gender Bender', *The Face*, November 1980, 20–2.
68. Savage, *England's Dreaming*, 185.
69. Savage, *England's Dreaming*, 252.
70. Wilson, *Bohemians*, 38.
71. Marshall, *Berlin Bromley*, 117–9.
72. Savage, *England's Dreaming*, 183.
73. Marshall, *Berlin Bromley*, 141.
74. Paul Morley, 'In Defence of Siouxsie and the Banshees', *NME*, 23 December 1978, 39.
75. Savage, *England's Dreaming*, 183.
76. Marshall, *Berlin Bromley*, 21.
77. Marshall, *Berlin Bromley*, 63.
78. Paul Baker, *Fantabulosa: A Dictionary of Polari and Gay Slang* (London: Bloomsbury, 2004).
79. Pierre Bourdieu, *The Field of Cultural Production* (New York: Columbia University Press, 1993).
80. Marshall, *Berlin Bromley*, 113.
81. Alan Sinfield, *On Sexuality and Power* (New York: Columbia University Press, 2004), 77.
82. Marshall, *Berlin Bromley*, 108.
83. Marshall, *Berlin Bromley*, 67.
84. Jon Savage, *London's Outrage*, 1 December 1976.
85. Savage, *England's Dreaming*, 484.
86. Anon., 'In This Issue We Talk To A Lesbian About Her Homosexual Life', *Guttersnipe* 5 (1979).
87. *Temporary Hoarding* (1978).
88. See CHE's website at http://www.c-h-e.org.uk (accessed 13 November 2014).
89. Andrew Shaw, 'Ever Fallen In Love With A Buzzcock?', 12 April 2013, http://gaynewsnetwork.com.au/entertainment/ever-fallen-in-love-with-a-buzzcock-10842.html (accessed 27 May 2014).
90. Chris Brazier, 'Cocks of the North', *Melody Maker*, 10 December 1977, 14.
91. Robinson, *Gay Men and the Left*, 106.
92. Gay Liberation Front activist Michael Brown quoted in Power, *No Bath But Plenty of Bubbles*, 25.
93. *Plaything* 2 (1978).
94. Anon., 'The Joys of Oppression – By Mouth Or By Rectum', *City Fun* 3, no. 3 (March 1982).
95. Halberstam, *The Queer Art of Failure*, 110.
96. Halberstam, *The Queer Art of Failure*, 106.
97. David Harvey, 'Their Crisis, Our Challenge', *Red Pepper*, April/May 2009, http://www.redpepper.org.uk/Their-crisis-our-challenge/ (accessed 1 June 2014).

Queer Romances with Fascism
David Alderson

Abstract: The claim that there may be a privileged connection between male homosexuality and fascism has been persistent, and has recently been renewed in some surprising quarters. It is an ahistorical assertion, however, because it relies on a sense that both fascism and homosexuality are fixed terms. This article considers the erotically charged figure of the skinhead and his connections with neo-Nazism. It offers readings of two recent subcultural works – the Danish film *Brotherhood* and Max Schaefer's novel *Children of the Sun* – but also provides a historicisation of the skinhead that situates him in relation to both Nazi ideology and its contradictions, and the shifting conditions of postwar Britain. Beyond this, the article interrogates the terms of the skinhead's 'queer' appropriation, and takes issue with the supposedly progressive, yet indeterminate, principles of antinormativity.

*

In 2008, the gay journalist, Johann Hari, posted an article in *The Huffington Post* claiming that 'the twisted truth is that gay men have been at the heart of every major fascist movement that ever was – including the gay-gassing, homo-cidal Third Reich. With the exception of Jean-Marie Le Pen, all the most high-profile fascists in Europe in the past thirty years have been gay'.[1] The claim is both dubious and sensationalist and, while Hari makes some attempt to justify it, he makes no attempt to account for the connection. Moreover, it isn't clear why Hari thinks there's anything audacious about the claim that there is something basically homosexual about fascism: the allegation has been persistent, and the refutation of it provided one motivation for the adoption of the pink triangle as a symbol by gay men back in the seventies.[2]

Judith Halberstam also writes about the connection between male homosexuality and fascism as if breaking some kind of taboo,[3] though she is a great deal more circumspect than Hari, and has to be, given that she is writing in an academic context and must acknowledge something at least of the extensive reflection that has taken place on the topic. Still, Halberstam is intent on demonstrating both that the suffering of male homosexuals under the Nazis has been exaggerated, and that their participation in the regime has been underestimated in order to justify the gay liberation narrative of more recent decades. It's probably true that all liberation movements can be convicted of exaggeration – though the revisionist 'correction' is rarely innocent – but the evidence for serious denial in this case is scant. Richard Plant, for instance, was the first to attempt a full treatment of Nazi 'homophobia', but he also included a chapter on Ernst Roehm and discussed the homoeroticism of proto-Nazi thinkers such as Ernst Bücher.[4] Plant emphasised what is now generally acknowledged to be the case: that the Night of the Long Knives put an end to whatever tolerance there had been of homosexuality by Hitler, marking the start of a more general and fairly determined persecution whose precise scope and severity nonetheless has been a matter of debate. Throughout this article, indeed, I draw on an abundance of academic work, much of it written by gay men, that evinces a consistent preoccupation with the relations between masculinity, homoeroticism and Nazism. Moreover, there have been numerous subcultural reflections on these topics in various forms, two recent instances of which I consider here.

Halberstam insists on the need to historicise the relationship, so her willingness to resort anachronistically to talk of 'gay men in the [Nazi] regime'[5] perhaps betrays a certain purpose. If, as she argues, the deployment of the pink triangle served to emphasise the status of homosexuals as historic victims during the period of gay liberation, talk more recently has focused on the assimilation of white gay men in particular. 'Homonormativity' is on the agenda, promoted in particular by the campaigns for lesbian and gay marriage and participation in the armed services. Neoliberals such as Andrew Sullivan see a sexual liberation movement and culture to which they were always hostile as now virtually obsolete;[6] radicals, by contrast, suggest that norms have shifted but still serve to reinforce power relations in other respects. In her arguments about homosexuality and fascism, Halberstam is perhaps asserting that homonormativity has a history.

The irony of queer radicalism, however, may be that it asserts anti-normativity itself as a norm. Since, of course, there could be no form of human interaction, collectivity or society without norms, this also often renders that radicalism both essentially negative and romantic: what, positively and concretely, do queers stand for? Michael Warner, however, is more specific in outlining an anti-normativity that targets middle-class respectability and the desire to assimilate to this at the expense of those who remain queer by contrast.[7] This is welcome, but the history of opposition to bourgeois norms is itself complex and relevant to the history of fascism's attractiveness in all sorts of ways that I focus on in this article. The kinds of 'complicity' that Halberstam discusses are, I think, more complex than she registers.

My responses to Halberstam's provocation, however, have been prompted by the two works I want principally to focus on: without them I doubt I would have thought to write on this topic. Both strike me as powerful works in instructively different ways. The first, a Danish film, *Brotherhood* (Donato, 2009), is in some ways the more conventional in that it powerfully develops a thesis about homophobic violence that was pioneered by gay liberation movements and theorists, though here it is articulated in relation to a contemporary neo-Nazi group: it insists that same-sex passion is ultimately incompatible with Nazism. I then attempt a complex historicisation of the figure of the skinhead in ways that were significantly prompted – even where this is not explicitly acknowledged – by the text I subsequently consider, Max Schaefer's extraordinary novel, *Children of the Sun*.[8] This focuses on the erotic fascination with skinhead neo-Nazism in ways that invite a reappraisal of that figure's significance. Finally, I return to the questions of anti-normativity, politics and (corporeal) form.

Politics Against Desire: *Brotherhood*

Brotherhood focuses on the figure of Lars, who is passed over for promotion in the Danish army because of rumours that he has made a pass at one of his own men. He drops out, and is subsequently talked into joining a neo-Nazi group that assaults immigrants, non-whites and gay men. The army ethos, we infer, has prepared him for this, but his new affiliation is also a response to his mother's attempts to organise his life for him. We only see her dominate the domestic sphere, including Lars's mostly silent father, but she is also a successful and well-connected local politician prepared to pull strings on Lars's behalf. After his initiation into the neo-Nazi group through his assault on an immigrant man in a local shelter, Lars taunts his disbelieving mother with the possibility that he was responsible when she reads about the incident in the newspaper: his rebellion is directed at her. It is subtly suggested, then, that there is a continuity for him between the maternal authority of his own home and the norms that dominate Danish politics: life has been domesticated through a liberal tolerance that he finds oppressively respectable. Neo-Nazism, by contrast, appeals to Lars's masculine sense of adventure. There is perhaps a hint that the opposition between mother and son is not so clear cut, since his mother encourages Lars's army career: the prevailing social order is itself ultimately dependent on force, and Danish politics have shifted increasingly to the right in recent decades, along with those of much of Europe. Still, Lars rejects domestication.

Lars's middle-class background, intelligence and military training mark him out as a potential leader of the neo-Nazi group, if also as potentially too smart for his own good (he provokes discomfort, for instance, by raising the topic of Roehm at one stage in the group's discussions). He is entrusted to the skinhead, Jimmy – also an ex-soldier, though working class – for training. In the secluded isolation of the country retreat of one of the middle-class leaders of the group that Jimmy is renovating, the two end up having a sexual relationship that is ultimately exposed to the others in the gang by Jimmy's brother, Patrick, out of complex motives: Patrick is bitter at Lars for having been preferred over him for promotion in the group, but we also discover at the outset that he, like his brother, is in some sense queer. Indeed, one way of viewing the drug-taking that makes Patrick insufficiently disciplined for responsibility in the eyes of the group's leaders is that it represents solace for unmet erotic needs.

Excruciatingly realistic presentations of violence are used at five key points in a film that might otherwise risk becoming an ethically problematic conventional romance, and in order to develop a complex sense of homosocial dynamics. In the first of these Patrick is on a cruising ground at night, 'pretending' to be gay. He gets one young man to expose himself, and tells him that he is 'very beautiful'. Diegetically, this is not a signal but a frank acknowledgement; extradiegetically, at the level of the film's analysis of homophobia as internalised repression,[9] it is a cue for the group's assault to begin. Jimmy is the one who ends this with a vicious kick that we later learn has hospitalised the man and is regarded as excessive even by the group's middle-class leaders. Thus, violence functions to repress erotic possibilities that are not exactly unconscious in the characters, and that violence is most zealously dealt out by the figure whose self-discipline will later lapse: the kudos that Jimmy enjoys on the basis of such viciousness is proportional to his self-denial.

This function of violence is explored and elaborated through subsequent manifestations of it. First, there is Lars's initiation into the group in a way that establishes the racial constitution of the group's homosociality: the male immigrant who feebly attempts to defend his family with a knife is ineffectual, unmanned, humiliated. Later, Jimmy insults a younger, very muscular Asian man in the kind of self-consciously 'contemporary' bar that looks as if it might exclude a group of skinheads like this. Jimmy lingers in order to make the insult as the others leave, rendering himself vulnerable. When the Asian guy punches Jimmy in the face, Jimmy spits blood back at him. This highlights once again the *self*-directedness of Jimmy's aggression, since he thereby solicits the further beating he duly receives. But the disconcerting thing about this moment, for both Asian character and viewer, is the intimacy suggested by that blood whose supposed purity is fetishised by neo-Nazis as it now vividly covers the Asian's face, 'built' torso and pristine white t-shirt, defiling cosmopolitan homosocial formalities. Partly because of this, and because within the protocols of male-on-male violence it is so outrageous – a moment of aggressive surrender – the exchange even seems oddly erotic, and the furious beating Jimmy receives resembles some of those he has dealt out.

The true extent of Jimmy's self-destructiveness, though, is made apparent, first through the way the group finally forces him to assault Lars once the pair's secret has been revealed, and then in the revenge finally taken on Jimmy by the young gay man he hospitalises at the outset, frustrating Lars and Jimmy's attempt at escape. At the end, Jimmy is in a coma and may not survive.

The violence is consistently presented through shot-reverse shot sequences that focus on the faces of those confronting each other, rendering that violence expressive and affecting as well as realistic. Head butts feature especially prominently, audibly as well as visually. If the sequences seem conventional in one sense – think, for instance, of the western, or adventure movies in general – we are not presented here with a 'free' contest between idealised and autonomous men. At the start, the victim is constrained, first to hit his assailant in a way that is inevitably half-hearted because fearful, and then to accept the rigorous beating he knows his own feeble attempts are intended to 'justify'. However, the formal, visual emphasis this produces of a clearly distinguished fear on the one side, and aggression on the other, is finally disturbed when Jimmy is forced to assault Lars by the group once the couple's secret has been discovered: Jimmy's face is now filled with pained confusion through this defamiliarisation of his role as ringleader.

The ending of the film is instructive. It sustains the central thesis that the subjective agent of violence is also its object, and thereby withholds from the two lovers the happy ending that is one narrative possibility for them. This is surely because the film's thesis is also bound up with its sense of justice: these two have committed appalling crimes and *must* not escape and find satisfaction if the film is to be exonerated of an inappropriate sympathy for them. That such sympathy is one danger the film risks is highlighted by the utterly crass publicity blurb for it, in which we are told that 'Lars proves he is a fast learner and rises quickly through the ranks while simultaneously developing closer bonds with the other members, especially the sexy Jimmy'. Thus, this film's complex meditations on violence and the erotic in their broadest senses are reduced to the banality demanded by a gay subculture industry on behalf of its audiences. In fact, however, such sex as there is in the film tends to present the corporeal manifestations of Jimmy's ideological convictions as a problem.

Most neo-Nazi violence takes place within and against urban settings, since these are the centres of migration and 'impurity', but also of the kinds of poverty and alienation that feeds far-right recruitment. Neo-Nazi ideology makes positive appeals to nature, the supposed constancies of blood and soil, as part of its critique of a degenerate modernity, and *Brotherhood* signals its awareness of this at various points. Lars, for instance, taunts Jimmy for drinking organic beer, as if such apparent sentimentality contradicted his hard 'Paki-bashing' image. However, nature is also enlisted by the film as the appropriate context for a sexual expression that is at odds with ideology. The setting for the relationship is the Scandinavian landscape and, while it possesses a bleakness that is continuous with the film's more general sense of desolation, it nonetheless functions symbolically to purify Jimmy and Lars: isolated from the city and the rest of the group, they first kiss after drunkenly swimming naked together and taking a shower.

The ensuing, inexplicit sex scene avoids cliché by *not* positioning Jimmy straightforwardly as the audience's object of desire. Instead, the Nazi tattoos that cover his body – and notably the Third Reich eagle across his shoulders – fill the screen, as if to suggest the incongruity of his having sex with a man at all. Subsequently, the contradiction is handled somewhat differently, since sexual relations necessarily take place in private and by contrast with the violence that serves to bond the group. Patrick, for instance, discovers the relationship by secretly observing Lars tend Jimmy's wounds through a window. Same-sex passion, then, is at odds with ideology, and progressively in all senses directs Jimmy and Lars beyond it.

However, the pathos of the film's realism centres primarily on Patrick, and it ends with him posing uncomfortably for photographs with the group's middle-class leadership, no longer dressed in skinhead garb, but in 'respectable' clothing. And it is in relationship to him that the film's title acquires the most profoundly ironic inflections. Patrick's desire to fit in somewhere is mediated by his admiration for a brother whose betrayal of him prompts Patrick's self-persecuted vengeance. This, in turn, secures his promotion within the very group that demands the renunciation of the kind of sexual relations that might have provided some satisfaction in his otherwise bleak existence.

Patrick's incongruity, the pathos that attends him and even the sense of an erotic potential betrayed in these final scenes all seem to me to demand a more complete historicisation of the figure he cuts. To establish this, we need to set that figure in a longer history because it is only in doing so that his contemporaneity, specificity and peculiar affective charge make sense. The categories of formality and respectability that I have been merely alluding to so far are absolutely central to our understanding of him.

Skinheads: A Rough Genealogy

George L. Mosse has argued that the late-nineteenth- and early-twentieth-century Germanic cult of the male body that was taken up by Nazism was complex and contradictory, emerging out of a Pietistic emphasis on respectability that demonised the sexual, abstracted a national principle of masculine brotherhood – the so-called *mannerbund* – from a prior cult of localised friendship and consequently discovered in the symbolism of the healthy, often naked, male body the index of self-control. Moreover, the various medical sciences, with their integrated moral, racial and biological anxiety over degeneration, reinforced this agenda. That this physical ideal was based on Greek models is an irony that serves to highlight the precariousness of its emphasis on purity. But it also testifies to that ideal's supposed transcendence of liberal, commercial, industrial and urban modernity – conditions often held responsible for biological and racial degeneracy.[10] Fritz Stern, for instance, highlights the powerful influence of the so-called conservative revolutionary, Julius Langbehn, on the German Youth Movement that emerged in the 1890s through his romantic anti-intellectualism and vitalism.[11]

Hence, a striking tension in the way this model of manliness was invoked that rendered it multi-accentual: it was anti-bourgeois to the extent that it highlighted and disdained the 'inorganic' qualities of modernity, but it was bourgeois to the extent that it promoted respectability. Paradox suffuses the discourse: its combined romanticism and classicism made it available to one rapturous theorist of the *Wandervogel*'s, Hans Blüher, who argued that its homoerotic potential was integral to its political significance: sexual relations, he claimed, cemented both State and militaristic bonds between men (the Theban band, for instance).[12] Blüher was influential on Roehm, who inveighed in his memoirs against the narrowness of bourgeois norms.[13] But Roehm's arch opponent, Himmler, had also read Blüher, and his response was more in keeping with normative limits to homosociality: 'That there must be male societies is clear. If one can call them erotic, I doubt. In any case, the pure physical homosexuality is an error of degenerate individualism that is contrary to nature.'[14]

Roehm's purge in 1934 was therefore significant: it marked Hitler's and the Third Reich's ultimately overriding commitment to respectability,[15] even if it has been argued elsewhere that the importance the Reich attached to racial purity, continuity and expansion led to an emphasis on heterosexual reproduction that itself vindicated a licentious masculinity by encouraging sexual activity outside marriage where 'necessary'.[16] If no-one suggests on this basis that heterosexuality was in reality 'behind' Nazism, this is because heterosexuals haven't needed to be secretive in principle, or to find justification in 'perversions' of dominant ideas.

One of the forms Roehm's commitment to masculine militarism took was his involvement with the Freikorps, those volunteer armies whose activities and propaganda after 1918 did so much to prepare the way for Nazism proper. Their novels and memoirs have been analysed by Klaus Theweleit as distillations of fascist subjectivity in its purest form.[17] Theweleit's Deleuzian argument – too complex and nuanced to summarise anywhere near adequately here – is that these texts express a need to shore up a territorial integrity that is at once psychic, corporeal and political, and directed against the threatening, deterritorialising 'floods' of working-class and communist revolutionaries whom the Freikorps associated with a feminine principle of disorder.

The account is compelling, but I am as much concerned with it here for its context. It emerges out of the desire of German radicals of the sixties and seventies to settle accounts with the Nazism of their parents' generation in a way that served to lend greater point and urgency to the more general countercultural tendency to see 'fascism' in order as such. Hence, Theweleit's genealogy of fascism as a masculine principle extends from the highly specific writings of the Freikorps to encompass not only Western history in general, but even early human evolutionary development.[18] Theweleit's anti-fascist commitment is to the liberation of a 'desiring production' that is itself romantically conceived and anarchically disordering.[19] Hence, it will have little truck with the conventional organised resistance of the left because this manifests a discipline that may itself be described as fascistic: 'it seems to me', he writes, 'that the battle lines between men are repeatedly blurred by the elements of masculinity they have in common.'[20] To this extent, therefore, the politics Theweleit gestures towards – but, of course, cannot substantially articulate because this would entail rendering them normative and thereby give them form – might be said actually to reinforce 'fascism' by vindicating its paranoia about potential dissolution.

Theweleit's focus on the relations between corporeal and political form makes it tempting to apply his analysis to the neo-Nazi skinheads who emerged in Britain in the seventies and eighties on the grounds that they manifested a physical and political 'hardness' that facilitated uniformity and integration against various others they regarded as degenerate and/or effeminate. We might also remark on their opposition to 'floods' – though, in the skinheads' case, this was mostly directed at 'immigrants', some of whom had actually been in Britain for decades by that point. However, skinheads also emerged out of social, political, cultural and subcultural contexts that were quite different from those that conditioned the emergence of the Freikorps.

They were, for instance, typically, self-consciously and even militantly 'working class'.[21] They did define themselves in part against a feminised principle of disorder, but a distinctive one: the middle-class 'hippies' of the counterculture, with their freedom-loving rejection of 'fascism'.[22] Skinheads, by contrast, emerged initially out of ska and rude boy subcultures, a fact often emphasised by those who seek to challenge the automatic association of them with racism and neo-Nazism.[23] This, though, is somewhat disingenuous: 'Paki-' and queer-bashing were present from the start. Moreover, the ideologically Nazified skinhead emerged in one sense quite consistently out of punk, which Dick Hebdige has described as speaking for 'the neglected constituency of white lumpen youth',[24] albeit in viciously ironic and nihilistic terms that often

David Alderson

embraced Nazi symbols and terminology in order to shock the respectable of all classes.

If a belief in the pointlessness of existence such as the punks' is a difficult pose to sustain, it may condition a subsequent commitment to alternatives that are nonetheless continuous with its romanticism. 'I hate the world', sang the early, punk incarnation of Ian Stuart's band, Skrewdriver ('Antisocial', 1977); in 1981, he confirmed the rumours already circulating about him by performing 'Tomorrow Belongs to Me' on stage. Stuart went on to collaborate with the National Front in promoting 'white power rock' through the promotional institutions of Rock Against Communism and the White Noise Club, and subsequently with the more marginal, explicitly violent Combat 18 through Blood and Honour. Through the organisation of gigs, festivals and recordings, he became crucial in promoting, consolidating and sustaining the skinhead subculture as a specifically neo-Nazi phenomenon.

The world Stuart hated was one that demanded specific sorts of socialisation and subservience:

> I don't wanna go to work another day
> I wanna be somebody
> I don't wanna wear no dinner suit
> I don't wanna family (*sic*)

Each of these lines is a cliché expressed in a fraudulent accent (Stuart was a Lancastrian), but collectively they are instructive because they express a rejection of conformity in terms of aspiration ('I wanna be somebody'), and thereby precisely delineate a social contradiction highlighted by Alan Sinfield in his account of postwar Britain. The welfare capitalism that was breaking down at the time Stuart sang these words had sought, and failed, to reconcile its claims to promote inclusiveness and national community with an economic growth through individual consumption whose benefits were inevitably felt more by some than others. Resentment was, and still is, expressed in terms of being 'left out'. 'Hence', writes Sinfield,

> the persistent, though incoherent, strain of disaffection and aggression in postwar British society. We may observe it in youth cultures, in disputes and lack of co-operation at work and in education; in vandalism and other abuses of the environment; in indifference towards the official political system (including trades unions); in hostility to minorities such as Blacks, Asians and gays; in lack of consideration towards the disabled, the sick and the elderly; in drug abuse and civil disorder.[25]

Ian Stuart was somebody in the end, but his aspirations paradoxically led not so much to commercial success; rather, he sought to uphold the 'rights' of a 'community' whose essential decency he felt could only be restored by violently (re-)establishing it as coterminous with the nation the state had betrayed, notably through decolonisation and its postwar sponsorship of immigration. Stuart's biography, *Diamond in the Dust*, written by members of Combat 18, is a distillation of British neo-Nazi skinhead sensibilities, combining veneration for Hitler with violent anti-Semitism and hostility to non-whites and homosexuals, while nonetheless absurdly asserting a belief in 'English' freedoms of speech and action that are specifically denied to white nationalists.[26]

A sense of white victimhood is not confined to neo-Nazis, however. In an interview about his novel, *Skinheads*, left-wing and self-consciously working-class writer John King suggests that multiculturalism 'has been promoted by too many careerists with a chip on their shoulder, England-haters who have been brainwashed at university. When the white British are told they don't even have a culture, and see their way of life and beliefs constantly belittled and sneered at, well, it's surprising there hasn't been more of a backlash'.[27] Such sentiments manifest a defensiveness and sense of pathos about 'white English/British' marginality[28] that merge all too clearly with appeals made by various forces on the right. King's leftist sense of Englishness as evident in all his writings is allied to the postwar settlement: people fought a war against Nazism for something that has subsequently been betrayed. This is a powerful narrative; the problem is the implication it may carry that that settlement was and is an achievement by and for the white English/British. Paul Gilroy has highlighted similar problems in others' attempts to reclaim patriotism for the left that are perhaps epitomised by the nuances in meaning of the very word 'settlement'.[29]

And yet, if we were to risk distorting Sinfield's point somewhat by imagining a single figure cumulatively becoming visible through his description of the various kinds of disaffection welfare capitalism has generated, he would surely be the presumptively straight, white working-class male; subliminally, at least, he is present. And he has become increasingly visible to the extent that he is now variously regarded perhaps as the modern epitome of that characteristic sixties figure, the social problem, but also as the despised chav or scally.[30] Indeed, practically the only time in which class gets mentioned in official discourse these days is in conjunction with him.[31] What this suggests is that those who might discern this figure in Sinfield's account – cosmopolitans should we call them? – are themselves implicated in the socio-cultural distinctions he is effectively describing.

To the extent that the skinhead has epitomised the figure of the straight white working-class male in his time, he has also generated an instructive confusion. David Leland's extraordinary TV drama, *Made in Britain* (Clark, 1982), focuses on the adolescent skinhead, Trevor. The swastika in the centre of his forehead projects his unpacifiable rage, not only towards British Asians, but to the welfare capitalism on which he is dependent (for a bed, food, spending money: for the duration of the drama he is 'on probation'). At the outset, in court, a posh, offscreen JP speaks to him in the voice Trevor knows to be authority-in-general: 'You do not invite leniency do you?' This is rhetorical, meant to put Trevor in his place, but he replies: 'No.' The exchange perfectly accounts for the inevitability of all that follows.

For all his racist violence, there is a romantic appeal to Trevor that registers with the left: he recognises the system as such, and will not be reasonable, will not be understood; he is anything but a 'docile body'.[32] Moreover, his absolute refusal to compromise propels him inevitably towards the police violence and incarceration that is also the system's – rather than his – ultimate indictment: though Trevor's almost preternatural and articulate malevolence appears unconditioned, the drama's title apportions blame, alluding ironically to the lack of employment available at this time, as well as to the peculiar 'patriotism' this has generated in people like Trevor. There is a tension even here, though: Trevor's persona surely casts that way of framing him as itself too understanding, too normative. Form and content are far from balanced, and those enamoured of his violence get a thrill out of Tim Roth's performance as Trevor.

Trevor's body, then, refuses imprisonment by the modern soul: he pisses on his probation file. But he is also for this very reason sexy – and putting it in words like that I know I risk casting myself as the middle-class, middle-aged queer Trevor would beat up in recognition of that truth. The skinhead's rebelliousness, like that of other subcultural groups, was characterised by sexual self-consciousness in ways that nonetheless facilitated differentiation from the counterculture. In the skinhead's case, this was through a style that made a fetish of aggressive, white working-class masculinity: a specific look was turned into an expression of authenticity through its defiance of the effeminate ephemera of fashion. The skinhead, then, is a particular erotic configuration: all accounts of him stress the sensuality of boots, skintight jeans and haircut (the feel of it, not just the appearance) – and the *homo*erotic potential of skinheads resides in their mutual acknowledgement of that fact (dancing topless, arm-in-arm together at gigs, for instance, as both *Brotherhood* and *Children of the Sun* emphasise).

'Hitler was a skinhead.' This favourite chant of theirs flaunts its own anachronistic implausibility because the skinhead is in so many ways an affront to Nazi ideals. Was the skinhead really the manifestation of racial superiority? He appeared to many as its dissolution.[33] Far from being the heroic Greek ideal of Nazi propaganda, his defining feature invited comparisons rather with Nazi victims; he certainly did not project futurity by any of the conventional images of optimism. Even if skinheads of various political hues have often claimed to stand for British decencies, they appear to middle-class onlookers to invert all those related moral and physical prioritisations of high over low that have been encoded and subjectively instilled in us as *uprightness*.[34] There is one further corollary to this: to the extent that he now lurks, along with others such as the chav, behind any invocation of the specifically ethnic category of 'whiteness',[35] he has sullied its purity, not least because he foolishly still believes in it. He is hated and feared; he fascinates and is desired.

Political Desire: *Children of the Sun*

It is the skinhead's specifically sexual appeal with which Max Schaefer's novel is largely concerned. And the role played by desire in part determines its form. In one sense, it is clearly a realist novel. Not only does it seek to recreate a plausible world, but its narratives trace a route through specific historical events, incorporating figures from them, along with clippings from newspapers, anti- and neo-fascist publications, the music press, hand-printed 'zines and the like. Indeed, in part the novel forms a history of neo-Nazi factions as well as anti-fascist activity from 1970 on. If the result of this very process is paradoxically to disturb fixed distinctions between fact and fiction, I am less concerned with whether this makes the novel technically postmodern than with its effects. After all, its subject matter makes us acutely aware of the dangers of relativising history into different possible narratives, since this might give legitimacy to those the novel implicitly critiques. Rather, I would say that it is concerned with establishing and reflecting on the social determinations of the erotic in history as the erotic has been incorporated into the contemporary reality principle to often disorienting effect.[36]

It is important, then, that the novel's first person narrator, James, is a middle-class creative writer with liberal left values who mixes in similar circles. He picks up a skinhead boyfriend, Adam, on the 2003 London demonstration against the invasion of Iraq. Adam manages to separate skinhead style from any political convictions it might be presumed to carry, but his attractiveness to the more intellectual James is symptomatic of the latter's more general seduction by the image that determines his research into the neo-Nazi past, including its more esoteric branches and their potential further to disturb his rational sense of proportion and connection. Indeed, James's horrified romance with neo-Nazism gradually determines the breakdown of his actual relationship with Adam precisely because James loses his grip on reality. The historical figure who so fascinates James is the iconic skinhead who appeared topless on the notorious *Strength Through Oi!* album and became bodyguard to Ian Stuart during the 1980s, Nicky Crane. Crane rejected neo-Nazism when he came out very publicly in 1992.

James's loss of control, however, is partly a consequence of the fantasies reality now pervasively incites. Hence, the scene in a skinhead fetish club at which Adam is a regular. It is James's first visit, and he can't handle either the ease with which Adam negotiates their open relationship or the equally easy disavowal of racism by the club's punters, one of whom he challenges then later dismisses implausibly on both counts as a '"racist prole"'.[37] As James's friend, Philip, points out, it is precisely this possibility that excites him sexually: the white working-class, James imagines, lacks inhibition. Adam's naivety, by contrast, is rather too indebted to liberal assumptions: he suggests that people's problems with his appearance are simply down to their prejudices. The taste for fetish and SM scenes to which his skinhead identity is connected is hardly just a matter of private preference, though: it entails the eroticisation of a danger with which the skinhead is associated.

This is emphasised through the way that the narrative of James contrasts, but ultimately converges, with the history of Tony, who becomes a skinhead himself after being seduced by one in a cottage in 1970 when he is 14. In Tony's case, the distinction between the desire to be and the desire for is elided at the outset through the appeal to him of the skinhead's embodiment of transgression: symbolically, he initially asserts his power by scaring off an older, hesitant middle-class cottager whom Tony first approaches. The mood of the cottage itself is highlighted by graffiti on the wall: 'On a window above the sink someone has drawn a penis and balls, in three loops like a cartoon cactus. Spraying from it are the words PAKI'S OUT.'[38] Not only is the cottage associated by its nature with the lower parts from which the upright body ideally distances itself, but in this sketch the political demand is expressed in the form of sexual climax and expulsion, rather than through formal, corporeal integrity: racism is rebellious.

The social possibilities for the queer appropriation of the skinhead's potential are highlighted in the early stages of the novel by the willingness of Tony and his first boyfriend, Dennis, to pose for a gay photographer for cash. Indeed, for most of Tony's life, skinhead and gay subcultures remain distinct, if not entirely separate, and what we might describe as Tony's sexual capital thrives on that distinction. At one point, he picks up a student who insists on role play with him even after being abused by Tony's skinhead friends on the tube. Moreover, Tony's acquaintance with James occurs through an online hookup site on which Tony – now in his fifties – advertises as 'arealnazi'. His profile is without pictures, a spur to the fantasy further encouraged by a text that promises violence ('*Nazi skinhead thug, fat, middle aged, tats, will abuse worthless scum*').[39] James finds this a turn on: at one point, while he exposes himself by webcam at arealnazi's direction, he is instructed to draw a swastika on his cock. He protests, but his cock leaps 'disloyally'.[40]

The potential climax to the novel, however – the final meeting of Tony and James – is also necessarily its disappointment. What, after all, might satisfy James's desire? Certainly not the financially hard up, ageing and therefore humanised, actual person of Tony who finally arrives. The two end up watching one of the porn films Nicky Crane was rumoured to have made in the eighties, but it is corny, a further turn off.

Conclusions

Murray Healy's insightful and provocative discussion of the skinhead stresses his absorption into queer subcultures to the extent that this has eroded the popular perception of his primarily ideological significance; a politics of resignification has taken place that has seen him become one among a number of recognisable queer types. At the same time, he is queer, Healy claims, because he challenges some of the respectable aspirations that were already a feature of gay politics in the nineties: the skinhead 'was a misfit, and it was that very outsider-ness to the world which "gay" had become that queer championed'.[41] So the skinhead had now become divorced from his neo-Nazi image and yet continued to cut an edgy figure in a world of increasing homonormativity. There is plausibility to this claim, but it is perhaps too neat, because the romantic abstractions ('misfit', 'outsider') function to disavow any connection to a more socially specific figure who lurks in a way that must continue to determine the prospects for his resignification. Moreover, if the neo-Nazi skinhead was made in Britain, he has been a successful export, and is still very much with us, attacking both immigrants and queers in Germany, Russia,[42] Greece and elsewhere, as *Brotherhood* reminds us.

There is, nonetheless, a certain abstraction to the skinhead's appeal. He visibly rejects normalcy, the rules and repressions of upbringing, even if this entails a possibly militant conformity. Aggression, in this sense, is indivisible from him, however personally agreeable and decent any individual skinhead may be. But socialisation of some sort is inevitable, and its romantic, merely 'antinormative', disavowal should not be mistakenly regarded as progressive in itself. Some are privileged enough to be able to play around with fantasies of rebellion, especially under contemporary conditions of expanded subcultural space and technological stimulation. In *Children of the Sun*, James's fantasies are of a kind of desubjectification, or deterritorialisation, that extends to his liberal-left sensibility. In *Brotherhood*, Lars is in flight from a bourgeois domestication that now includes 'political correctness', but he never becomes a skinhead himself. This remains the sign of a white working-class frustration and affirmation that generates fantasies of political transcendence.

If there is a general relationship between male same-sex passion and fascism it is a loose one, attendant on the ambiguity and contradiction that are characteristic of all predominantly homosocial movements and institutions, as well as fascism's apparent anti-bourgeois promise where bourgeois societies have been repressive. The figure of the skinhead, however, was distinctive because he gave a class inflection to more general conditions of youth rebellion and 'desublimation', the same conditions ultimately that gave rise to the sexual liberation movements. Given this common origin, and the mobility of commodified identities, it should not be so surprising that the significations of the skinhead have proved multi-accentual. To say that, however, is precisely not to suggest that meaning has become plural and may be put to various uses, but rather that it is governed by social tension and conflict of which the illusion of (cosmopolitan) autonomy and indeterminacy are symptoms. *Brotherhood* and *Children of the Sun* may offer different perspectives, but they are ultimately perspectives on the same world.

University of Manchester

Notes

1. Johann Hari, 'The Strange, Strange Case of the Gay Fascists', 25 May 2011, http://www.huffingtonpost.com/johann-hari/the-strange-strange-story_b_136697.html (accessed 25 June 2014).
2. Erik N. Jensen, 'The Pink Triangle and Political Consciousness: Gays, Lesbians, and the Memory of Nazi Persecution', in *Sexuality and German Fascism*, ed. Dagmar Herzog (New York: Bergahn Books, 2005), 322–3.
3. Judith Halberstam, *The Queer Art of Failure* (Durham, NC: Duke University Press, 2011), 147–71.
4. Richard Plant, *The Pink Triangle: The Nazi War Against Homosexuals* (New York: Henry Holt, 1986), 53–69.
5. Halberstam, *The Queer Art of Failure*, 148.
6. Sullivan is the author of *Virtually Normal: An Argument About Homosexuality* (London: Picador, 1996); see, more recently, his essay 'The End of Gay Culture: Assimilation and Its Meaning', in *The New Republic*, 24 October 2005, http://www.newrepublic.com/article/politics/the-end-gay-culture (accessed 20 June 2014).
7. Michael Warner, *The Trouble With Normal: Sex, Politics and the Ethics of Queer Life* (Cambridge, MA: Harvard University Press, 2000).
8. Max Schaefer, *Children of the Sun* (London: Granta, 2011).
9. Jonathan Dollimore examines psychoanalytic and materialist accounts of this dynamic in *Sexual Dissidence: Augustine to Wilde, Freud to Foucault* (Oxford: Clarendon Press, 1991), 242–8.

10 George L. Mosse, *Nationalism and Sexuality: Middle-Class Morality and Sexual Norms in Modern Europe* (Madison: University of Wisconsin Press, 1985).
11 Fritz Stern, *The Politics of Cultural Despair* (Berkeley: University of California Press, 1961), 176–80.
12 Andrew Hewitt, however, argues that Blüher's emphasis on Eros was cultural, rather than biological and racial. His anti-Semitism emerged from his counterposition of the family (heterosociality) with the State (homosociality), and a belief that stateless Jews identified principally with the former. *Political Inversion: Homosexuality, Fascism and the Modernist Imaginary* (Stanford: Stanford University Press, 1996), 104–29.
13 Ernst Roehm, *The Memoirs of Ernst Roehm*, trans. Geoffrey Brooks (London: Frontline Books, 2012), 170–1.
14 Cited in Geoffrey J. Giles, 'Same-Sex Incidents in Himmler's SS and Police', in *Sexuality and German Fascism*, ed. Herzog, 261.
15 Giles, 'Same-Sex Incidents in Himmler's SS and Police', 289.
16 See Dagmar Herzog, 'Hubris and Hyprocrisy, Incitement and Disavowal', in *Sexuality and German Fascism*, ed. Herzog, 8–13.
17 Klaus Theweleit, *Male Fantasies*, 2 vols, trans. Erica Carter and Chris Turner (Minneapolis: University of Minnesota Press, 1987 and 1989).
18 See his discussion of Elaine Morgan's controversial work, *The Descent of Woman* (London: Souvenir Press, 1972), in *Male Fantasies*, vol. 1, 288–94.
19 For a more trenchant analysis along similar lines, see Michael Rothberg's critique in 'Documenting Barbarism: Yourcenar's Male Fantasies, Theweleit's Coup', *Cultural Critique* 29 (1994–5), esp. 98–108.
20 Theweleit, *Male Fantasies*, vol. 2, 407–8.
21 The inverted commas here acknowledge that I am not using this term in any precise economic or sociological sense, but am accepting the tellingly less discriminating cultural use of it.
22 On the distinction between counter- and specifically working-class subcultures, see John Clarke, Stuart Hall, Tony Jefferson and Brian Roberts, 'Subcultures and Class', in *Resistance Through Rituals: Youth Subcultures in Postwar Britain*, ed. Tony Jefferson and Stuart Hall (London: Routledge, 1996), 65–71.
23 As, for instance, throughout John King's novel, *Skinheads* (London: Jonathan Cape, 2008), which I discuss below. In Trevor Griffiths's drama, *Oi for England* (1982), politics divides a skinhead band, and in *This Is England* (dir. Shane Meadows, 2006) the specifically neo-Nazi figure, Combo, is distinguished by his pathological predisposition to violence.
24 Dick Hebdige, *Subculture: The Meaning of Style* (London: Methuen, 1979), 63.
25 Alan Sinfield, *Literature, Politics and Britain in Postwar Britain*, 3rd edition (London: Continuum, 2004), 319.
26 See http://www.skrewdriver.net/diamond.html (accessed 10 July 2014).
27 http://www.bookdepository.com/interview/with/author/john-king (accessed 15 July 2014).
28 I don't have the space here to interrogate the obviously significant and problematic elision King (and others) make between English and British.
29 Paul Gilroy, *There Ain't No Black in the Union Jack* (London: Unwin Hyman, 1987), 51–3.
30 For the dimensions and extent of this disdain, see Owen Jones, *Chavs* (London: Verso, 2012).
31 Kjartan Páll Sveinsson highlights this: 'Introduction. The White Working Class and Multiculturalism: Is There Space for a Progressive Agenda', in *Who Cares About the White Working Class*, ed. Kjartan Páll Sveinsson (Runnymede Trust, 2009), 3–7.

32 This is Michel Foucault's term for the quiescent modern subject. See *Discipline and Punish: The Birth of the Prison*, trans. Alan Sheridan (London: Allen Lane, 1977), 135–69.
33 Walter Laqueur touches on some of the negative responses to skinheads by older fascists and those elsewhere in Europe in *Fascism: Past, Present, Future* (Oxford: Oxford University Press, 1994), 128.
34 The best analysis of this process I know comes in Peter Stallybrass and Allon White, *The Politics and Poetics of Transgression* (Ithaca: Cornell University Press, 1986), 125–48.
35 The classic exploration of the symbolism of whiteness is Richard Dyer's *White* (London: Routledge, 1997).
36 I am following Herbert Marcuse's critique of Freud here in suggesting that the reality principle into which we are socialised is historically variable. See *Eros and Civilization: A Philosophical Inquiry Into Freud* (London: Routledge, 1956), esp. 11–54.
37 Schaefer, *Children of the Sun*, 256.
38 Schaefer, *Children of the Sun*, 4.
39 Schaefer, *Children of the Sun*, 164, emphasis original.
40 Schaefer, *Children of the Sun*, 212.
41 Murray Healy, *Gay Skins: Class, Masculinity and Queer Appropriation* (London: Cassell, 1996), 173.
42 See Hilary Pilkington, Elena Omel'chenko, and Al'bina Garifzianova, *Russia's Skinheads: Exploring and Rethinking Subcultural Lives* (London: Routledge, 2013) for a detailed account.

People of the Black Mountains and the Politics of Theory
John Connor

Abstract: In this essay I situate Raymond Williams's historical novel trilogy, *People of the Black Mountains*, in a late-century historical conjuncture and structure of feeling. I address Williams's attempt to solve the problem of genre: how, as he saw it, to write a historical novel that was neither 'period fiction', the recreation of a past time 'remaining enclosed within that period', nor one with the emerging metafictional forms of postmodernism. The search for precedent and inspiration for 'a historical novel of a different kind' led Williams to revisit the cultural production of the mid-century United and Popular Fronts; and it is from these examples, specifically the workers' theatre plays of Bertolt Brecht and the fiction of Welsh fellow-traveller Gwyn Thomas, that Williams found the formal means to do with the novel what he was also attempting to do in his essays in critical theory and socialist strategy: help us to rediscover the political in moments of local capacity and to find in ourselves our own best 'resources for a journey of hope.'

*

'I Don't Take Easily to Detachment'[1]

Raymond Williams resented the label the 'English Lukács'.[2] To a border-countryman and 'Welsh European', the adjective 'English' rankled, as did the identification with a career he saw as quite unlike his own.[3] Lukács signified, for Williams, 'a very specific and important kind of mind', 'the mind of one kind of high intellectual, who knows and accepts and keeps his distance from what others see as substantial everyday life'. A conception of the philosophical project as one 'from which merely personal matters are excluded' could never be Williams's, nor could the pride with which Lukács claimed only second-hand knowledge of emotional disturbance.[4] 'I can say that I have never felt frustration or any kind of complex in my life. I know what these mean of course, from the literature of the 20th century, and from having read Freud. But I have not experienced them myself.'[5] This is the boast of the intellectual who has shed their bourgeois skin, who is no longer prey to the liberal affliction of believing themselves special or their private life of any general significance. Of its sort, the abnegation is admirable: we appreciate the impulse to cauterise the personal, to transcend the limitations of the individual and so enter unblinkered into critical understanding of the social whole. Lukács takes Heraclitus at his word: those who are awake have a world in common, every sleeper has a world his own.[6] But Williams sees also the blind spot of such a wide-awake world, for our feelings are never quite so private or our dreams only ours alone.

Indeed, Williams's most celebrated conceptual innovation was to compound the cognitive 'aspiration to totality' with an affective register, comprising 'all the known complexities, the experienced tensions, shifts, and uncertainties, the intricate forms of unevenness and confusion' that make up daily life.[7] The 'structure of feeling' was a plea for a kind of criticism, indeed for a kind of socialist strategy, that would dare approach the world so commonly 'specialized as "emotional"', the world 'where people actually live', 'that world in which people live as they can as themselves'.[8] It too was aspirational: from its first mention in *A Preface to Film* (1954, with Michael Orrom) to its full theoretical elaboration in Williams's *Marxism and Literature* (1977), the 'structure of feeling' was a reaching for reconciliation between the competing claims of social constructionism and socialist humanism, the necessity and the benefit of doubt.[9] It was an expression of desire for a different ethical and temporal relationship to the object of study: not the presumed insight of hindsight or the easy distance of critique, but a wager on closeness and co-presence.

Williams was repudiating what he saw as the dominant critical tendency to turn 'contemporary life' and 'the always moving substance of the past' into 'finished products' and 'fixed forms', 'formed wholes rather than forming and formative processes'. It was a method mimetic, he argued, of a capitalist imperialism presumed always to have already colonised, by ideology and incorporation, our human creativity and capacity for resistance.[10] The structure of feeling promised instead an opening onto emergence, onto a process of becoming in the 'generative immediacy' of 'the true social present'.[11] Williams had in mind 'characteristic elements of impulse, restraint, and tone; specifically elements of consciousness and relationships; not feeling against thought, but thought as felt and feeling as thought: practical consciousness of a present kind, in a living and interrelating continuity'.[12] To privilege practical knowledge of this sort, though situated 'at the very edge of semantic availability', though partial, personal and subject to all manners of mistaking, was not to abdicate the aspiration to totality but to recognise that analysis takes time and in the meantime we must manage. Nor was it to deny the impress of ideology on our powers of historical response, but rather to credit, under duress, our ordinary ability to adapt and to improvise, to feel our way in time. For the structure of feeling reveals a present in play, crossed by impulses not yet fully legible and by possibilities not yet foreclosed: it shows the social '*in solution*', 'at once interlocking and in tension'.[13] It signals the point of departure for a poetics and politics of everyday life, and a line of approach to where Williams would have us be, implicated in and intimate with the lives and relationships we discuss.

Lukács, it should be noted, had also been hostile to critical and creative practices that reify the world. In 'Narrate or Describe' (1936) and in the essays that comprise *The Historical Novel* (1937–38), he celebrates the great realist writers for transcribing the dynamic tendencies and contradictions of the historical process; a 'real historical fidelity to the whole' manifests in their novels' 'faithful artistic reproduction of the great collisions, the great crises and turning-points of history'.[14] Whence the famous rejection of description for rendering this larger logic of development static and so concealing our own labour of becoming; whence in turn the praise of narrative for its power of cognitive estrangement, revealing in the alienated order of things an image of man making his destiny, albeit not under conditions of his choosing. The criticism stands, however, that in Lukács the discovery of Marx too little modifies the early matrix of *Lebensphilosophie* and Fichtean metaphysics, giving only a Left-ethical inflection to a narrative of man moving through history from sinfulness to salvation.[15] The work of the critic and critical realist is then to supply the 'unmasking mirror' that, when held up to contemporary society, illuminates the course of a Left-Hegelian *Via Crucis* towards 'the Calvary of Man's totality'.[16] In such a certain teleology there is little need for the contingencies and everyday resistances of history: the focus falls on the 'big occasions', 'crisis periods' and 'deep disturbances of the social' that then 'lay bare those vast, heroic, human potentialities which are always latently present in the people'. 'The possibilities for human upsurge and heroism' require the catalyst of a clarifying catastrophe to lift us out of the ordinary to where History appears.[17]

History is what hurts, we have been well taught, but the argument of the 'structure of feeling' is that it can hurt without the state of exception, without war as such and as a proxy for revolution.[18] In this essay, I follow the implication of Williams's affective turn for the historical novel he wrote across the final decade of his life. Unfinished at his death in 1989, Williams's *People of the Black Mountains* trilogy is a study of survival, of successive adaptations and improvisations told across the discontinuous present of twenty-five thousand years of history in his familiar border country of Wales. I examine the trilogy as a renovation of the genre most famously theorised by Lukács for the age of the Popular Fronts and as a counterblast to the historical novel's late-century emergence as the privileged literary form of postmodernism.[19] I approach its attempt at a realism of the 'true social present' as a challenge to the then dominant poststructuralist critique of the 'classic realist' text and as anticipating more contemporary efforts to revive the mode after the moment, now past, of postmodernism. The most notable forms of this return to realism have been Lukácsian. Fredric Jameson's 'aesthetic of cognitive mapping' is the rubric under which projects as diverse as Allan Sekula's late-career photowork, the HBO television series *The Wire* (2002–08) and Roberto Saviano's 'unidentified narrative object' *Gomorrah* (2006) have come to be read.[20] But alongside the cognitive ambition to narrate the social whole I see Williams's fidelity to feeling, to social life as a scene of affective attachment, negotiation and projection, anticipating developments in critical theory that counterpose a 'depressive realism' to more ordinarily optimistic ways of being in the world and hoping for the future.[21] What resources can we draw for a journey of hope, Williams will ask in this last novel, from reading scenes of 'substantial everyday life', dedramatised and marked more often by failure than by success? It is a question that in its earnest inclusion of 'merely personal matters' distinguishes Williams from the postmodern impulse towards detachment and irony as it does from Lukács's tactical subordination of individual response to the standard of 'objective (historico-philosophical) correctness'.[22]

Seeing a Man Crying

In 1978, Williams emerged from a series of interviews with the editors of the *New Left Review* in 'a condition of almost overwhelming anxiety'.[23] The interviews had ranged freely over many days and four hundred published pages through Williams's life and work, and as they drew to a close he found himself paralysed with the same 'inexplicable kind of sadness', the same 'extreme distress', that he described himself in conversation as having witnessed in others. He had been speaking then of some of his activist friends:

> [...] people I know very well and deeply respect, who have fought and fought and quite clearly had expected that in their lifetime, their active lifetime even, there would be decisive breaks into the future. I have seen one or two of these men actually crying, from some interfused depth of social and personal sadness, and knowing why and knowing the arguments to be set against such a feeling and still in some physical sense absolutely subject to it.[24]

They know — as do we, too well — the dangers of feeling down, where to temporise with negativity risks unfitting us for the struggle. Left melancholy lapses into Left traditionalism, Left conservatism: the terms are ready to hand to punish attachments that appear backward and to elect sadness over hope.[25] The struggle demands that melancholy pass promptly into mourning, that meditation upon the lost object detain us no longer than is necessary to fire us up again to fight. Now, however, it was Williams who was feeling, 'for the first time, some of the states out of which defeatist and reactionary ideologies have so often been built'. And however much 'years of analysis enable me quite easily to reject the projections and conclusions: what they don't help in is getting rid of the states themselves'. Williams determined that the only way to fight this state was by 'going beyond it, not back from it', which in turn meant 'passing through the shadows of the devastating experiences', spending time with the sadness.[26]

Attuned to an emergent structure of feeling, Williams turned again to the question of revolution and the experience of defeat. Williams was fond of the lines in *When We Dead Awaken* that describe 'a tight place, where you stick fast' and where 'there is no going forward or backward'.[27] What Ibsen had framed as personal and thence as 'the essential tragedy of the human situation', Williams transposed to the social and historical: the moment when a movement can no longer move freely, when however much betrayed by circumstance it will not abandon the cause.[28] In theory, at least, we have only to make this transposition, to recognise our feelings as public and the suffering as social, to comprehend and complete 'the tragic action', whose common name 'in our own time […] is revolution'. 'We make the connections, because that is the action of tragedy, and what we learn in suffering is again revolution, because we acknowledge others as men and any such acknowledgment is the beginning of struggle, as the continuing reality of our lives.'[29] But in the final decade of Williams's life, this revolutionary cycle felt stalled at the point of crisis. The 1979 'Afterword' to *Modern Tragedy* describes 'a specific contemporary sadness' no longer the monopoly of a movement culture but a function of the culture at large. The failures of the Soviet experiment and the colonial liberation movements, the breakdown of the postwar consensus, the rise of the New Right and 'the terrible disintegration of what was once a labour movement' only point to a more devastating development: the 'widespread loss of the future', 'the loss of hope; the slowly settling loss of any acceptable future'.[30] The future that once empowered the socialist project has shrunk to the short-term projections of the election cycle and the commodities trade; whatever remains of our power to imagine the future has been colonised by figurations of catastrophe: mass unemployment, environmental collapse, 'the millennium as apocalypse; the final crisis as nuclear holocaust'.[31]

The influential account of this reorganisation of time and tense comes in the analogy Fredric Jameson draws between the temporal logics of schizophrenia and late capitalism. The model derives from Deleuze and Guattari, and behind them from Lacan, and describes 'a breakdown of the signifying chain' that strands the subject in 'a series of pure and unrelated presents in time'.[32] Each moment comes before the patient 'with heightened intensity, bearing a mysterious charge of affect', the lack of coherent sequence and indexical relation to a world outside the subject more than made up for by feelings of 'intoxicatory or hallucinogenic intensity'.[33] Like the schizophrenic, the postmodern subject inhabits a world of delaminated moments, colour-saturated images and distracting intensities, utterly unable to map the world system that envelops them and so restore to it a sense of 'the activities and the intentionalities that might focus [the present] and make it a space of praxis'.[34] This is not the place to attempt the 'parallel study' of Jameson and Williams for which Peter Brooker has rightly called, but we may note in passing one difference, no doubt a function of their different social locations: that whereas for Jameson, late capitalism's 'emotional groundtone' appears the 'liberation from anxiety' to 'a peculiar kind of euphoria', for Williams, this anxiety overwhelms.[35] The same reduction of the temporal manifold to the narrow place of the present produces not a 'waning of affect' but its tragic surcharge: the lost object – hope, the future horizon – shapes a present immobilised by 'deadlock and stalemate', 'a blocked and [...] static period', whose apparent 'vitality in mimicry, parody and pastiche' is a palliative for the pain.[36]

Williams reads critical theory as likewise in flight from the pain of first-person implication and involvement: abstemious and untrusting, the contemporary idioms of critique betray the ethos or affective stance we have already seen him attribute, not altogether fairly, to Lukács.[37] In the linguistic turn, the abstraction of semiotics, sign systems and signifying practices Williams reads the need to speak of processes without subjects and of subjects spoken only by the systems in which they speak; conceding, as he must, that 'these systems, as systematic analysis reveals them, have great explanatory power', he nevertheless insists that 'the form and language of their explanations' is anaesthetic: bracingly cold, 'ice-cold', a guard against the pain of self-discovery in the new crisis-ordinary of the impasse.[38] The invitation is for theory to return to room temperature and to entertain other interpretative possibilities.[39] Williams maps out two. For a critical theory that has come to disregard the present as the domain of ideological interpellation and false consciousness, a reminder that the dominant 'never in reality includes or exhausts all human practice, human energy, and human intention:' the present is always also a time of emergence, of the improvisation of 'new perceptions and practices of the material world'.[40] For a socialism that finds itself fixed in time, frozen in attitudes of action and analysis that no longer work, a reminder that 'the dynamic movement' lies in coming to terms with and 'gaining confidence in *our own* energies and capacities'.[41]

In the late essays on socialist strategy, Williams scans the contemporary for signs of popular 'self-management': strikes and sit-ins, worker occupations, 'various kinds of community organizations' and volunteer work.[42] He offers these as moments in the long revolution, the learning-by-doing, through active planning, decision-making and implementation, through error and correction, of a 'sharing socialism'.[43] But as the trilogy will underscore, collective militancy and self-organisation cannot be the only narrative of the Left: survival, the process of maintaining and repairing solidarity, has also to be told, because it too, and crucially, has always happened. Rather than project a possible future to motivate political desire, *People of the Black Mountains* suggests that we draw our conclusions from 'the sheer duration of the struggle for alternatives; the repeated postponements of hope'.[44] 'The defeats have occurred over and over again, and what my novel is then trying to explore is simply the condition of anything surviving at all.'[45] The fact, and the feat, of survival is the trilogy's true theme, a statement of faith in our ability to invent, and continually to reinvent, from within the scene of survival, new idioms of the social. It is, perhaps, a bleak lesson to draw from the past and from our own blocked present: a refiguration of the cultural revolution as 'long, hard, contentious and untidy – its one criterion of success, for as far as we can see, being a possible majority of successes over its many failures'.[46] The temporal orientation is towards the chastened optimism of the present of possibility and what, within the structural dominant of an epoch, is always emergent.[47] Williams will have us remember that 'the moment of transition to an idea of socialism […] comes not once and for all but many times; is lost and is found again; has to be affirmed and developed, continually, if it is to stay real'.[48] *People of the Black Mountains* commits to this labour of affirmation and development, where with each new defeat it is not the pain of loss that comes to the fore but rather the assurance that despite it, and at whatever minimum, we survive and so preserve the possibility of social change. It is this 'shared belief and insistence that there are practical alternatives' that 'has been, from the beginning, the sense and impulse of the long revolution'.[49]

'The Realist Project Today'[50]

Williams came at the trilogy no stranger to the genre. His first attempt at publication had been a novel of the English Revolution (a manuscript submitted to Victor Gollancz when he was sixteen and politely declined), and the long struggle with what became his first published novel *Border Country* (1960) involved the writing and rejection of a draft novel – 'Between Two Worlds' (1958) – set at the time of the 1926 General Strike. But like other forms shaped in lasting ways 'within a bourgeois world', he found the historical novel initially ill-suited to his purpose.[51] The form seemed only to invite a simple contrast – 'what it was like yesterday; not like today' – and to show the past, 'enclosed in its time', as 'an object – often colourful – of spectacle'.[52] What the form did not seem set up to do, Williams felt, was capture 'the continuity of working-class life', 'the lives of working people who continue, as real men and women, beyond either victory or defeat'.[53]

With its 'twenty-five thousand years, a thousand generations', *People of the Black Mountains* maps the span of our attention to the long revolution's very *longue durée*.[54] The trilogy shares with the *Annales* school historians, who coined the term, something of the same suspicion of the chronology of crisis and the eventful history of state politics and social elites. Drawing likewise upon traditions of geohistory and historical geography, Williams states his intention to write 'a true historical novel', 'a historical materialist novel', to show man located in a milieu and in habits shaped by his natural environment.[55] Together with his wife Joy, Williams undertook 'long research' and wide reading in the titles of archaeology, palaeology, environmental, economic and social history that append the second volume, and then took his thinking about 'the base' 'away from [the] books' to 'the actual ground, however altered, where it all happened'. *In situ*, the earth offered up its own 'authentic information, stressing every syllable of that word'. Up on the mountains, ground and base, natural and social history, came 'into some kind of contact', some kind of felt and mutual 'information'.[56] The trilogy is tailored, therefore, to the 'form of human relationships within a physical world'. Its idiom is one of 'livelihoods', of 'direct and practical ways of life' forged in concert with nature. And so, although geography, climate, mentality matter, they do so to inculcate 'a broader sense of human need and a closer sense of the physical world'.[57] Not for Williams the *Annales* school fantasy of an immobile history, a history without people.[58]

People of the Black Mountains unfolds as a series of sixty-plus projected episodes, each one suggesting some new adaptation, some change in livelihood or startling new capacity of thought. The stories converge upon, and are interwoven with, a present time in which a young man, searching for his grandfather fallen in the hills, retraces the old man's steps and the history that lies beneath them. As Glyn walks the 'heart line' of the mountains, the earth stirs memories of the people who have made their lives on it.[59] This frame narrative also gives us Glyn's commentary, the commentary of a university student with a 'well certified education': it is he who must parse, for himself and for us, the different levels of abstraction and kinds of knowing, the distance between his grandfather's amateur interest in the local history and his own professional training, the further distance between the 'touch and breath' of the 'mind' on the mountains and the 'record and analysis' of the academy, between 'history as narrative [and] stories as lives'.[60]

One episode, for example, takes place some five and a half millennia before the Common Era and tells of a boy, too frail to hunt with his tribe, who conceives instead the plan to trap a piglet and to feed it up for food in the winter months when the hunting is lean. He is foiled, and the story ends with his disappointment. Had he succeeded, we are to understand, the Neolithic Revolution would have come early to the Black Mountains. As Glyn then reflects: 'What had happened, and failed, in the case of Aaron and his pig, must have happened, failing or briefly and intermittently succeeding, many hundreds of times. Two thousand years were to pass, eighty generations, before another hunter […] saw the decisive change from hunting to herding and cultivation.'[61] 'Many hundreds of times': we hear in this Williams's 'one criterion of success' in living the long revolution, the possible preponderance of successes over defeats.[62] We hear in it Williams's note to the socialist novelist: 'the necessary inclusion of defeats and failures, and the relations between these and subsequent adaptations. Possible only in the historical novel […]'[63] At stake in the story, then, is less the local signification of the struggle (the domestication of a pig) than the drama of improvisation and the assurance, within what Williams calls 'the endlessly repeated present', of 'subsequent adaptations'.[64] Against the once and for all revolutionary conjuncture, with its providential teleology and single, unilinear model, Williams argues for a change of pace and scale, a sort of devolution from the destiny-driven grand narrative of the great collective project to the moments of small drama that constitute the interleaved episodes of the trilogy. 'The true pace, always, was local and day by day', concludes Glyn of the story of Aaron's pig.[65]

People of the Black Mountains is history 'written very much, as it were, from below', its episodes of labour and livelihood all told 'from the point of view of the people who were using this often very unpromising land to make a living'.[66] As Glyn reflects of the early chronicles of the kings, with their epithets '"the Good", "the Evil" or "the Bald"', the problem was 'not in the assigned names' nor even 'in seeing past them to an indecipherable scramble of rulers and kingdoms'; the problem lay 'in seeing under this starlight the crowded history of unrecorded and anonymous men and women, through generations of repression and war', their relations always more complex and their means of survival more subtle.[67] But the trilogy is also critical of what Williams sees as a tendency in Left social history to rest content with the rescue of history's lost 'myriads of eternity', to narrate 'the making, the struggles, the defeats of a class' without framing those defeats 'as springboards for new struggles or as lessons for final victory'.[68] As Williams remarks in the 1979 'Afterword' to *Modern Tragedy*, there have indeed been 'significant and understandable new connections with periods of our own popular struggles, and especially with some of the most heroic and invigorating periods', but this positive development can also 'be seen as one of the more active forms of the loss of a future. For there is a sense in which the reproduction of struggle is not primarily, whatever may be claimed, a production of struggle'.[69]

The two terms discover the tension in Williams's long-standing 'defence of realism' between what he calls its indicative and subjunctive modes. There are 'social realities that cry out' for realism's 'serious detailed recording and diagnostic attention', its 'challenging selection of the crises, the contradictions, the unexplored dark areas' of the social: 'our central commitment', writes Williams, 'has always to be to those areas of hitherto silenced or fragmented or positively misrepresented experience'.[70] But what if 'the mere reproduction of an existing reality' becomes 'a passivity, even an acceptance of the fixed and immobile?'[71] Realism can indeed state powerfully 'that this is what reality is like, these were the impulses that emerged and these were the impulses that were thwarted'; it can stand powerful testament to 'a social situation in which at one level or another all roads have been blocked'.[72] But we have then to move beyond 'the more bystanding and incidental versions of realism' towards a more dynamic mode of aesthetic and political production.[73]

At an 'ordinary realistic level', writes Williams of the British Left in the 1980s, there has been, there continues, a 'repeated failure, under extraordinary provocation, to generate sufficient collective action'; 'one opportunity after another' has been 'missed, even at times rejected'. The Left has not yet learnt that 'the problem of action is now within a changed set of social relations, in which the obvious lines of action are not simply to be recovered from some past repertory, where people know what the forms of action are'.[74] Left traditionalism has been taken to name the libidinal attachment to a 'past repertory' of analyses and action plans, to the point where a kind of narcissistic identification with an antiquated orthodoxy prevents us from recognising the present state of emergency. The challenge for a socialist art, Williams argues, in consequence, is to model scenes of learning, to familiarise a Left whose own habits of historical responsiveness appear to have stalled with what it looks like to learn, to venture hypotheses, to risk new strategies within a world more ordinary than otherwise. Instead of the preponderant structure of an *Annaliste* 'immobile' history and the crisis-marked hot chronology of the traditional and mid-century Left historical novel, Williams directs attention to the slow processes of adaptation, adjudication and improvisation that play out provisionally and often unsuccessfully within the 'true social present'.[75] For the historical novel, this becomes a prescription not only to include 'defeats and failures' but also to portray the 'learning from defeat', 'the actual learning of lessons, the attainment of a new consciousness by analysis of what has happened'.[76]

In the essays and lectures that became *Politics of Modernism* (1989), Williams claimed that the innovations of the late nineteenth- and early twentieth-century avant-gardes had become 'the new but fixed forms of our present moment' and that the only way 'to break out of the non-historical fixity of *post*-modernism' would be to rewrite our literary history. Specifically, he instructed writers of the Left to 'search out and counterpose an alternative tradition' to the canon of Cold War 'international' modernism, to find precedent for a literature of social engagement from among the 'neglected works left in the wide margin of the century'.[77] The collection sounds the call for criticism and creative practice to exit 'the long and bitter impasse of a once liberating Modernism' and to surpass the limitations of an unrevised realism.[78] It calls on realism to re-enter the space of learning and for modernism to reconnect 'its revolt against the fixed image and the conventional sequence' with 'those areas of shared reality where we are all uncertain, crossed by different truths, exposed to diverse and shifting conditions and relationships, and all these within structures of feeling [...] which can be reached as common'.[79] *People of the Black Mountains* is the consequence of this critical revisionism; from the twentieth century's wide non-canonical margins the trilogy draws inspiration from the experimental workers' theatre of Bertolt Brecht and from a mid-century Welsh historical novel.

In 1986, Williams oversaw the reissue of Gwyn Thomas's fictional account of the 1831 Merthyr Rising, *All Things Betray Thee* (1949) and wrote for it a remarkable introduction. There, he treats the novel as a work of exemplary literary realism in that, though it chronicles a defeat, it transposes the pain and despair to an idiom in which learning becomes ordinary and everyday, part of a political and creative practice. Plot-wise, the rising in the novel's fictional South Wales iron town of Moonlea is suppressed and its leaders killed. But though the movement's 'best voices' are silenced, Thomas assures us at the end that 'The silence and the softness' left by their deaths 'will ripen. The lost blood will be made again. The chorus will shuffle out of its filthy corners and return. The world is full of voices [...] practicing for the great anthem but hardly ever heard. We've been privileged' – and the 'we' includes the reader along with the harpist-protagonist to whom this speech is addressed – to have had 'our ears full of the singing. Silence will never for us be absolute again'.[80] The novel closes with the harpist, Alan Hugh Leigh, walking away from Moonlea 'full of a strong, ripening, unanswerable bitterness, [and] feeling in [his] fingers the promise of a new enormous music'.[81] Williams glosses the conceit: 'The music can be felt in the fingers because the singing has been heard and silenced but also remembered; it is there to be practiced for the next time.'[82] Pointing to a future beyond its time, *All Things Betray Thee* undoes the terms of its title, for 'what comes through' is 'the true promise of that music'. Beyond victory and defeat there remains, for Williams, 'the certainty of the composition: not only the remaking of the lost blood, but the memory of voices which is also a finding of voices: the vast struggle out of silence into a chorus which is at once being practiced and composed'.[83] However belaboured, the musical metaphor initiates for Williams a formal shift from 'representation – the common currency of fiction – [to] rehearsal and performance'.[84]

These elements of composition and practice, rehearsal and performance lift us from the realist mode Williams called 'indicative' (fiction's 'common currency') to the realm of 'subjunctive possibility'. They supply what Williams calls the 'transforming relationships', the process-based 'transformations', that make over the merely mimetic into a mode of 'production of struggle'. Williams credits the 'distinction' to Brecht, and what he came to emphasise – against the popular 'English Brecht' of 'tough talk and open stagecraft' – as 'the most important Brechtian invention'.[85] Williams has in mind the teaching plays Brecht wrote in the period of his 'deliberate movement away from the experimental bourgeois theatre towards a possible working-class theatre'. It was a moment (1926–33) then 'overborne by political history'. Largely left behind after 'the coming to power of the Nazis', the teaching plays offer an alternative to Brecht's subsequent move – in method and subject material – 'towards new and deliberate forms of distance'.[86] The decision to set 'so many of his major plays back in time', the epic drama's 'enthronement of the critical spectator', represent for Williams the reversion, under impossible circumstances, to a less generative and less generous mode of anti-bourgeois or bourgeois avant-garde critique. The teaching plays, by contrast, attempt to abolish the distance between the performance on the stage and the people in the stalls.[87]

At stake in the two Brechts is a critical sensibility: a mode of engagement no longer suspicious or adversarial but open to attachment and approach and willing to work with the people and materials to hand. Herein lies Williams's objection to the Brechtian 'lessons' invoked with such force in the British realism debates of the 1970s.[88] For while he shared with the *Screen* critics a rejection of what Colin MacCabe called the 'fashionable way of receiving and recuperating Brecht' operative in Britain 'since the beginning of the Cold War' (in which Brecht's plays become satires on the possibility of meaningful social change and his techniques turned 'into pure narcissistic signals of an "intellectual" work of "art"'), Williams could not endorse the *Screen* critics' prescription: a more radical art of alienation, a more thoroughgoing complication of artwork and audience in the place of contradiction. A properly revolutionary art, MacCabe claimed, would find itself 'always concerned with an area of contradiction beyond the necessity of the present revolution'.[89] Williams thought the risk simply too great that, in learning to detach themselves from the action, the audience-member and desired reader would pass on to disenchantment or lapse into a self-congratulating sophistication, premised on the abdication of first-person connection and present-political implication. Williams champions the *Lehrstück* for the sake of a political pedagogy that would draft the audience not as critics but as actors and students in the open improvisation of the production itself. The pieces require of their players the adoption of postures, the repetition of speeches, the criticism and adaptation of alternative modes of playing: performance is of a piece with rehearsal, where what is being practiced is the reinvention of daily life and the prefiguration of a socialist society. They place us, writes Williams, 'where we have always in fact been – on the stage and in the action, responsible for how it comes out'.[90]

The Coming of the Measurer

Williams finds especially provocative those instances in the *Lehrstücke* when a scene is 'played and then replayed', when an action that has been played out one way and brought to term is then 'restarted' and 'played differently'.[91] This repetition with a difference models for Williams how a movement might begin to move again within the 'tight place' of the impasse. One such sequence of practice and performance follows from the episode 'The Coming of the Measurer' in the first volume of the trilogy. The story stands out, in part because it reads as a variation on the theme so familiar in Williams's writings of the return of the native, and in part because it is so clearly a parable of the politics of knowledge and power. Here the native is an old man returning home after thirty-four years in Menvandir, one of the Wessex stone-circle settlements that stand 'at the growing point of the world' and at the cutting edge of its 'modernity'.[92] In Menvandir, the little boy from Wales has risen to become one of the elect 'Dalen' of the 'Company of Measurers'; he has learned their ways and taken a new name, Mered. The measurers are the ancient astronomers who oversaw the building of the megaliths; but the 'importance' of Menvandir, for all that it stands as 'the most honoured, the most respected [centre of learning] within the island and beyond', 'is not the place'. 'It is not even the Company, it is the idea. The idea of true measuring.'[93] Menvandir embodies the scientific revolution of its Neolithic time, and the story Williams tells of it carries allegorical significance for the revolutions, including aesthetic and political, of our own. As in Brecht's own allegory of the use and abuse of this idea in his *Life of Gallileo* (1943; 1947), where the revolution in question is at the literal and historical level Copernican, but again also aesthetic and political, what is at stake in the tale is the value of the New.

Mered, we learn, has turned his back on Menvandir because Menvandir has turned its back on the 'idea', abusing its relationship with the community that sustains it for the pursuit, not of knowledge, but of wealth and power. Science has succumbed to the giving of signs and the mystification of the people. As Mered at one time explains, there are 'many orders and forms of order:

of power in learning and learning in power: there are essential differences'.[94] Menvandir has forsaken one form of order for another, learning the ways of power to control a people whose consent, though once willingly given, is now taken by force. 'What had once been community became order, and what had once been gift, tribute.'[95] Shadowing, then, this tale of ancient druidry are the lessons to be drawn from Stalin's appropriation of the idea of communism and from the Cold War West's appropriation of the idea of modernism. Glyn reflects on the fate of this Stone-Age Renaissance, whether it did indeed play out as this story, and as the two ones that follow, have seemed to imply:

> [...] that the highest knowledge of its time [became] so closely connected with power and exploitation that it would at last be rejected, walked away from by people whose suffering, both habitual and sudden, had bred new kinds of fear and belief? Could there have been a generation which learned to see these lords of the sun and moon as evil, turned wilfully away from the common life of water and earth? Turned away also from the old human law, in which all were of a family, and all families of a family, linked by willing and customary gifts and exchange?[96]

This is the benefit of a four-thousand-year hindsight, but it carries consequence for a twentieth-century science, and for conceptions of modernism and socialism, that have failed to nurture the links between their priests and the people, to close the gap between their standards of learning and the general understanding.

In *Life of Galileo*, it is the parallel between Galileo's astronomy and the theoretical physics of Robert Oppenheimer that forces the question. Williams turned often to the play's final scene, which shows Galileo's *Discorsi* being smuggled out of Italy in a carriage, the message in a bottle of a suppressed science, to be printed and distributed among Europe's *illuminati*.[97] Those who read in the scene the power of information to escape controls (and seated in the dock sit the Vatican and Kremlin) miss the larger meaning: for while the carriage crosses the border, the 'boys whom Galileo might have enlightened are still talking about witches'. In leaving the children untutored, Galileo has ill-equipped the world to use for peaceful purpose and the common good a science that will later split the atom and deliver the bomb. The 'highest value', writes Williams, 'is not knowledge, or even, in that limited sense, truth. The central question is what the knowledge is used for, and Galileo's deepest betrayal, in Brecht's version, is to cut the links between knowledge and the education and welfare of the people'.[98]

In Galileo, as in Mered's false colleagues of the Company, we meet a monopolist of knowledge. The academy knows many of their kind. Cambridge

English was one such lapse from 'shared search and discovery' 'to an appropriation, through practical control, of the body of knowledge'; Williams sees the elevation of the professional theorist as another.[99] Williams describes the modernist project as falling likewise into the hands of its 'intellectual agents and dealers', who in the Cold War turned it into 'a dominant and misleading ideology', 'the decisive culture of an international capitalist world'.[100] And the pattern extends to the sciences. Like others of his moment – one thinks of John Lachs on the 'mediation of action' and Zygmunt Bauman on the 'flotation of responsibility' – Williams attends to the political consequence of scientific specialisation, what happens when each field is allowed to develop its own 'operational equations' independent of moral calculus and, due to its high technical specificity, unavailable to popular understanding and democratic oversight.[101] Williams traces the connections between monopolies of knowledge and a state's monopoly 'of overt or threatening violence', concluding that in order 'to refuse nuclear weapons, we have to refuse much more than nuclear weapons' – we have to refuse the privatisation of knowledge and the centralisation of decision-making processes.[102]

Specifically, Williams frames the politics of nuclear disarmament in terms of 'a struggle for a new international information order'.[103] The novel *Loyalties* (1985) maps the emergence of computer-assisted missile systems and automated market-trading systems, and follows the shadowlines that connect the advertising and broadcast media to the university and to the government intelligence agencies, nodes in what would seem an entirely hostile information order. But as Williams also insists, 'no policy of merely defensive exclusion can stand against this. Only the positive recovery, development and open exploratory use of the new forms and technologies by actual societies, for their own diverse purposes, can make new socialist cultures'.[104] The challenge is then the education deficit, the asymmetry, as he calls it with reference to English studies, between 'literature' and 'literacy'.[105] A democratisation of learning would require that the 'relatively enclosed and distanced academies' become 'outward-looking, taking their own best knowledge and skills to a wider and more active society'.[106] Williams means by this the 'taking [of] what has been learned in necessarily difficult work on to testing encounters with all those men and women who have only ever intermittently and incompletely been addressed: going to learn as well as to teach, within a now dangerous unevenness of literacy and learning [...]'.[107]

Just such a testing encounter supplies the conclusion of 'The Coming of the Measurer', as we watch Dal Mered do what Galileo failed to do and teach the child at hand. This scene of instruction corrects for Galileo's compromise and for all the other intelligence professionals (whether professors or spies) who have at one time or another restricted the flow of information.[108] In dramatising an action that has been played before and playing it to a different end, Williams also takes this story into the subjunctive. Dal Mered shows the boy how to draw a perfect circle and to measure the middle of the day; together they mark out the shortest day and set a watchstone for the winter solstice. Within the time of the story, the mothers, who have charge of the traditional midwinter ceremony, stick to their old and inexact way of measuring the seasons, and Mered defers to them. But in a subsequent story, we hear again of Mered and his pupil Karan; they are remembered as 'wise men' and their winter and summer solstice stones are known and used. Of the Karan we met as a boy, it is told how he went on to Menvandir and there learned the higher arts of measuring; it is told how he returned, estranged from the old religion of the mothers but still determined to serve his people. As Mered's private study had been the movements of the planet Mars, Karan's became the ground beneath his feet. 'He walked the mountains, always measuring' for a place of safety from 'the earthstorm', and he died in them alone. Four hundred years have passed and his memory now is fading, but the later story tells of a young man – no measurer, but a practical and observant mind – who completes the search for a shelter from the earthquakes in the mountains. The community build a circle of stones around it, and they consider it sacred.[109]

'To Learn as Well as to Teach'[110]

Told across these several stories is a parable of pedagogy and the politics of theory whose application, beyond the immediate question of solstices and seismic activity, is to socialist strategy broadly conceived. The fate of Menvandir, walked away from by the very people its 'idea' was supposed to serve, is a cautionary tale for all professional intellectuals and proprietors of knowledge. But Dal Mered's course of action is also exemplary, as he turns his back on the university in ruins to teach a curious child, setting a stone to more precisely mark the year's turning but then deferring to the mothers' local and sufficient knowledge. His sensitivity is an acknowledgement that knowledge obtains under different circumstances and material conditions of possibility, shaping specific kinds of solidarity, and that there are real social consequences to thinking in different idioms and at different levels of abstraction. Between the knowledge of Menvandir and the knowledge of the mothers there is a distance that must itself be measured. Reading this story of the measurer, we recall the closing lines of Williams's first novel, *Border Country* (1960), where the resolution to a life divided between the rival claims of knowable community and educated intelligence, local knowledge and critical distance, is said to lie in 'measuring the distance' between them. This is not quite a solution for the novel's returning native, a choice of exile over homecoming or the other way around, but rather a willingness to inhabit the impasse for what it might still have to offer of difficult integrity and political possibility. 'Not going back, but the feeling of exile ending [...] By measuring the distance, we come home.'[111]

Throughout his career, Williams was at pains to underscore that high theoretical abstraction and the most particular, practical knowledge have each their part to play in the socialist struggle. It was the 'unique and extraordinary character of working-class self-organization', Williams reflected, to try 'to connect particular struggles to a general struggle' and so to vindicate 'the extraordinary claim that the defence and advancement of certain particular interests, properly brought together, are in fact the general interest'.[112] The difficulty lies in the bringing together. A struggle that begins 'as local and affirmative, assuming an unproblematic extension from its own local and community experience to a much more general movement', will be unprepared to face 'the quite systematic obstacles' that stand in its way; but the point of view of totality and the systemic perspective tends also to corrode the feeling of affirmation, introducing 'necessarily' its own 'politics of negation', 'politics of differentiation' and 'politics of abstract analysis'.[113] What local experience cannot know abstract analysis can, but only at the expense of what makes an active politics feel most possible in the moment: the immediate experience of collectivity and common purpose. David Harvey glosses this moment in Williams's thought:

> The move from tangible solidarities understood as patterns of social life organized in affective and knowable communities to a more abstract set of conceptions that would have universal purpose involves a move from one level of abstraction – attached to place – to another level of abstractions capable of reaching out across space. And in that move, something was bound to be lost.[114]

The inevitable loss plays out also in the reverse movement, when critical theory enters a given community 'to learn as well as to teach'. If we cannot do without the local and the global as concurrent political goals, habits of thought and structures of feeling, the challenge must be to find ways to cultivate the connectivity within and between militant particularisms and the social totality. No act of measuring, no move between locations, comes without cost, without compromise or betrayal; but neither can the particular or the universal valency be held entirely sufficient unto itself.

In polemic, to be sure, Williams tended rather to indict 'the bracing cold' and 'inherent impersonalities and distances' of the professional intellectual, implying an unfair equivalence between the critic's theoretical pose, the executive's decision to lay off a workforce and the 'sovereign power to order war': they all share, he at one point suggests, in a 'latent culture of alienation, within which men and women are reduced to models, figures and the quick cry in the throat'.[115] The preference for the warmth of 'living presence' and the militant particular comes in despite of Williams's recognition that a politics of place, whether organised around the point of production or the encroachments of capitalist imperialism, tends rather to conserve a status quo than address larger and long-run questions of social and ecological justice; parochial in ambition, a local struggle risks also reproducing existing patterns of social exclusion. Whence again the importance, in Williams's theoretical vocabulary, of measuring distances, negotiating loyalties and orchestrating 'testing encounters'. In finding a way to teach the boy the method of Menvandir while still respecting the local authority of the mothers, Mered accepts, as Williams would have social theory do, the ethical and epistemological conflict between global ambition and local commitment. For Mered, as for the other scholarship boys of Williams's fiction, these competing claims create a tension to endure; but what is experienced in one man's lifetime as contradiction and even failure assumes then the 'subsequent adaptations' of the long revolution, the possible preponderance of success and by gestures such as Mered's to the mothers the survival of that 'idea of value' Williams calls our faith 'in the possibilities of common life'.[116]

Colgate University, New York State

Notes

1. Sue Aspinall, 'This Sadder Recognition: Interview with Raymond Williams', *Screen* 23 nos 3–4 (1982), 145.
2. Terry Eagleton links Williams's 'intellectual provincialism' to Leavis and Lukács in *Criticism and Ideology* (London: Verso, 1976), 36; Edward Said considers the nexus of ideas Williams shares with Lukács and Lucien Goldmann in *The World, the Text and the Critic* (Cambridge, MA: Harvard University Press, 1983), 226–47. It is perhaps a symptom of the 'English' uncertainty as to the existence or role of its own intellectuals that Williams should so often be named as a national variation upon a Continental theme. Tony Pinkney describes Williams as an English Bloch; *The Times* calls him 'our nearest British equivalent to Sartre'. Pinkney, introduction to Raymond Williams, *Politics of Modernism: Against the New Conformists* (London: Verso, 1989), 28–31; 'New Books', *The Times*, 15 June 1989, 19. On the English assumption that 'Intellectuals begin at Calais', see Stefan Collini, *Absent Minds: Intellectuals in Britain* (Oxford: Oxford University Press, 2006).
3. Williams declares his identity as a 'Welsh European' in *Politics and Letters: Interviews with the New Left Review* (London: New Left Books, 1979), 296.
4. Raymond Williams, *What I Came To Say*, ed. Neil Belton, Francis Mulhern and Jenny Taylor (London: Hutchinson Radius, 1989), 269–70.

People of the Black Mountains and the Politics of Theory

5. Georg Lukács, 'Interview: Lukács on his Life and Work', *New Left Review* 68 (1971), 58.
6. Lukács offers the Heraclitus fragment as an epigraph to the essay 'The Intellectual Physiognomy in Characterization', in *Writer and Critic, and Other Essays*, trans. Arthur David Kahn (London: Merlin Press, 1970), 149.
7. Lukács addresses the 'aspiration towards totality' in *History and Class Consciousness*, trans. Rodney Livingstone (London: Merlin Press, 1971), 149–222. Williams discusses the 'structure of feeling' at greatest length in *Marxism and Literature* (Oxford: Oxford University Press, 1977), 128–35.
8. Raymond Williams, *Towards 2000* (Harmondsworth: Pelican, 1985), 266; Williams, *Politics of Modernism*, 116.
9. Sean Matthews examines the long development of the term and its autobiographical connection in 'Change and Theory in Raymond Williams's Structure of Feeling', *Pre-Texts: Literary and Cultural Studies* 10, no. 2 (2001), 179–94.
10. Williams, *Marxism and Literature*, 128.
11. Williams, *Marxism and Literature*, 134; 133; 132.
12. Williams, *Marxism and Literature*, 132.
13. Williams, *Marxism and Literature*, 133; 132.
14. Georg Lukács, *The Historical Novel*, trans. Hannah and Stanley Mitchell (London: Merlin, 1962), 166.
15. See Darko Suvin, 'Lukács: Horizons and Implications of the "Typical Character"', *Social Text* 16 (1986–7), 97–123.
16. Georg Lukács, *Probleme des Realismus III: Balzac und der französische Realismus* (Neuwied and Berlin: Luchterhand, 1965), 440.
17. Lukács, *The Historical Novel*, 52–3.
18. Fredric Jameson, *The Political Unconscious: Narrative as a Socially Symbolic Act* (Ithaca: Cornell University Press, 1981), 102; and Fredric Jameson, 'The Historical Novel Today, or Is It Still Possible?', in *The Antinomies of Realism* (London: Verso, 2013), 259–313.
19. Brian McHale examines 'the pertinence of the historical novel to postmodernism' in *Postmodernist Fiction* (London: Methuen, 1987). Linda Hutcheon treats as 'paradigmatic' of postmodernism 'those well-known and popular novels which are both intensely self-reflexive and yet paradoxically also lay claim to historical events and personages' in *A Poetics of Postmodernism: History, Theory, Fiction* (London: Routledge, 1988), 5; and *The Politics of Postmodernism* (London: Routledge, 1989). At the beginning of it all is Fredric Jameson's treatment of E.L. Doctorow and the allied 'nostalgia film' in 'Postmodernism, or The Cultural Logic of Late Capitalism', *New Left Review* 146 (1984), 53–92.
20. Fredric Jameson, 'Postmodernism', 40. See, for example, Gail Day, 'Realism, Totality and the Militant *Citoyen*: Or, What Does Lukács Have To Do With Contemporary Art?', in *Georg Lukács: The Fundamental Dissonance of Existence. Aesthetics, Politics, Literature*, ed. Timothy Bewes and Timothy Hall (London: Continuum, 2011), 203–19; David Cunningham, 'Capitalist Epics: Abstraction, Totality and the Theory of the Novel', *Radical Philosophy* 163 (2010), 11–23 and 'Here Comes the New: *Deadwood* and the Historiography of Capitalism', *Radical Philosophy* 180 (2013), 8–24; Alberto Toscano and Jeff Kinkle, *Cartographies of the Absolute* (London: Zero Books, 2015).
21. See, for example, Lauren Berlant, 'Starved', *SAQ* 106, no. 3 (2007), 434; and Earl McCabe, 'Depressive Realism: An Interview with Lauren Berlant', *Hypocrite Reader* 5 (2011), http://hypocritereader.com/5/depressive-realism/ (accessed 29 November 2014).
22. Georg Lukács, *Tactics and Ethics: Political Writings 1919–1929*, trans. Michael McColgan (London: New Left Books, 1972), 7.
23. Raymond Williams to Perry Anderson, cited in Fred Inglis, *Raymond Williams* (London: Routledge, 1995), 255.

24 Williams, *Politics and Letters*, 295.
25 Walter Benjamin coined the term 'Left Wing Melancholy' in a 1931 review of poems by Erich Kästner; Wendy Brown returns to Benjamin in her essay 'Resisting Left Melancholy', originally presented as a paper at the 'Left Conservatism' conference, organised by Chris Connery in January 1998 at the University of California, Santa Cruz. Proceedings gathered in *boundary 2* 26, no. 3 (1999).
26 Inglis, *Raymond Williams*, 255; Williams, *Politics and Letters*, 294.
27 First adopted as a motto for his refusal, postwar, to recant the Cultural Front politics of the 1930s, Williams later addresses the lines to the 'blockage' of the 1970s and 1980s and to the challenge of keeping faith with a long revolution. Raymond Williams, *Drama from Ibsen to Eliot* (London: Chatto & Windus, 1952), 54; *Modern Tragedy* (London: Chatto & Windus, 1966), 100; and *Drama from Ibsen to Brecht* (London: Chatto & Windus, 1968), 59; 74.
28 Williams, *Politics and Letters*, 62–3.
29 Williams, *Modern Tragedy*, 83–4.
30 Williams, *Politics and Letters*, 294–5; Williams, *Politics of Modernism*, 96–7.
31 As Monk Pitter, the quondam Cambridge spy turned freelance market analyst in Williams's 1985 novel *Loyalties* observes, these are 'the only futures they think are left'. Raymond Williams, *Loyalties* (London: Hogarth, 1989), 162. On the political timescale in which 'four or five years is usually as far as the future goes', see Raymond Williams, *Resources of Hope: Culture, Democracy, Socialism*, ed. Robin Gale (London: Verso, 1989), 281.
32 Jameson, 'Postmodernism', 72.
33 Jameson, 'Postmodernism', 73.
34 Jameson, 'Postmodernism', 73.
35 Peter Brooker, 'Modernism under Review: Raymond Williams's *The Politics of Modernism*', *Modernist Cultures* 6, no. 2 (2011), 213; Jameson, 'Postmodernism', 61; 64.
36 Williams, *Politics of Modernism*, 132; 104.
37 The cultivation of distance further connects the Marxist theorist who imagines that 'by an act of intellectual abstraction' he can place himself 'above the lived contradictions' of the world and be himself beyond 'question' to the Cambridge critic (with his 'idealized and projected "authors" and "trained readers" who are presumed to float, on a guarded privilege, above the rough, divisive and divided world of which yet, by some alchemy, they possess the essential secret'). Both are versions of the dissident bourgeois culture that found in the modernist metropolis a home and a hero: 'the lonely writer gazing down on the unknowable city from his shabby apartment'. Cold War modernism pressed this image into service as the universal truth of our modernity. This 'late-born ideology of modernism' Williams would accuse in turn of paving the way for the New Right's 'dissolution and deregulation of all bonds and all national and cultural formations' for the sake of the 'sovereign individual', the free market and the 'open society'. Terry Eagleton, 'Two Interviews with Raymond Williams', *Red Shift* 2 (1977), 12; *Writing in Society* (London: Verso, 1983), 189; and Williams, *Politics of Modernism*, 33–4; 62; 76.
38 Williams, *Writing in Society*, 223. Lauren Berlant has repurposed the term 'impasse' to describe what she calls 'a space of time lived without a narrative genre', 'a holding station that doesn't hold securely but opens out into anxiety, that dogpaddling around a space whose contours remain obscure'. It is, she suggests, the affective dominant of our historical present, the time sandwiched between Fordist capitalism and whatever will follow neoliberalism. Berlant, *Cruel Optimism* (Durham, NC: Duke University Press, 2011), 199. In 'Depressive Realism' and again in *Cruel Optimisim*, Berlant confesses her debt to Williams for his defence of the structure of feeling as that 'collective sense of the historical present' which 'presents itself first affectively then through mediations that help or induce people

to navigate worlds whose materiality is overdetermined by many processes (means of production, social relations of production, normative traditions etc.)'.
39 In so doing, Williams anticipates what has become a mainline of contemporary critical reflection. See Amanda Anderson, *The Way We Argue Now: A Study in the Cultures of Theory* (Princeton: Princeton University Press, 2005); Timothy Bewes, 'Reading With the Grain: A New World in Literary Studies', *Differences* 21, no. 3 (2010), 1–33; Judith Butler, 'The Sensibility of Critique: Response to Asad and Mahmood', in *Is Critique Secular? Blasphemy, Injury and Free Speech*, ed. Talal Asad, Wendy Brown, Judith Butler and Saba Masood (Berkeley: Townsend Center for the Humanities, 2009), 101–36; Rita Felski, 'Suspicious Minds', *Poetics Today* 32, no. 2 (2011), 215–34; and Eve Kosofsky Sedgwick, 'Paranoid Reading and Reparative Reading, Or, You're So Paranoid You Probably Think This Essay is About You', in *Touching Feeling: Affect, Pedagogy, Performativity* (Durham, NC: Duke University Press, 2003), 123–52.
40 Williams, *Marxism and Literature*, 125–6.
41 Williams, *Towards 2000*, 268.
42 Raymond Williams, *Culture and Materialism: Selected Essays* (London: Verso, 1980), 262–3.
43 Williams, *Resources of Hope*, 284–7.
44 Williams, *Politics of Modernism*, 98.
45 Williams, *Resources of Hope*, 322.
46 Williams, *Culture and Materialism*, 272.
47 Williams, *Marxism and Literature*, 126.
48 Williams, *Resources of Hope*, 249.
49 Williams, *Towards 2000*, 268–9.
50 Williams, *Politics and Letters*, 223.
51 Williams, *Politics and Letters*, 271. 'I could not get *Border Country* right', he later explained, 'until it was more than the past', until the General Strike stood framed within a subsequent history of change. 'What interested me most […] was a continuing tension, with very complicated emotions and relationships running through it, between two different worlds that needed to be rejoined' – worlds of class and perspective, to be sure, but worlds of change in time as well. 'With the degree of change after 1945 the problem was to find a fictional form that would allow the description both of the internally seen working-class community and of a movement of people, still feeling their family and political connections, out of it.' Williams, *Writing in Society*, 62; Williams, *Politics and Letters*, 272.
52 Williams, *Who Speaks for Wales? Nation, Culture, Identity*, ed. Daniel Williams (Cardiff: University of Wales Press, 2003), 156–7
53 Williams, *Politics and Letters*, 271–2; Williams, *Politics of Modernism*, 116.
54 Raymond Williams, *People of the Black Mountains*, vol. 1, *The Beginning* (London: Paladin, 1990), 10.
55 Williams, *Who Speaks for Wales?*, 158; 165.
56 Williams, *Writing in Society*, 262.
57 Williams, *Towards 2000*, 265–7.
58 See Fernand Braudel, *The Mediterranean and the Mediterranean World in the Age of Philip II*, trans. Siân Reynolds (Berkeley: University of California Press, 1995), I. 20–1. More pointedly, see Emmanuel Le Roy Ladurie's *The Peasants of Languedoc*, trans. John Day (Urbana: University of Illinois Press, 1974); and 'History Without People: The Climate as a New Province of Research', in *The Territory of the Historian*, trans. Ben and Siân Reynolds (Chicago: University of Chicago Press, 1979), 287–319.
59 Williams, *People of the Black Mountains*, vol. 1, 6.
60 Williams, *People of the Black Mountains*, vol. 1, 9; 12.
61 Williams, *People of the Black Mountains*, vol. 1, 83.

62 Williams, *Culture and Materialism*, 272.
63 Williams, *Who Speaks for Wales?*, 157–8.
64 Williams, *Who Speaks for Wales?*, 163.
65 Williams, *People of the Black Mountains*, vol. 1, 83.
66 Williams, *Who Speaks for Wales?*, 168–9;
67 Raymond Williams, *People of the Black Mountains*, vol. 2, *The Eggs of the Eagle* (London: Paladin, 1992), 159.
68 Williams, *Who Speaks for Wales?*, 154. E.P. Thompson credits Blake's myriads with nourishing 'for fifty years, and with incomparable fortitude, the Liberty Tree' in *The Making of the English Working Class* (New York: Vintage, 1966), 832.
69 Williams, *Politics of Modernism*, 104.
70 Williams, *Politics of Modernism*, 115–6; 85.
71 Williams, *Politics of Modernism*, 116.
72 Williams, *Politics and Letters*, 218.
73 Williams, *Who Speaks for Wales?*, 108.
74 Aspinall, 'This Sadder Recognition', 147.
75 For the 'classic form' of the historical novel, see Lukács's treatment of Scott in *The Historical Novel*; for its Popular Front revival, see my own article, 'Jack Lindsay, Socialist Humanism and the Communist Historical Novel', *Review of English Studies* 66, no. 274 (2015), 342–63.
76 Williams, *What I Came To Say*, 235.
77 Williams, *Politics of Modernism*, 35.
78 Williams, *Politics of Modernism*, 139.
79 Williams, *Politics of Modernism*, 117.
80 Gwyn Thomas, *All Things Betray Thee* (London: Lawrence & Wishart, 1986), 311.
81 Thomas, *All Things Betray Thee*, 318.
82 Thomas, *All Things Betray Thee*, ix.
83 Thomas, *All Things Betray Thee*, viii.
84 Williams, *Who Speaks for Wales?*, 109
85 Williams, *Politics and Letters*, 217–8; Williams, *What I Came To Say*, 262.
86 Williams, *Politics of Modernism*, 89–90.
87 Williams, *Politics and Letters*, 216.
88 Notably, the journal *Screen* devoted two special issues to Brecht in Summer 1974 (15, no. 2) and Winter 1975 (16, no. 4), the second a transcript of discussions held during the 1975 Edinburgh International Film Festival on the topic 'Brecht and Cinema/Film and Politics'. Two of Williams's Cambridge colleagues led the charge in the critique of the 'classic realist text': Colin MacCabe, in 'Realism and the Cinema: Notes on Some Brechtian Theses' and Stephen Heath, 'Lessons from Brecht' (both in *Screen* 15, no. 2).
89 MacCabe, 'Realism and the Cinema', 25.
90 Williams, *What I Came to Say*, 266.
91 Williams, *Politics and Letters*, 218; Williams, *What I Came to Say*, 265.
92 Williams, *People of the Black Mountains*, vol. 1, 158.
93 Williams, *People of the Black Mountains*, vol. 1, 161–3.
94 Williams, *People of the Black Mountains*, vol. 1, 161.
95 Williams, *People of the Black Mountains*, vol. 1, 237.
96 Williams, *People of the Black Mountains*, vol. 1, 238.
97 Williams, *Drama from Ibsen to Brecht*, 287–8. Williams, *Modern Tragedy*, 201; Williams, *What I Came to Say*, 263–4; Williams, *Culture and Materialism*, 253
98 Williams, *What I Came to Say*, 263.
99 Williams, *Writing in Society*, 220.
100 Williams, *Politics of Modernism*, 130; 31. Williams, *Writing in Society*, 223.

101 John Lachs, *Responsibility and the Individual in Modern Society* (Brighton: Harvester, 1981); Zygmunt Bauman, *Modernity and the Holocaust* (Ithaca: Cornell University Press, 1989), 24–7; and Bauman, *Postmodern Ethics* (Oxford: Blackwell, 1993), 132; Williams, *Loyalties*, 318–9.
102 Williams, *Resources of Hope*, 204; 209.
103 Williams, *Resources of Hope*, 311.
104 Williams, *Resources of Hope*, 311.
105 Williams, *Writing in Society*, 212–26; Williams, *What I Came To Say*, 153–4.
106 Williams, *Politics of Modernism*, 139.
107 Williams, *Writing in Society*, 225.
108 See Bruce Robbins, 'Espionage as Vocation: Raymond Williams's *Loyalties*', in *Intellectuals: Aesthetics, Politics, Academics*, ed. Bruce Robbins (Minneapolis: University of Minnesota Press, 1990), 273–90.
109 Williams, *People of the Black Mountains*, vol. 1, 218–9.
110 Williams, *Writing in Society*, 225.
111 Williams, *Border Country* (Harmondsworth: Penguin, 1964), 334.
112 Williams, *Resources of Hope*, 249.
113 Williams, *Resources of Hope*, 115.
114 David Harvey, 'Militant Particularism and Global Ambition: The Conceptual Politics of Place, Space and Environment in the Work of Raymond Williams', *Social Text* 42 (1995), 83–4.
115 Raymond Williams, *What I Came to Say* (London: Hutchinson, 1989), 43.
116 Williams, *Resources of Hope*, 322.

Uses of Shelley in Working-Class Culture: Approximations and Substitutions

Jen Morgan

Abstract: This article engages with Raymond Williams's theories of cultural traditions in order to challenge the critical commonplace that Percy Bysshe Shelley's poetry exerted a dogmatic influence on Chartism and Owenite socialism. After reviewing the terms of this orthodoxy, the article goes on to focus on a period between December 1838 and July 1839, in which the movements' periodical cultures developed 'Shelleys' with quite different characters in response to a specific political context. I situate the appearance of poems such as *The Revolt of Islam* and 'Song: To the Men of England' in Owenite periodicals and Chartist newspapers in terms of major events in Chartism's history. When these audiences' relationships with Shelley's poetry are viewed in terms of active engagement with the text, rather than acceptance of a dogmatic influence, a more complex picture emerges. Such usage, I suggest, bears out arguments in *Marxism and Literature* on the political valency of emotion in the formation of structures of feeling. To focus on the use of 'residual' culture in the formation of particular 'emergent' structures is also to be concerned with historical rather than epochal questions. Williams's own comments in *Politics and Letters: Interviews with New Left Review* on working-class use of Shelley's poetry in this period, however, suggest that he did not believe that such creative use by working-class movements was possible in this period. In those interviews, Williams described the presence of Shelley's phrases in working-class culture as 'approximations or substitutions' for a genuinely working-class structure of feeling. I conclude the article by arguing that 'approximations' recognises cultural change and is closer to the truth of the formations' relationships with Shelley.

*

Introduction

It has become something of a critical orthodoxy that the nineteenth-century political and social movements Owenite socialism and Chartism held the Romantic poet Percy Bysshe Shelley in high esteem. While it serves as a useful shorthand indicating the importance of Shelley to the movements, to refer to his poem *Queen Mab* as their 'gospel' or 'bible' risks courting a limiting perspective on the relationship between the poet and these audiences. In order to challenge this orthodoxy, I focus in this article on a period between the winter of 1838 and the summer of 1839 as one in which Owenism's and Chartism's main publications – the *New Moral World* and the *Northern Star*, respectively – used Shelley's poetry as a resource in responding to the same political context but in different ways. Clear differences between Owenite and Chartist 'Shelleys' emerged dialectically in this period as the Owenite 'Shelley' took the form it did, in part, because it was not the Chartist 'Shelley', and vice versa. I argue that this use evidenced a critical and creative process of reception rather than a passive transmission of Shelley's ideas at the expense of their own.

A cluster of related concepts from Raymond Williams's *Marxism and Literature* helps illuminate these developments: his concepts 'selective traditions' and 'structures of feeling' acknowledge the possibility of admiration and influence co-existing with critical thought. His definitions of 'residual', 'dominant' and 'emergent' elements as historical indicators of cultural developments underpin my section 'Shelley in Context: December 1838 to July 1839'. This part of the article shows how Shelley's poetry provided the Owenites and Chartists with material to argue for values they wished to endorse and to challenge dominant ones. Despite the potential that Williams's concepts offer my research, however, his own comments on the relationship between Shelley and the working class of the 1830s betray a less confident perspective on their capacity for critical independence. I conclude the article by considering these comments in *Politics and Letters: Interviews with New Left Review*, a record of interviews conducted by members of the periodical's editorial committee.

Queen Mab as the Owenites' 'Gospel' and the Chartists' 'Bible'

The critical orthodoxy I want to question is grounded in undeniable material facts of early nineteenth-century publishing and has impressive credentials. Pirated extensively from 1821, Shelley's poem *Queen Mab* was a key weapon for radicals asserting the right to read and circulate ideas that challenged political, social and religious hegemonies.[1] Owenism's and Chartism's intellectual cultures grew out of this milieu, and members of the movements produced their own editions of the poem in the 1830s.[2] In his account of meeting Robert Owen and some of his followers, Thomas Medwin, Shelley's cousin, described *Queen Mab* as 'the gospel of the sect'.[3] According to Medwin, Owen described Shelley's assertion in *Queen Mab* that marriage ought not to outlast affection as 'the basis of [Owen's] chief tenets'.[4] At the end of the century, George Bernard Shaw and members of Marx's circle reported similar claims for the poem's centrality to Chartism. The now infamous claim that *Queen Mab* 'was known as The Chartists' Bible' originated in Shaw's account of a lecture, an occasion on which an 'old Chartist' remembered that Shelley's poetry had given him 'the ideas that led him to join the Chartists'.[5] The lecturer, the Fabian Henry S. Salt, cited Eleanor Marx on her father's opinion that Shelley 'had inspired a good deal of that huge but badly managed popular effort called the Chartist Movement'.[6] She also informed Salt that, according to Engels and the Chartist George Julian Harney, the Chartists were given to 'Shelley-worship'; Engels had said 'we all knew Shelley by heart then'.[7] The material record, people close to Shelley and the movements and members themselves all confirm *Queen Mab*'s importance in the history of working-class movements.

The most frequently cited modern sources on the subject themselves rest on the testimonies of Medwin, Shaw and Eleanor Marx. Bouthaina Shaaban's frequently cited article 'Shelley in the Chartist Press' originated in doctoral work seeking to provide 'specific evidence to support [the] truth' of Medwin's and Shaw's claims.[8] While her work began to establish the extent of Shelley's presence in Chartist newspapers and periodicals, it also sought to explain their '"worshipping" Shelley more than any other Romantic poet' rather than to question this characterisation of the relationship.[9] Shelley was 'loved and honoured by the Chartists', and this love and honour resulted 'not surprisingly, in the Chartists echoing Shelley's arguments and ideas in their own writings'.[10] M. Siddiq Kalim argued that Shelley's poetry was valuable for Owenism because emotionally engaging poetry sugared the theoretical pill for Owen's followers. Shelley 'alone was in perfect accord' with Owenism and strategic use of his poetry in Owenite propaganda enabled Owenite truths to 'go deep down into the heart' of the 'ignorant worker [who] may not be able to grasp the real meaning of the verse even when explained to him'.[11] The Owenites 'loved, adored, and idolized [Shelley] as a poet, thinker, and man'.[12] For both critics, the movements found Shelley's poetry doctrinally valuable because it stimulated emotion and his influence on them was characterised by strong affection reaching its zenith in 'idolization'.

More recent scholarship has cited Shaaban and Kalim, often wishing only to note Shelley's popularity among these audiences, but David Duff made the orthodoxy's ramifications explicit by arguing that 'as a didactic poem, history had judged *Queen Mab* to have been a remarkable success, ultimately achieving positively dogmatic status as the "gospel" of the Owenites, and later the "Chartists' Bible"'.[13] It is this perception of a 'dogmatic' authority endowed on Shelley by Owenism and Chartism that I want to question. It suggests that Owenites and Chartists accepted Shelley's politics, via his poetry, wholesale and uncritically. I do not wish to deny the importance of Shelley but to argue that respect and admiration could and did co-exist with healthy powers of discrimination. I argue that the movements' journals and newspapers show that they emphasised or downplayed various aspects of Shelley's poetry as suited contributors in particular contexts. In my analysis of such examples, I approach the transmission and reception of Shelley's poetry within Owenism and Chartism in terms of an active hermeneutics rather than a passive acceptance of his poetics, politics or both. If we think in terms of an active and creative reception in which faith can be compatible with critical inquiry, then characterisations of these movements as engaging in 'Shelley-worship' may no longer convince.

The 'Selective Tradition' and 'Structures of Feeling'

As a concept, the 'selective tradition' enables me to reconceive the supposed canonical status of *Queen Mab* and Shelley's other poems in working-class culture of this period. As *The Long Revolution* had it, literary traditions were not natural and given but the result of 'a continual selection and reselection of ancestors'.[14] This selection was, moreover, an 'interpretation' on which rested 'particular contemporary values'.[15] Williams developed these ideas in *Marxism and Literature*, introducing a much sharper sense of class difference by moving away from *The Long Revolution*'s proposal that the agents creating 'selective traditions' were successive 'generations' producing 'a general human culture'.[16] The purpose of a hegemonic selective tradition was to function as 'an actively shaping force' offering 'a version of the past which is intended to connect with and ratify the present'.[17] Counter-hegemonic selective traditions, therefore, would have to make the same move but in the service of different values. Shelley's work thus emerges as a self-selected 'bible' for the radical culture of the 1820s from which Owenism and Chartism developed. Shelley had by no means been embraced by his own class or 'respectable' middle-class readers, so the pirating of *Queen Mab* in the 1820s really was a choice signifying rejection of hegemonic values rather than recognition of a generally celebrated writer. This sense continued in the 1830s and '40s, as the Owenites and Chartists developed their own versions of Shelley while members of Shelley's circle, such as Mary Shelley and Leigh Hunt, were fighting a rear-guard action in attempting to restore Shelley's literary and moral reputation.[18]

The radical or working-class selective tradition emerging in the 1820s and '30s, then, was constructed consciously in order to articulate distinct literary and political values.[19] Given this active relationship with the texts of a working-class canon, I suggest it is unlikely that working-class readers received Shelley's *Queen Mab* and his other poems as if they were holy writ demanding submission to the letter. Even if the Owenites and Chartists themselves had accepted descriptions of *Queen Mab* as their gospel or bible, we need not assume that a text functioning as a 'Bible' or 'gospel' for a social or political movement had a positively dogmatic status. We know from studies on the relationship between religious nonconformism and working-class literacy that the Holy Bible was not only (or even necessarily) a source of gospel truth for autodidacts, it was also an intellectual resource and a starting point for discussion rather than an end. In *Bread, Knowledge and Freedom*, for instance, David Vincent shows how 'tiny libraries [...] largely composed of works connected with the Protestant religion [...] constituted an essential foundation for the pursuit of knowledge'.[20] If the Bible enabled working-class people to acquire literacy, and thus a greater stock of knowledge from other sources, then its own status as a source could be undermined by this process. While a shift from faith to free thought was not guaranteed – Vincent notes the existence of 'layers of secularization which the pursuit of knowledge engendered' – what was fundamental to that Protestant, and especially dissenting, tradition was commitment to an active rather than a passive relationship with the Bible.[21] In other words, even those who did not renounce Christianity retained the right to read and interpret their Bible without deference to authority. As a 'bible' in this sense, Shelley's poetry provided his Owenite and Chartist readers with tools for understanding and argumentation rather than a programme to follow.

Recognising this process is not to deny an emotional response in Owenites or Chartists reading Shelley's poetry. Rather, it is to reject the premise that evident emotional responses signify the absence of an intellectual (perhaps a critical intellectual) response. *Marxism and Literature*'s iteration of Williams's recurring concept 'structure of feeling' is useful in this respect. What was at stake for him in the late 1970s was recognition of class rule as a phenomenon saturating 'the whole process of living', experienced emotionally and intellectually, as well as the continuing relevance of his concept during a period in which Antonio Gramsci's theory of 'hegemony' was being read and taken seriously by Anglophone intellectuals.[22] Gramsci's 'hegemony', for Williams, was distorted by theorists tending to use the term as a synonym for 'ideology' or 'superstructure' subordinated to the more important material 'base'.[23] In other words, using 'hegemony' to denote a fixed analytical structure rather than a dynamic process effectively squandered the term's promise. If the concept was to be a Marxist one then it could not be content to recognise and describe the hegemonic via critical analysis but must facilitate the development of a counter-hegemonic project able to challenge the terms of the dominant formation successfully.

One of the biggest dangers faced by those with an interest in challenging prevailing hegemonic practices, therefore, was an inability to draw connections between present experience identified as personal and subjective and the social formation on which that experience depended. Williams proposed that his concept 'structure of feeling' would encourage recognition of lived experience:

> The term is difficult, but 'feeling' is chosen to emphasize a distinction from more formal concepts of 'world-view' or 'ideology'. It is not only that we must go beyond formally held and systematic beliefs, though of course we have always to include them. It is that we are concerned with meanings and values as they are actively lived and felt.[24]

The importance of stressing 'feeling' was that it allowed the 'affective elements of consciousness and relationships' to have critical value. The concept did not oppose emotion and thought but understood cognition as 'not feeling against thought, but thought as felt and feeling as thought: practical consciousness of a present kind, in a living and interrelating continuity'.[25]

I suggest that the Chartists were operating with a similar sense of the importance of 'subjective' feeling in motivating the development of 'objective' political programmes. A characteristically Chartist expression of the political value the movement found in emotion and poetry occurred in a lecture on poetry reported in the Chartist newspaper the *Charter*.[26] For the lecturer, Mr Spencer, the 'Value of Poetry' lay in its ability to 'regenerate mankind. Poets [...] were the representatives of the undeveloped parts of human nature, as leaders in the career of progression. This view was illustrated by references to the poetry of Shakspeare (*sic*), Byron, and Shelley'. Poetry's remit went beyond the aesthetic narrowly conceived: 'poetry, to fulfil its end, must pursue the perfect in all things – in the regions of philosophy it must seek unadulterated truth; in politics, justice; in religion, charity'. In its link to the social and political, Spencer does not conceive poetry as a world apart but as a source of inspiration depending on human action to achieve its ends:

> Surely among the millions who groan and sweat and toil, there are some less overcome than others who will seize the harp of prophecy, and sing the great truths that time has wrought out to be a joy and deliverance to the people. We need to be touched to be awakened; the trammels of custom must be broken, the net-work of conventionalism destroyed.[27]

In his definition of poetry's social role, Spencer suggests it has the capacity to articulate hopes for the future and to inspire people to reach for them. He stresses the importance of feeling for political movements – 'we need to be touched to be awakened' – and that the feeling subject both came from and spoke to 'the millions'. The agents of this change will be the subordinated (those who 'sweat and groan and toil'), and the change will be qualitative – customary restrictions will be 'broken' and conventional values 'destroyed'. I suggest that this example evidences a conscious attempt by Chartists to grasp the potential of the aesthetic and political in order to challenge the hegemonic.

Spencer did not propose that his audience take their political programme from Shakespeare, Byron and Shelley but that they take on the poet's role of awakening others and provoking action.[28]

Shelley in Context: December 1838 to July 1839

1839 was an especially active year for Chartism both politically and in terms of publishing. Major events such as the presentation of the first National Petition to Parliament in May and August's planned but curtailed General Strike were followed by the Newport Insurrection in November. It was also a boom period for Chartist publishing, with the already established *Northern Star* being joined by smaller newspapers and journals around the country, such as the Welsh *Western Vindicator*, the Scottish *Chartist Circular* and the metropolitan *London Democrat*. Chartist newspapers played an important role in sustaining the movement politically, helping it to cohere nationally around shared values and aims.[29] They also helped to develop the movement's literary practices: publishing original poetry, favourite poems by Shelley and others and literary criticism.[30]

Shelley's presence in Chartist discourse in this period was not incidental to Chartist politics and publishing but central. Firstly, Shelley's poetry became more readily available to Chartists via their own newspapers and editions of his poetry. 'Song: To the Men of England', for example, was written in 1819 but published for the first time in the Mary Shelley edited collection of 1839, *The Poetical Works of Percy Bysshe Shelley*, which cost twenty shillings for four volumes.[31] When the *Northern Star* printed the poem in April 1839, it made the poem available to readers with less disposable income than was necessary to purchase *Poetical Works*.[32] Chartists subsequently used phrases from the poem to articulate their political positions in editorials, letters and speeches appearing in their newspapers and journals. Chartists valued Shelley's poetry, therefore, as both literature and as a resource for political rhetoric.

It was in this sense that Shelley belonged to a counter-hegemonic selective tradition: connecting with present concerns in order to challenge the hegemonic rather than to ratify it. Shelley's centrality to the most urgent events and questions of Chartist strategy in 1839 proves that his writing contributed semantic figures for Chartists developing their own structures of feeling. Focusing on the specificities of this usage, not only recognisably Chartist but specific to particular historical moments, also bears out Williams's argument that we need a way of understanding political and cultural change on a historical (rather than an epochal) level. If 'hegemony' has too often been used to denote a reductive sense of 'ideology', then a related problem has been the tendency to view social change as the succession of epochs rather than as occurring within particular historical conjunctures.[33] Definitions of 'bourgeois society' and 'bourgeois art' could distract from the important issue of how to understand the present with all its inconsistencies in order to produce change. In order to tackle this problem, Williams offered the 'residual', 'dominant' and 'emergent' as categories able to name changes in the ongoing process of hegemonic self-reproduction, as well as opposition to hegemony, with greater historical precision.

Residual social and cultural forms are 'effectively formed in the past' but are 'still active in the cultural process'.[34] As Mike Sanders argues, while Williams 'privileges those artworks most closely connected with "emergent" formations', Chartist poetry shows how 'the residual facilitates working-class resistance in this period'.[35] I argue that this insight can also be applied to Chartist use of Shelley, and that his poetry was useful and inspiring for Chartists but required adjustment if it was to be relevant for their movement. Shelley's poem on exploitation of the working class at the point of production, 'Song: To the Men of England', is used in 1839 to argue for a concept elaborated more fully after Shelley's death, the General Strike, which the Chartists threatened if their political demands were not met.[36] In terms of chronological progression, Shelley's poem of 1819 was obviously prior to Chartism's strategy of 1839. It is evident, however, that the specificities of Chartist use of 'Song: To the Men of England' in 1839 means that their own version of the poem should be thought of in terms of the emergent: as an 'adaptation of form' if not as a significant new form in itself.[37]

Newspapers and periodicals not only provide evidence of such forms but must also be theorised as actively shaping the respective 'Shelleys' produced by Owenites and Chartists. While it is true that people in this period could be both Chartists and hold Owenite views regarding, for example, the desirability of religious secularism, it is not possible to claim that the Chartist *Northern Star* and the Owenite *New Moral World* had the same ideological commitments or discursive strategies. Print culture makes visible those differences, since formulations could be either welcome or unwelcome, and therefore published or not published. Owenism's main periodicals the *Crisis* (1832–34) and the *New Moral World* (1834–45) were not exact contemporaries of their Chartist equivalent, the *Northern Star* (1837–52). The period covered by this article, therefore, occurs in the overlap.

I argue that such differences between the *New Moral World* and the *Northern Star* set parameters enabling me to distinguish between Owenite and Chartist 'Shelleys'. The choices that Owenites and Chartists made within Shelley's oeuvre as it was available to them illustrate differences between them at the level of political and social commitments. The two movements' use of different poems in print, or different sections of the same poem, illustrates Owenism's commitment to the liberation of women and Chartism's greater attraction to a more robust and physical form of popular politics. British Owenites had been making use of Shelley's poetry in the *Crisis* and *New Moral World* from 1833, primarily to articulate their commitment to women's freedoms. The emergence of a provokingly different Chartist use of Shelley's poetry in 1839, I argue, threw into relief the Owenites' use and became its rival for the attentions of the working class. This dynamic relationship between the movements' presentation of Shelley makes the period under consideration especially significant.

Prometheus Unbound and *The Revolt of Islam* in the *New Moral World*

The *New Moral World* series 'A Review of Modern Poets, and Illustrations of the Philosophy of Modern Poetry' began on 1 December 1838. It aimed to address poetry 'which is identified with, and prophetic of, the redemption of the human race, from the present miserable system to one of intellect, virtue, and happiness'.[38] Shelley was in fact the only 'modern poet' to feature in the 'Review' over its seven instalments, the first five of which addressed his lyrical drama *Prometheus Unbound*.[39] Owenites believed that the route to social regeneration lay not in exploiting conflict between classes but in cultivating peace, and the 'Review' quoted *Prometheus Unbound* in support of this belief.[40] The crucial difference between Shelley's poem and Aeschylus's *Prometheus Bound*, which Shelley took as his model, was in Shelley's Prometheus's repudiation of the curse he had laid on his oppressor.[41] The series singled this act out for special notice; the journalist quotes those lines before stating: 'Here spoke the philanthropist, and, in Prometheus, Shelley spoke the feelings of his own benevolent bosom.'[42]

After a break of four months, the 'Review' went on to address another of Shelley's epic poems, *The Revolt of Islam*.[43] The poem is as Shelley described it in the Preface: a meditation on the events of the French Revolution. As Shelley saw it, the event demonstrated the great difficulty of realising the revolution's worthy principles while avoiding terror: 'Can he who the day before was a trampled slave, suddenly become liberal-minded, forbearing, and independent?'[44] The instalments covering *Revolt* describe the childhood of the two main characters, Laon and Cythna, before quoting liberally from passages in which Laon persuades soldiers to stop murdering revolutionaries and then the victorious revolutionaries to spare the life of the despot.[45] The other aspect of the poem valued by Owenites was the active role played by Laon's female counterpart, Cythna. The 'Review', therefore, quoted Cythna's 'splendid ode to equality' as well as the question she posed that appeared frequently in Owenite discourse: 'Can man be free if woman be a slave?'[46] Owenites found *Revolt*, especially Cythna's feminist statements, a valuable resource for their own articles and parables.[47]

The Revolt of Islam in the *Northern Star*

Chartists found *Revolt* less rhetorically useful, judging by the weight they gave the poem in relation to some of Shelley's other poems such as *The Mask of Anarchy* and 'Song: To the Men of England'. This section discusses the two references to *Revolt* I found in the *Northern Star* in 1839; it would not reappear in the paper before 1847.[48] Chartists were far less inclined than Owenites to use the poem, and Shelley's poetry generally, as a feminist resource. The only example of which I am aware was in the 'Address of the Female Political Union of Newcastle-Upon-Tyne to Their Fellow Countrywomen', published in the *Northern Star* in February 1839.[49] The 'Address' called for Chartist women to support men in their efforts to obtain the Charter, using the following lines from *Revolt* as its epigraph:

> Well ye know
> What woman is, for none of woman born
> Can choose but drain the bitter dregs of woe
> Which ever from the oppressed to the oppressors flow.[50]

The 'Address', however, did not quote the lines faithfully; it had the final two lines as 'Can choose but drain the bitter dregs of woe / Which ever *to* the oppressed *from* the oppressors flow'.[51]

In Shelley's version, oppression's negativity rebounds on the oppressors: in this instance husbands who enslave their wives by denying them equality. A month before the appearance of the Chartist women's address, a *New Moral World* article 'Woman as She is, and as She Ought to Be' had quoted the lines accurately in support of its argument that if women do not have 'equal rights, power, and importance in the social scale with man' then all of society, including men, suffers.[52] The Chartist version in the 'Address', however, changes the dynamic of the original lines by switching the prepositions 'from' and 'to'. This alteration reverses the direction of the woe's movement and de-genders Shelley's critique; the lines become a more straightforward description of oppression causing working-class suffering. The Female Political Union of Newcastle-Upon-Tyne demanded the right to occupy the 'field of politics' in order to 'help our fathers, husbands, and brothers to free themselves and us from political, physical, and mental bondage'. They did not also demand the extension of the franchise to women; as in Chartism more generally, a woman's right to the franchise was subordinated to a man's.[52] Alteration of Shelley's lines in this context suggests that suppression of an imbalance of power within the working-class family helped them to locate the source of oppression outside that family. This source of oppression acted on the family negatively as a unit; domestic disharmony was a result of political tyranny experienced by the working class as a whole.

If Chartists downplayed *Revolt*'s feminism, another use of the poem laid greater emphasis on the threat of popular violence in self-defence. Lines from *Revolt* appeared in the *Northern Star*'s poetry column of 20 July 1839 under the title 'The Arguments of Tyranny (From Shelley's *Revolt of Islam*)'.[54] The lines depict a battle between the forces of revolution and counter-revolution, a battle in which the former discover a cache of 'rude pikes / The instrument of those who war but on their native ground / For natural rights', to the 'shout of joyance'.[55] Laon, the great pacifist in Owenite readings of the poem, also experiences this joy and it appears as if they will repel their assailants. The counter-revolutionaries, however, are encouraged by the realisation that they are more powerful martially, 'and then the combat grew / Unequal but most horrible', until only Laon survives.[56] The fact that the *Northern Star* quoted these lines under the title 'The Arguments of Tyranny' then requires explication. It is plausible that the scene is supposed to illustrate the idea that 'might is right' is a tyrannical argument. While it is possible to defend Shelley's avowed commitment to non-violence in the poem's Preface on the basis that an oppressed people must also reject this argument of tyranny, the lines the *Northern Star* chose to print do not suggest that Laon and his comrades were wrong to defend themselves.

Much then depends on what a legitimate counter-argument to tyranny might be, since the Chartists were clearly not minded to accept tyrannical arguments. The immediate political context for Chartists reading these lines in the *Northern Star* included the violent disruption of the Chartist Convention in Birmingham by the London Metropolitan Police just two weeks earlier.[57] Key debates in the Convention at that point were on the right to bear arms and the related issue of what 'ulterior measures' ought to be taken in the (expected) event that Parliament would reject the first national petition in July. One of these measures was preparation for a 'sacred month', or General Strike, in August which Chartists believed the state would attempt to break. As Malcolm Chase argues, in these circumstances: 'the sacred month was [...] not an action short of outright insurrection, it *was* insurrection'.[58] The *Northern Star*, therefore, offered its readers Shelley's description of war between those who fought for 'natural rights' and the forces of 'tyranny' sixteen days after the state attacked the Convention and eight days after Parliament had rejected their petition. The next anticipated milestone in Chartism was strike action that Scottish Chartists expected would cause 'nothing short of physical revolution'.[59] When the *Northern Star* quoted these lines from Shelley's *Revolt* in this context, it was clear that they were intended to speak to this moment.

Contemporary Chartist readers, however, could have drawn several conclusions from the lines in this context. On one level, the lines dramatised a confrontation between proponents of a just cause and oppression in a manner valorising the former. In this manner, the lines supported morale. On another level, the conclusion of the battle illustrated the costs that the people incurred in facing an enemy better prepared for the fight. The lines might therefore have been read as illustrating the lack of preparation for confrontation that some in the Convention argued necessitated the postponement or curtailment of the sacred month. The Chartist leader Feargus O'Connor's editorial in the *Northern Star* of 2 August argued that it was not the right time to embark on a sacred month, proposing a three-day strike instead: the people 'are not a tenth part of them in possession of the means of self-defence'.[60] This inequality meant that the arguments of tyranny, if this did mean 'might is right', could not be answered in kind by Chartists with any prospect of success. Use of these lines in this context was possibly also preparing the ground for a recovery before the defeat had occurred. If the Chartists were the equivalent of Laon's righteous army then a short-term defeat did not reflect on the cause's worthiness. Injustice was temporary – as *Revolt*'s conclusion had it, 'all power and faith must pass' – while the memory of the defeat sustained faith in values that were eternal: 'to long ages shall this hour be known; / And slowly shall its memory, ever burning, / Fill this dark night of things with an eternal morning'.[61] For all of these readings, Shelley's lines in this context upheld the principle of self-defence; the question for Chartism was a strategic one.

'The Arguments of Tyranny' is a possible response, therefore, to the reading offered by Owenites in the *New Moral World*, since the 'Review' did not deliver on its promise in what transpired to be its final instalment to continue discussion of *Revolt* in future issues. The 'Review' had covered the content of *Prometheus Unbound* from the poem's beginning to its conclusion over five instalments. Discussion of *Revolt*, on the other hand, was limited to discussion of the Preface and the first five cantos, meaning that the 'Review' did not cover the poem's final seven cantos. As 'The Arguments of Tyranny' appeared in the *Northern Star* a month after the last instalment of the 'Review' appeared in the *New Moral World*, it is possible that the *Northern Star*'s editors deliberately picked up the baton by excerpting lines from *Revolt*'s sixth canto.

Cian Duffy has described a 'persistent – one might go so far as to say a *defining* – tension at the heart of Shelley's political writing between gradualism and revolutionism, quietism and violence'.[62] I concur with this reading of Shelley, and suggest that this is precisely the kind of ambiguity in his poetry on the subject of political violence that Owenites would have found troubling. The *New Moral World* of 10 August 1839 (when Chartist strike action was imminent) printed 'Extracts from Our Contemporaries', newspapers such as the *Morning Chronicle*, which speculated on the 'connection between the two bodies'.[63] The editor of the *New Moral World* responded to this in an afterword, stating that 'the objects of the Chartists and the Socialists, as well as the means adopted by each for their advancement, are totally opposed to each other'. The *New Moral World* criticised the Chartists' conduct and stressed the differences between that movement and Owenism frequently throughout 1839.[64] It is not surprising, therefore, that the 'Review' ended when it did, on 22 June 1839, without discussing the lines that Chartists went on to use the following month in a manner that would have offended Owenite principles. Owenism and Chartism were in this period using the same poem by Shelley in order to imagine opposing actions: conciliation and confrontation, respectively, between the oppressed and their political opponents.

Duffy's insight also allows us to avoid concluding that the reason Shelley's poetry could be made to illustrate different political positions is that it had no coherent policy of its own. In this view, Shelley's poetry could be the 'gospel' or 'Bible' of Owenism and Chartism because they were faithful in their own ways to different aspects of his oeuvre. If, on the other hand, Owenites and Chartists can be shown to have abstracted either quietist or aggressive aspects from a whole that existed in tension, then what we have are truly creative responses to Shelley's poetry. These responses have characters different to that of the original source, as well as to one another.

'Song: To the Men of England' in the *Northern Star*

The same issue of the *Northern Star* in which 'The Arguments of Tyranny' appeared also featured what I argue is another motivated use of Shelley's poetry, this time in the context of a political speech rather than a poetry column or article on poetry. The article 'Meeting of Chartists at Stockport' reported a number of speeches made by Chartists in response to Parliament's recent rejection of the national petition on 12 July and in expectation of the sacred month in August.[65] At a meeting on 15 July 1839 the Chartist Bronterre O'Brien used images similar to those in Shelley's 'Song: To the Men of England' in presenting the strike as a decisive crisis. Without mentioning the poem by name, O'Brien said:

Let not the anvil be struck within the length and breadth of the land. Let not a needle nor a spade be used unless to dig some tyrant's grave. Let not a shuttle move, unless to weave the winding sheet of some monster-robber, some profit-monger, who dared to attack the People's Parliament. All will then soon be over.[66]

In his poem, which Michael Scrivener described as representing an 'uncompromising view on labour alienation', Shelley depicts the appropriation of wealth produced by the working class: 'The robes ye weave, another wears; / The arms ye forge, another bears'.[67] He then recommends its members stop participating in their own exploitation: 'Weave robes – let not the idle wear: / Forge arms in your defence to bear.'[68] This last line could be adduced as evidence for Stephen Behrendt's claim that 'this poem comes as close as Shelley ever comes to sanctioning violence as a last resort'.[69] The poem appeared frequently in the Chartist press over the course of 1839.[70] By using Shelleyan images in reference to an anticipated general strike, O'Brien applied the economic logic of Shelley's lines to the immediate conditions faced by Chartists. He even engaged with the poem's final stanza, in which Shelley described the consequences of the workers not doing as he recommended:

> With plough and spade and hoe and loom
> Trace your grave and build your tomb,
> And weave your winding-sheet – till fair
> England be your Sepulchre.[71]

In transforming Shelley's final stanza O'Brien not only counters its pessimism, he might also have been suggesting that Chartists take revenge for the recent attack on the Convention in Birmingham. In O'Brien's formulation, the grave and winding-sheet were to be cut to the shape of the 'tyrants' and 'profit-monger', to those 'who dared to attack the People's Parliament', rather than to the people themselves. For all the ambiguity in poems such as *Revolt* or *The Mask of Anarchy* on the use of violence in self-defence at critical moments, Shelley was quite clear that he thought vengeance unequivocally wrong. As *Mask*, the other poem very popular in Chartism, had it: 'Blood for blood – and wrong for wrong – / Do not thus when ye are strong.'[72] In their frequent use of the poem, Chartists did not quote these lines and they exaggerated *Mask*'s aggressive aspects. According to my findings, use of 'Song' comparable to O'Brien's did not occur in the *New Moral World*; I found no references to the poem in the Owenite journal though it was still in print six years after 'Song' was published for the first time.

What matters, if we are to take Shelley's poem seriously as concerned with questions of political strategy, is what constitutes a position of strength. A possible reading of the line in *Mask* is that Shelley equates the position of strength with unequivocal victory and that his injunction against revenge, therefore, is not incompatible with use of violence in self-defence at the moment of confrontation. It would then become a question of whether responding in kind to the state's 'attacks' on the Convention, which was still meeting when O'Brien spoke, constituted self-defence or revenge. Such questions recognise the lack of straightforwardness inherent in Shelley's images of political struggle; his poems do not give unambiguous instructions to his intended readers. There was no clear didactic content for Owenites and Chartists in this period; interpretation in such circumstances was always creative.

The analysis of deliberate use of Shelley in the Owenite and Chartist press offered above demonstrates the importance of considering omissions as well as presences of Shelley in the movements' cultures. The Chartists did not 'echo' Shelley's poetry faithfully if they omitted his celebrations of women's political agency or represented it as a force benefitting men in the first instance and women only secondarily.[73] Women's liberty was at least as important in Shelley's politics and at least as prominent in his poetry as his denunciations of political, economic and religious tyranny over the many by the few. Such facts evidence clear critical selection among Shelley's poetry, determined by the wider concerns of Chartism, which did not prioritise the emancipation of women in the way that Owenite ideology did explicitly. This is no straightforward 'echoing' of Shelley, but a deliberate and selective use of his poetry within specific contexts. Likewise, it cannot be claimed that Owenites were in 'perfect accordance' with Shelley if they presented him in such a way that suggested he, like them, was against violence in every circumstance.[74] Owenites had to suppress the ambiguity regarding political violence in Shelley's poetry if they were to present him as 'a philanthropist in fullest sense of the word, who warred not against men, but false principles', and a poet whose 'every line [...] breathes a spirit of love and affection for the whole human race'.[75] This not only suppressed Shelley's mixed feelings regarding the use of violence in self-defence and his recognition of class interests, but also overlooked his frequent use of invective levelled at figures such as 'The King, the wearer of a gilded chain / That binds his soul to abjectness, the fool / Whom courtiers nickname monarch'.[76] Where Owenism, under the direction of Owen, felt moved to exclude the unpalatable aspect of Shelley, Chartism effectively suppressed it by including it in a reconfigured form.

Williams on Shelley and the Working Class in *Politics and Letters*

While working-class appreciation of Shelley's poetry has been celebrated by some as a laudable affective response to a Romantic genius, a critic like Williams, committed to working-class agency, viewed their use of Shelley as problematic. Interviews with the *New Left Review*, published in the volume *Politics and Letters*, feature the only comments to my knowledge that Williams made on concrete instances of working-class responses to Shelley in the period I consider.[77] In those interviews Williams suggested that the appearance of Shelley in working-class culture of the 1830s was a 'paradox' and evidence that their structure of feeling was only partially articulated:

> a dominant set of forms or conventions – and in that sense structures of feeling – can represent a profound blockage for subordinated groups in a society, above all an oppressed class […] For example, it seems probable that the English working class was struggling to express an experience in the 1790s and 1830s which in a sense, because of the subordination of the class, its lack of access to means of cultural production, but also the dominance of certain modes, conventions of expression, was never fully articulated. If you look at their actual affiliations, what is striking is a great grasping at other writings. Working people used Shelley; they used Byron, of all people; they responded very strongly to Mrs Gaskell. Should they or should they not have? These works could only have been approximations or substitutes for their own structure of feeling.[78]

For Williams, the existence of an identifiably working-class experience with at least the potential for articulation in the 1830s (and even the 1790s) was not in doubt. What was in question was the adequacy of existing linguistic formulations and registers to articulate that experience. While Williams posits use of Shelley by working people as an open question worth considering, he also stated that working-class people 'struggled' to express their experience because 'certain modes, conventions of expression' were hegemonic, and that these were drawn from 'other writings'.

By this point in his development of the 'structure of feeling' as a concept, Williams wanted 'to use the concept much more differentially between classes'; this statement appears a few pages before his comments on working-class use of Shelley.[79] The implication here, given Williams's desire to make the subject of his latest iteration of the 'structure of feeling' a class subject rather than a generational one, was that a working-class culture worthy of the name had to break links with the cultural products of other classes. The class origins of Shelley, Byron and Gaskell's works, then, rendered them inadequate as resources for the expression of a working-class structure of feeling. This view is obviously unfruitful for my study as it meant, if correct, that establishing Chartist use of Shelley disqualified them as working-class subjects. The terms 'approximation' and 'substitution', however, are not synonyms. An approximation can be very close to the original, but its difference from the source can be productive in the sense of the emergent as 'adaptation of forms', as noted above. What is useful in the original can be retained and augmented with what is necessary in the new historical context. Approximations can also change further over time, if necessary. A substitution, on the other hand, could only be the replacement of one thing for another.

One reason that Williams could make these comments was the lack of available research showing, for example, that Chartists did not lack 'access to means of cultural production' but had a serviceable outlet for political poetry in the *Northern Star*.[80] Williams also appears to have mistaken Shelley in the 1830s as an example of work encoding 'a dominant set of forms or conventions', whereas he was actually not part of the dominant literary tradition in this period. As St Clair and others have since shown, although Shelley was an aristocrat, his reputation was very far from secure in respectable circles, which did not see him as articulating their own values.[81] Williams's statement above conflates class origins and the 'dominant tradition'. As he stated himself in *Marxism and Literature*, a hegemonic formation can incorporate facets of working-class culture into its own version of the selective tradition in order to 'recognise' it, thereby neutralising any threat it posed. Similarly, there is nothing to prevent working-class cultural expropriation of middle- or upper-class culture in an oppositional manner; analysis of this phenomenon was a concern of classic early texts in British cultural studies.[82] Williams also, I argue, conceded too much to his interviewers' searching questions on the validity of 'structure of feeling' as a concept.[83] As Christopher Norris noted, the interviewers placed a great deal of pressure on Williams to defend his theories from the perspective of structuralist Marxist positions he had disavowed.[84] On his own terms, Williams could not reasonably require 'full articulation' of working-class experience in this period. It was his dissatisfaction with the concept of ideology, in which 'it is the fully articulate and systematic forms which are recognizable as ideology', that led Williams to propose the structure of feeling as better able to register 'tensions, shifts, and uncertainties' while recognising resistance to class rule.[85] The potential of his theories for studies such as my own, however, outweighs the significance of these local problems and Williams can hardly be held responsible for failing to do the primary research that his own theoretical work made possible.

Acknowledgement

This essay is based on research funded generously by the Arts and Humanities Research Council.

Notes

1. See Iain McCalman, *Radical Underworld: Prophets, Revolutionaries and Pornographers in London, 1795–1840* (Oxford: Clarendon Press, 1993) and William St Clair, *The Reading Nation in the Romantic Period* (Cambridge: Cambridge University Press, 2004).
2. Notable editions are John Brooks's Owenite editions of 1829 and 1833, and Chartist editions published from 1839 onwards by John Watson and Henry Hetherington.
3. Thomas Medwin, *The Life of Percy Bysshe Shelley* (London: Humphrey Milford, 1847), 100.
4. Medwin, *Percy Bysshe Shelley*, 98.
5. George Bernard Shaw, 'Shaming the Devil about Shelley', in George Bernard Shaw, *Pen Portraits and Reviews* (London: Constable and Company, 1949), 244.
6. Shaw, 'Shaming the Devil', 244.
7. Henry S. Salt, *Company I Have Kept* (London: George Allen & Unwin, 1930), 51.
8. Bouthaina Shaaban, 'Shelley in the Chartist Press', *Keats-Shelley Memorial Bulletin* 34 (1983): 41–60 and 'Shelley's Influence on the Chartist Poets with Particular Emphasis on Ernest Charles Jones and Thomas Cooper' (PhD diss., University of Warwick, 1981), viii.
9. Shaaban, 'Chartist Press', 42.
10. Shaaban, 'Chartist Press', 52, 56.
11. M. Siddiq Kalim, *The Social Orpheus: Shelley and the Owenites* (Lahore: Government College, 1973), i.
12. Kalim, *The Social Orpheus*, 121.
13. David Duff, *Romance and Revolution: Shelley and the Politics of a Genre* (Cambridge: Cambridge University Press, 1994), 70–1 (original emphasis). Shaaban's article in particular has attracted citations in works important and influential in the field, such as Paul Thomas Murphy, *Toward a Working-Class Canon: Literary Criticism in British Working-Class Periodicals, 1816–1858* (Columbus: Ohio State University Press, 1994), 12; St Clair, *The Reading Nation*, 336; and James Bieri, *Percy Bysshe Shelley: A Biography* (Baltimore: Johns Hopkins University Press, 2008), 673.
14. Raymond Williams, *The Long Revolution* (Cardigan: Parthian, 2011), 73.
15. Williams, *The Long Revolution*, 74.
16. Williams, *The Long Revolution*, 72.
17. Raymond Williams, *Marxism and Literature* (Oxford: Oxford University Press, 1977), 115, 116.
18. Leigh Hunt's Preface to the first edition of *The Mask of Anarchy* (1832) and Mary Shelley's notes to *The Poetical Works of Percy Bysshe Shelley* (1839) were important milestones in this history.
19. See Murphy, *Toward a Working-Class Canon*.
20. David Vincent, *Bread, Knowledge and Freedom: A Study of Nineteenth-Century Working Class Autobiography* (London: Europa, 1981), 110–1. See also Jonathan Rose, *The Intellectual Life of the British Working Classes* (New Haven: Yale University Press, 2001), 9.
21. Vincent, *Bread, Knowledge and Freedom*, 178. For an account of dissenting religion as an intellectual tradition informing the development of political radicalism, see E.P. Thompson, *The Making of the English Working Class* (Harmondsworth: Penguin, 1968), 28–58.

22 Williams, *Marxism*, 110.
23 Williams, *Marxism*, 112.
24 Williams, *Marxism*, 132.
25 Williams, *Marxism*, 132.
26 'Lambeth Mutual Instruction Society', *Charter*, 8 March 1840, 11.
27 'Lambeth Mutual Instruction Society', 11.
28 There is a possible indirect reference here to Shelley's essay *A Defence of Poetry*, which ends with the famous description of poets as 'the unacknowledged legislators of the World'. When the *Charter* printed Spencer's lecture, the essay had recently been published for the first time in the collection *Essays, Letters from Abroad, Translations and Fragments* (1840). However, I found no direct reference to the essay in any of the Chartist newspapers and periodicals that I examined. 'A Defence of Poetry', in *Shelley's Poetry and Prose: Authoritative Texts, Criticism*, ed. Donald H. Reiman and Neil Fraistat (New York: Norton, 2002), 535.
29 Dorothy Thompson, *The Chartists* (London: Temple Smith, 1984), 16–7.
30 Mike Sanders, *The Poetry of Chartism: Aesthetics, Politics, History* (Cambridge: Cambridge University Press, 2009), and '"Tracing the Ramifications of the Democratic Principle": Literary Criticism and Theory in the *Chartist Circular*', *Key Words: A Journal of Cultural Materialism* 8 (2010), 62–72.
31 St Clair, *The Reading Nation*, 682.
32 For analysis of such material aspects of the *Northern Star*, see James Epstein, *The Lion of Freedom: Feargus O'Connor and the Chartist Movement, 1832–1842* (London: Croom Helm, 1982), 68.
33 Williams, *Marxism*, 112.
34 Williams, *Marxism*, 122.
35 Sanders, *The Poetry of Chartism*, 25.
36 See Iorwerth Prothero, 'William Benbow and the Concept of the "General Strike"', *Past and Present* 63 (1974), 132–71.
37 Williams, *Marxism*, 126.
38 'A Review of Modern Poets, and Illustrations of the Philosophy of Modern Poetry', *New Moral World*, 1 December 1838, 83.
39 See the *New Moral World* issues of 1, 8, and 22 December 1838; 5 January 1839 and 16 February 1839.
40 Eileen Yeo, 'Robert Owen and Radical Culture', in *Robert Owen: Prophet of the Poor. Essays in Honour of the Two Hundredth Anniversary of His Birth*, ed. Sidney Pollard and John Salt (London: Macmillan, 1971), 84–114.
41 Cian Duffy, *Shelley and the Revolutionary Sublime* (Cambridge: Cambridge University Press, 2005), 152.
42 'A Review of Modern Poets, and Illustrations of Philosophy of Modern Poetry', *New Moral World*, 8 December 1838, 103. The lines quoted from Prometheus Unbound were I, 262–305 in P.B. Shelley, *The Poems of Shelley*, vol. 2, ed. Kelvin Everest and Geoffrey Matthews (London: Longman, 2000).
43 'Review of Modern Poets and Poetry. Shelley's Revolt of Islam', *New Moral World*, 15 June 1839, 533–5.
44 *The Poems of Shelley*, vol. 2, 36.
45 'Modern Poets: Shelley's Revolt of Islam. Act II', *New Moral World*, 22 June 1839, 550–2.
46 *Revolt*, ii, 36 in *The Poems of Shelley*, vol. 2, where the poem is included under its original title *Laon and Cythna*.
47 See 'For the Crisis', *Crisis*, 9 November 1833, 83–4; W.W. Pratt, 'On the Necessity and Pleasures of Agricultural Employment', *New Moral World*, 16 June 1838, 265–6; 'Woman as She is, and as She Ought to Be', *New Moral World*, 26 January 1839, 210–1; and 'The

Pleasures and Advantages of Knowledge', *New Moral World*, 12 September 1840, 166–8; John Goodwyn Barmby, 'The Inferiority of Fourier's Classification of Society', *New Moral World*, 5 December 1840, 355–6.

48 Thomas Frost, 'Scott, Byron and Shelley', *Northern Star*, 2 January 1847, 3.
49 'Address of the Female Political Union of Newcastle-Upon-Tyne to Their Fellow Countrywomen', *Northern Star*, 9 February 1839, 6.
50 *Revolt*, VIII, 3330–3.
51 My emphasis. Consulting the editions of the poem available to the Female Political Union of Newcastle-upon-Tyne suggests it is likely that this alteration to Shelley's line was their own (or the *Northern Star*'s compositor's) and was not merely copied from an unfaithful edition. John Brooks's 1829 edition of *Revolt*, popular among Owenites, and *Poetical Works* agree that the line is 'Which ever from the oppressed to the oppressors flow'.
52 Pratt, 'Woman as She is', 177.
53 Jutta Schwarzkopf, *Women in the Chartist Movement* (London: Macmillan, 1991), 89.
54 'The Arguments of Tyranny (From Shelley's *Revolt of Islam*)', *Northern Star*, 20 July 1839, 7; *Revolt*, VI, 2425–60, 2473–8, 2488–96.
55 *Revolt*, VI, 2444–6.
56 *Revolt*, VI, 2456–7.
57 For a history of this period in Chartism, see Malcolm Chase, *Chartism: A New History* (Manchester: Manchester University Press, 2007), 57–87.
58 Chase, *Chartism*, 80, emphasis in original.
59 Chase, *Chartism*, 81.
60 Chase, *Chartism*, 86.
61 *Revolt*, XII, 4704, 4708–10.
62 Duffy, *Shelley and the Revolutionary Sublime*, 10, emphasis in original.
63 'Extracts from Our Contemporaries', *New Moral World*, 10 August 1839, 669–70.
64 See 'The Chartists and the Socialists', *New Moral World*, 2 March 1839, 296; James Lindsay, 'Chartism v. Socialism', *New Moral World*, 8 June 1839, 516–7; 'Birmingham Town Mission', *New Moral World*, 22 June 1839, 552–4; 'Mr Owen to the Social Missionaries', *New Moral World*, 11 July 1839, 593–7; W. Hawkes Smith, 'Chartism and Socialism', *New Moral World*, 10 August 1839, 670–1; 'Physical, *versus*, Moral Revolution', *New Moral World*, 7 December 1839, 929–31.
65 'Meeting of Chartists at Stockport', *Northern Star*, 20 July 1839, 1.
66 'Meeting of Chartists at Stockport', 1.
67 Michael Scrivener, *Radical Shelley: The Philosophical Anarchism and Utopian Thought of Percy Bysshe Shelley* (Princeton: Princeton University Press, 1982), 232; 'Song: To the Men of England', 19–20 in P.B. Shelley, *The Poems of Shelley*, vol. 3, ed. Jack Donovan, Cian Duffy, Kelvin Everest and Michael Rossington (London: Longman, 2011).
68 'Song: To the Men of England', 23–4.
69 Stephen Behrendt, *Shelley and his Audiences* (Lincoln: University of Nebraska Press, 1989), 195–6.
70 Percy Bysshe Shelley, 'To the Men of England', *Northern Star*, 27 April 1839, 7; '*Tait's Magazine* for April, 1839', *Brighton Patriot*, 7 May 1839, n.p.; 'Poets our Best Teachers', *London Dispatch*, 12 May 1839, 6; Shelley, 'Song to the Men of England', *Northern Liberator*, 5 October 1839, 7; 'Percy B. Shelley', *Chartist Circular*, 19 October 1839, 16; and Shelley, 'To the Men of England', *Western Vindicator*, 14 December 1839, 6.
71 'Song: To the Men of England', 29–32.
72 *Mask*, 195–6 in *The Poems of Shelley*, vol. 3.
73 Shaaban, 'Chartist Press, 56.
74 Kalim, *The Social Orpheus*, i.

75 'A Review of Modern Poets', *New Moral World*, 1 December 1838, 84.
76 *Queen Mab*, III, 30–2 in P.B. Shelley, *The Poems of Shelley*, vol. 1, ed. Kelvin Everest and Geoffrey Matthews (London: Longman, 1989).
77 Raymond Williams, *Politics and Letters: Interviews with New Left Review* (London: Verso, 1979), 100–3, 110–2, 164–5. Williams's comments were in response to questions about his discussion of Shelley in 'The Romantic Artist' in *Culture and Society: 1780–1950* (New York: Anchor Books, 1960), 33–52.
78 Williams, *Politics and Letters*, 111, 164–5.
79 Williams, *Politics and Letters*, 158.
80 Sanders, *The Poetry of Chartism*, 69–86.
81 Besides St Clair and McCalman, see Neil Fraistat, 'Illegitimate Shelley: Radical Piracy and the Textual Edition as Cultural Performance', *PMLA* 109 (1994), 409–23; and Stephen C. Behrendt, 'Shelley and his Publishers', in *The Oxford Handbook of Percy Bysshe Shelley*, ed. Michael O'Neill and Anthony Howe (Oxford: Oxford University Press, 2013), 83–97.
82 See Tony Jefferson, 'Cultural Responses of the Teds', in *Resistance through Rituals: Youth Subcultures in Post-War Britain*, ed. Stuart Hall and Tony Jefferson (London: Hutchinson, 1976), 81–6; and Dick Hebdige, *Subculture: The Meaning of Style* (1979; London: Routledge, 2005).
83 Williams, *Politics and Letters*, 133–74.
84 Christopher Norris, '*Keywords*, Ideology and Critical Theory', in *Raymond Williams Now: Knowledge, Limits, and the Future*, ed. Jeff Wallace et al. (London: Macmillan, 1997), 28.
85 Williams, *Marxism*, 109, 129.

Back in the CCCS: Portraits of Alumni from the Centre for Contemporary Cultural Studies by Mahasiddhi (aka Roy Peters), University of Birmingham
Claire MacLeod Peters

Raymond Williams once remarked of a photograph taken at the 1977 Durham miners' gala, subsequently used for the cover of Working Papers in Cultural Studies 10, *On Ideology*, that 'it has it all'.[1] The image featured a banner of Harold Wilson, some people eating sandwiches, a snack van and a child wielding a sword looming large in the foreground. In this image Williams saw Gramsci, Lacan and Lukács as emerging from the photographer's selection and assembly of signifiers, revealing something profound about ideology, but moreover producing a meditation on the polysemic nature of the signifying practices themselves. In his structuralist analysis the photograph is not only a way of 'interrogating' the social relations but for Williams that image captures a crucial insight about the production of meaning that goes beyond the frame.

That photographer was Mahasiddhi, previously known as Roy Peters and a former student at the CCCS, whose recent exhibition, *Back in the CCCS* (4 June–30 July 2014), presented a series of portraits of some of the people who crossed his path during his time there between 1975 and 1979, as well as some that he met doing this project. Each image was accompanied by a few lines of text to frame it, each person reflecting on their time at the Centre and its effect on their trajectory. What emerged from this highly personal quest to reconnect with some of the scholars, thinkers, teachers, activists and friends was not an exhaustive and definitive homage to the Centre, but something of a working paper. Rebecca O'Rourke sits on the pavement in front of a Cambridge Road street sign, revealing Mahasiddhi's continued interest in playing with signs and signifiers whilst also pointing to (for that's what an indexical sign does) the significance of space and location here. Roger Shannon is captured in close-up, simultaneously crisp and blurry, looking out beyond the frame, in front of a chalk board, at a café perhaps, the out of focus writing appearing to say 'soupe des signes'. Richard Dyer appears with his hands against a pane of glass in his shower; the image is reflected and doubled in the adjacent mirror, but the mirror from a different angle also reveals the photographer himself divided at each edge of the image. Richard does not smile but looks at himself ahead. The set-up is revealed as just that – no attempt is made to efface the traces of normal life – the mirror reflection reveals shampoos and towels behind the photographer. The image is remarkable: it is clearly self-reflexive but like the 'On Ideology' image it is also a metapicture in the vein of Velazquez's *Las Meninas*, and the viewer is implicated in its production. Throughout the exhibition, the elements of negotiation and collaboration between photographer and subject were striking, and as Robert Lumley points out in his accompanying text, 'Individual Group Portrait or Group Individual Portrait', it is precisely this ethical dimension that accounts for the unique and captivating quality of the portraits. Mahasiddhi, it seems, like his subjects, was profoundly marked by his time at the CCCS, not least because of how it transformed his 'ways of seeing'.

'Birmingham Centre for Contemporary Cultural Studies 50 Years On' was held at the University of Birmingham on 24–25 June 2014 to mark the fiftieth anniversary of the CCCS. The conference set out to explore the legacies of the Centre, looking at the unique teaching and research methods it used as well as thinking about the political and cultural context in which it emerged and how that might illuminate something about today's pedagogical, intellectual and cultural climate both in an academic context and beyond. The event also marked the creation of a CCCS archive at the University of Birmingham, which houses material produced by former staff and students between its inception in 1964 and its closure in 2002. These events were part of an AHRC-funded project about the CCCS led by Dr Kieran Connell and Professor Matthew Hilton, born out of conversations with pioneering figures in its creation, Michael Green, who died in 2011, and Stuart Hall and Richard Hoggart, both of whom died last year.

The conference was shot through with a sense of conflict and ambivalence about the archive being located and indeed celebrated here at the University of Birmingham – the very place that shut down the final incarnation of the CCCS back in 2002 when it was part of the Department of Sociology. Many presenters commented on a sense of place that was integral to the Centre's identity – it represented a major cultural and academic research hub *outside* London, performing a decentring of the usual grip of the capital. Furthermore, a sense of the relationship of the Centre to the city was also a key element of the broader project's approach to its cultural history. However, as Professor Ann Gray pointed out in her excellent overview of the final years of the CCCS, the relationship of the Centre to the university is fraught. Her paper explored the peculiar and unpredictable vicissitudes of 'institutional memory', or rather forgetting. The university, it seems, having been quick to vouch for the 'continuity of a tradition' of intellectual engagement with the cultural sphere at celebratory and prestigious conferences quickly adopted the view that the 'unit' that was 'reorganised' in 2002 was not the CCCS. This 'airbrushing' of the Centre from the university's history, she argued, is a timely reminder of institutional power. In this way, she raised urgent questions about the closure of the CCCS in relation to pertinent pedagogical issues that affect all of us working in higher education – questions about the separation of teaching and research, new funding structures, staffing contracts and teaching practices – that constitute a veritable shift in the politics of education. Indeed, that first panel situating the Centre did more than simply outline a historiographical timeline, rather its contributors argued for a new 'people's history' contesting the grand narratives of the past and suggesting the need now more than ever perhaps for a critical engagement with these educational policies.

This was not like any other academic conference I have attended, partly because the scope and reach of the CCCS at the time was not traditionally 'academic'. It was involved in questioning precisely what academic pursuit should be; questioning how disciplinary boundaries and literary canons were constructed; challenging the delineations between what was or was not worth studying critically. Dick Hebdige's paper, for instance, was both a performance of cultural studies as well as being about it. There was a flavour of contestation throughout – any cultural history of the Centre has to be able to account for its internal divisions and contradictions, something touched on in Richard Johnson's contribution to the debate. The notion of praxis that was so crucial to the ethos of the Centre was also reflected in the programme of this two-day conference. Papers deeply grounded in serious and complex theoretical considerations, such as those by Paul Gilroy and Gregor McLennan, entered into a conversation with cultural practitioners themselves, such as the filmmaker and artist Isaac Julien, or indeed political activists. In each of the papers the separation between 'crude' politics and the theorising that goes on at academic institutions was no longer possible: just like Mahasiddhi's exhibition, the theory was part of the practice and the practice *was* in itself theoretical.

University of Birmingham

Note

1   Raymond Williams, Working Papers in Cultural Studies 10, *On Ideology*, *Times Higher Educational Supplement*, 10 June 1977.

Keywords

Radical

Radical has a long and interesting history in the English language, first appearing as an adjective in the fourteenth century and then as a noun from the seventeenth century. The derivation is ultimately from the Latin *rādīx* – root, usually in the physical sense of the root of a plant (retained in 'radish'). The material sense dominated the early use of the term, though there is a clear development in the first recorded examples of a more general meaning: fundamental to, or inherent in, the processes of natural life. Another early extension is evident in the use of the term to suggest origins or primacy and hence causation (the root of something). This general meaning appears in various branches of knowledge from the late sixteenth century: mathematics, the study of language and medicine in particular. And it is in relation to medicine that an important semantic shift takes place. From the seventeenth century, medical treatment directed towards the root, origin or cause of a disease could be described as a 'radical cure' (1633) (used today in 'radical surgery'). This sense developed at more or less the same time to mean an activity (often a change) that goes to the root or origin of something, or that concerns its essential or fundamental aspects, and which is therefore extensive.

The adjectival form appeared in political discourse in the late eighteenth century, often in the phrase 'Radical Reform' (with specific reference to the reform of Parliament under George III); the related noun form – 'a Radical' – is found commonly from the early nineteenth century. This marked a decisive development and the basis of this new, specific sense is clear: political change related to the very nature of society which is therefore far-reaching. Thus while it is evident that the older meaning of 'fundamental' has been maintained and remains significant, it is interesting to note that the political sense becomes prominent from this point and quickly produces the derivatives 'radicalism' and 'radicalise'. In the early to mid-nineteenth century, 'radical' was used to refer to more progressive forms of politics – in Britain the Liberal Party, in the US the anti-slavery Republican Party – and was later deployed in a sharper way to distinguish between the 'Parliamentary Left and the Radical Left' (1870). Towards the end of the century, however, the term was increasingly applied to parties of the right in order to differentiate them from those with liberal and, particularly, socialist tendencies. In continental Europe, 'radical' has typically referred to politics ranging from conservative centrism to (neo-)fascism.

This semantic flexibility continued in the twentieth century in important ways. From the late 1950s, 'radical' was used of, and indeed by, the New Left and related social movements. This was a response to the difficulty of the use of terms such as 'socialist' or 'communist' in the USA (but also elsewhere), particularly in the context of the discursive politics of the Cold War. This meaning remains current on the left in the US and is used in contrast to 'liberal', which can mean anything left-of-centre. In Britain this stronger political sense was often associated popularly with what became known as 'alternative' forms of social life, although in reality 'radical' politics tended to be inspired by Marxist and socialist thought. One significant example of the more emphatic use of the term was 'radical feminism', which draws on the historical sense of fundamental change while also signalling the means by which such change is to be brought about. Precisely because of its own historic achievements ('radical feminism' was actually an early twentieth-century coinage which meant, in effect, feminism), feminism is often now divided into 'liberal' and 'radical' modes, a distinction that derives from the discourse of the American left.

A more recent development has challenged the use of 'radical' as a term of the political left. As the dominant Keynesian model of mixed economies came under attack from the mid-1970s, a new form of right-wing politics appeared whose priorities were the defeat of organised labour, privatisation, market deregulation and the promotion of finance capitalism. Now known as neoliberalism, and currently the hegemonic economic order, this doctrine was such a departure from the post-Second World War consensus that its proponents were described as the 'Radical Right' (also the 'New Right'). Interestingly, the term is again inflected differently in the US and Britain. In America the 'Radical Right' sought fundamental change both to the economy and to social and cultural life (it was usually associated with extremely conservative forms of Christianity). In Britain, the 'Radical Right' has focused primarily on the economy (with the exception of its efforts to 'reform' education). In both cases the social effects of the neoliberal 'restructuring' of the economy have run counter to the ideological tenets of more traditional forms of conservatism.

Two contemporary uses of 'radical' indicate its continuing semantic complexity. The first, now often shortened to 'rad', derived from 1960s surfing culture and meant 'challenging' or 'risky'; it became by extension a general term of approbation – 'excellent', 'outstanding', 'impressive' (see also, 'awesome', 'cool', 'crucial'). The second and more significant use dates from the very late twentieth century and belongs to politico-cultural discourse. In the noun phrase 'Islamic radical', 'radical' occurs as a near-synonym for a number of other terms that are also semantically imprecise: 'militant', 'jihadi' and 'terrorist'. But the extension of the adjective is likewise unclear; is an 'Islamic radical' necessarily an adherent of 'Radical Islam' or simply Islam? Additionally, 'Radical Islam' is itself opaque. Does the phrase refer to a particular theological interpretation of Islam (often referred to as 'Islamic fundamentalism'), or to a political movement based on Islamic beliefs that rejects the socio-cultural order of

Keywords

'the West' (another unclear, homogenising, phrase)? All of these difficulties affect the deployment of the recently revived verb 'radicalise'. With regard to the contemporary uses of 'radical', it is clear that their discursive power often derives precisely from their lack of exact reference.

Tony Crowley
University of Leeds

Recoveries

Amy Dillwyn, *Jill* (1884)[1]

The republication of Amy Dillwyn's 1884 novel *Jill* is part of an attempt to recover the author as an important figure in women's literature and history, as well as a welcome contribution to the maturing field of the study of Welsh literature in English. Dillwyn (1845–1935) was a member of a prominent Victorian industrial family active in Liberal politics, science, literature and the arts in the Swansea area. After the death of her father in 1892 she became a pioneering female industrialist, successfully managing the family's metal works, as well as becoming active in local politics and campaigns for women's suffrage. In earlier life, however, she had published fiction during a relatively short but prolific career – six novels in twelve years – including a well-received historical novel, *The Rebecca Rioter* (1880).[2]

Jill, her fourth novel, is a story of unconventional adolescence, adventure, travel and rebellion against late-Victorian hypocrisy, as well as of unrequited same-sex desire. As Kirsti Bohata explains in her introduction, it draws on Dillwyn's own relationship with the woman she privately referred to as her 'wife', Olive Talbot (x–xi), but it also seems, in its spirited defence of entrepreneurial values, to foreshadow in some ways her later industrial career. It tells the story of Jill Trecastle as she escapes the family estate in protest at her stepmother's determination to impose the strictures of a conventional Victorian adolescence, disguising her class status to pursue an independent 'career', first as a governess, and later as a travelling maid – a situation in which she finds herself falling in love with her mistress, Kitty. The novel offers a number of overt reflections on the issues of 'natural' femininity and sexuality central to contemporary discussions around the 'woman question', as Jill, in her engaging and irreverent manner, proudly defines herself by her hard-headed disposition and her right to live according to her nature. She indeed ponders whether she was born or made, asking why an 'adventurous disposition' like hers comes from nature or experience, and whether her unconventional 'career' is simply the result of a 'natural deficiency' of affection inherited from her mother, whose tolerance of her daughter is apprehended as empty conformity to the '*covenances* of English life' (5).

---

1   Amy Dillwyn, *Jill* (London: Macmillan, 1884; Dinas Powys: Honno, 2013. xxiii + 108 pp. £10.99 pb. ISBN 978-1-906784-94-2).
2   Biographical information from Kirsti Bohata's introduction and from the Dillwyn Project of the Centre for Research into the English Literature and Language of Wales, Swansea University: http://www.swansea.ac.uk/crew/researchprojects/dillwyn/ (accessed 10 June 2015).

Recoveries

Questions of nature are at the heart of the novel's many contradictions, for while arguing for a liberalisation of gender norms that would free those of a different 'nature', like Jill, from irrelevant and absurd conventions, it does so through a plot that upholds and seeks to vindicate a naturalised order of property and class, culminating in Jill's inheritance of the family estate and her stabilised sense of identity as an ambiguously gendered but unequivocally classed 'lady squire'. While Jill successfully appropriates and manipulates the signifiers of class in pursuit of her 'career', she nonetheless maintains throughout an unshakeable sense of herself as a 'lady'. When confronted with the unwanted advances of the valet Perkins, she feels that 'to be taken liberties with by a man-servant was a humiliation not to be endured' (114). Bohata, noting the pejorative class terms of Jill's revulsion, suggests that it is men in general that are the real problem for Jill (xvi), but it is difficult to avoid the sense that it is working-class masculinity in particular that is so disturbing to her sense of self. The episode is couched in unusually intense language that contradicts Jill's characteristic coolness: 'intense horror and indignation'; 'humiliation'; 'degradation'; 'unutterably horrible'; 'dreaded and hateful' (110–1). Indeed, 'I think it's a great pity that there are any men at all in the world – or, anyhow, any except gentlemen' (109). The only character subject to comparable hatred is Jill's stepmother, a socially ambitious widow whose shopkeeper origins Jill is delighted to discover and torment her with.

It is in response to these two antagonisms, the 'irksome' authority of her stepmother and the sexual threat posed by Perkins, that intrude on her nature that Jill becomes a travelling maid on a tour of Europe, a career move that enables her to indulge her 'strange fascination' (115) with Kitty, 'the first person I had ever come across who possessed the gift of arousing the sluggish capacity for affection which lay dormant in my cold-blooded nature' (231). Exploiting the relatively under-policed space of intimacy between upper-class women and their maids, Dillwyn explores same-sex desire within the boundaries naturalised by the novel. Unable to reveal her true identity for fear of losing her position, Jill accepts that the (assumed) class difference means her feelings are not reciprocated, and the failure of the mistress-maid relation to become a romantic one 'contributed greatly to restrain my liking within reasonable limits' (116). Nonetheless, in one of the novel's picaresque episodes, in which Kitty and Jill are imprisoned by escaped convicts in a Corsican chapel, Dillwyn offers an image of equality: 'our separate identities were, for the time being, well-nigh merged into one. Whatever affected the condition of one of us must necessarily affect that of the other also'; 'Truly a queer sort of selfish unselfishness!' (180). The possibilities suggested by Jill's European adventures, however, are closed down on return to England, and the loss of Kitty to a conventional marriage. Another, less disruptive, relationship between women is offered in Jill's reforming friendship with a saintly nurse, Sister Helena, who is, naturally enough, 'unmistakably a lady by birth' (297).

In its explorations of relationships among women and its implication in debates over gender and nature the novel offers considerable interest to modern readers and critics. It is interesting, too, for its struggle to manage the contradictions its images of rebellion bring to light, a struggle registered in the disjointed, episodic plot. Most crucially, the outcome, triumphant for Jill, is completely disconnected from her enterprising pursuit of freedom. Her father abruptly dies, leaving her free to become the 'lady squire' (323) – a relief, since she has realised that such security is preferable to 'the halo of adventure and enterprise' that drew her to an independent living (319). This variation on a patriarchal property settlement, albeit one without a husband, positions Jill's adventures as a hiatus in the natural order, rather than an experiment in more enduring possibilities in late-Victorian life. Jill's amusingly bold narrative voice, and the fine satirical moments it makes possible, are major accomplishments of this work, troubled in revealing ways by the intersections of class and gender.

Elinor Taylor
University of Westminster

John Hampson, *Saturday Night at the Greyhound* (1931)[1]

John Hampson Simpson (1901–55) has been largely forgotten, but for a time during the 1930s he was known for the publishing success of *Saturday Night at the Greyhound*. The book rapidly went through three impressions and sold 3,000 copies, earning the praise of Graham Greene. In 1937 it was reprinted by Penguin, and sold a further 80,000 copies. The book marked a new direction for the Hogarth Press, which had not previously published a novel of provincial working-class life. Although it was Hampson's first novel to be published, it was not the first to have been read by Virginia and Leonard Woolf. They had already seen the manuscripts of *Go Seek a Stranger* and *O, Providence*, the latter of which followed from the Hogarth Press in 1932. It was the explicitly homosexual *Go Seek a Stranger* that the Woolfs thought was his most impressive submission, though they declined the chance to publish it as they felt that the content was too explicit in its account of a gay man's life to be published in Britain at that time. Hampson had submitted the manuscript in 1928, just at the moment that Radclyffe Hall's *The Well of Loneliness* was being banned for obscenity in spite of Virginia Woolf's protests. Leonard Woolf had

---

1 John Hampson, *Saturday Night at the Greyhound* (London: Hogarth Press, 1931; Richmond, Virginia: Valancourt Books, 2014. 108 pp. £9.99 pb. ISBN 978-1-941147-25-2).

written to Hampson on 13 October 1928 expressing his regret at not being able to publish the novel, stating that 'unfortunately we do not think that this would be possible under present circumstances'.[2]

Hampson was born in Birmingham in 1901 and he remained for much of his life in the West Midlands. His was a relatively wealthy home, but in 1907 the family brewing business failed and John's schooling was neglected after he suffered bouts of ill health. He worked in various hotels and public houses, and was briefly imprisoned for stealing books. In 1925 he found employment as a nurse and companion to a boy with Down's syndrome, and this provided him with sufficient security to begin writing fiction. Walter Allen, a friend and fellow 'Birmingham Group' writer, felt that his best work was published between 1931 and 1936, and included the novels *Strip Jack Naked* (1934) and *Family Curse* (1936) – the latter dedicated to Leonard Woolf – as well as several stories which appeared in limited editions from small presses and in John Lehmann's influential *New Writing*. In 1936 he married the Austrian actress Therese Gift (neither spoke each other's language), at the suggestion of W.H. Auden, so that she might escape the Nazi authorities with the use of a British passport.

There is something unique about these early works of fiction that is immediately recognisable, even if it is hard to classify. Allen notes that Hampson's fiction is characterised by 'the natural expression of an abhorrence of anything like fine writing or verbal decoration or the obviously charming. Its angularity reflects the angularity of a mind intransigently honest, not cynical but unillusioned and sardonic, stoic'.[3] The comment encapsulates both the qualities of the writing and the harshness and austerity of life during the Depression years.

The writing has clearly a deeply-felt sense of place. Indeed, the National Portrait Gallery website, where photos taken of Hampson by the fashionable photographer Howard Coster in 1935 can be viewed, defines Hampson's particular distinction as that of a 'writer on English life', a formulation that highlights the sociological aspect of his writing. In the same vein, his contribution to the Collins series of *Britain in Pictures* was *The English at Table* (1944), a book that drew upon his experience in the catering business. (Other contributors to the series, which aimed at boosting war-time morale, included Edith Sitwell, Graham Greene and Elizabeth Bowen.) Hampson's *A Bag of Stones* (1952) was a return to fiction, and developed his theme of the alienated male in a brutal family environment from which he seeks liberation. Here, the threatening father has returned to the family after service in the war and bullies his son, prompting rebellion. This novel was ahead of its time in drawing

---

2   Helen Southworth, '"Going Over": The Woolfs, The Hogarth Press and Working-Class Voices', in Helen Southworth, ed., *Leonard and Virginia Woolf, The Hogarth Press and the Networks of Modernism* (Edinburgh: Edinburgh University Press, 2010), 218.
3   Walter Allen, *Tradition and Dream* (London: Phoenix House, 1964), 226.

attention to the psychological impact that exposure to war can have, with its brutalising of ordinary human relations, an example of what we would today call post-traumatic stress. Although for Hampson it must have been an instance of the diminutive underdog (Hampson was extremely small bodied) fighting against oppression (the symbolism is taken from David slaying Goliath, hence the bag of stones) we can see that the narrative enacts the homosexual's fight against the denial of his right to be different.

Saturday Night at the Greyhound (1931) remains Hampson's best-known novel, reprinted in 1950 and 1986. It successfully conveys the conflicts and intense emotions of a small group of people struggling to grind out a living in rural Derbyshire, exploring the emotional conflicts that exist between Tom, his sister Ivy, and his brother-in-law Fred. Ivy and Fred have moved to the country to set up as landlords of the local pub. Although Ivy is in love with Fred, and he needs her sensible approach to life, the marriage is threatened by Fred's philandering. It is evident that he is a man with a masculinity that attracts the sexual interest of those he meets – perhaps even Tom, though this is not articulated in any way other than Tom's acknowledgement of Fred's physical prowess, which he finds both disturbing (suggesting desire) and intimidating. Tom, who, like Hampson and the character Alec in *Go Seek*, has worked in various hotels and public houses, has a practical understanding for the trade. He observes what is happening but is unable to prevent catastrophe. The struggles of this displaced group of people are set against impersonal economic forces and the frustrated lives and indifference of the local mining community, in particular the malevolent Mrs Tapin, whose daughter is the illegitimate offspring of the lord of the manor and the object of Fred's attentions. The action is concentrated in one evening, but nonetheless manages to range over the histories of the main protagonists through a series of flashbacks. The novel manages to maintain a fatalistic inevitability, systematically shattering the illusions of the characters as the impossibility of their dreams is gradually revealed. The autobiographical element in the fiction allows Hampson to explore his own sexuality in the context of a culture that is structured so as to deny him free expression of selfhood, although contemporary readers will read the repressed subtext in relation to Tom. Hampson's achievement is that he managed to experiment with fictional structures that expressed his feeling of sympathy for the underdog in a style that was uncompromising and retains its direct freshness after eight decades.

John Hampson died from a heart attack at the age of 54, leaving behind a body of writing which still needs to be properly reassessed.

Stephen Rogers

Reviews

Simon Dentith, *Nineteenth Century British Literature Then and Now: Reading with Hindsight.* Farnham: Ashgate, 2014. ix + 182 pp. £60 hb. ISBN 978-1-4724-1885-2.

'Hindsight', the key term in Simon Dentith's new book, is itself a nineteenth-century coinage. The first *OED* citation, from 1883, shows it as a neologism in inverted commas, yet by the time of the second citation in 1895 its advantages were already 'proverbial'. As for its meaning, the *OED* suggests 'Seeing what has happened, and what ought to have happened, after the event', and the *New Shorter Oxford Dictionary* simplifies this to 'wisdom after the event'. These definitions attribute a level of certainty, even of cocksureness, to hindsight that Dentith rightly rejects: hindsight for him is characteristically ambivalent, and its temptations are often suspect. We are not necessarily more clear-sighted than those we call the 'Victorians', nor are we as much their heirs as we sometimes like to think.

As Dentith observes in his opening chapter, hindsight at its broadest is the defining condition of historical knowledge, yet it is also a viewpoint we need to resist. As historians we may set out to rescue individuals, classes and social movements from what E.P. Thompson famously called 'the enormous condescension of posterity'; and as literary critics, while understanding novels and poems as historical products, we need to explain why they have not been superseded, why some of them can and do speak directly to our times. A significant reference point here is Robert Frost's poem 'The Roads Not Taken', with its sense of alternative historical paths and the possibility of recovering – primarily in imagination, but perhaps also in reality – what is excluded from our current self-understanding. Dentith's succeeding chapters on *The Mill on the Floss*, *David Copperfield*, Trollope, Ruskin and Morris pursue different kinds of critical recovery, a recovery that turns from the individual to the political sphere as the book goes on. His aim is always 'to mobilise the defamiliarising power of texts from the past' (99).

When, in *The War of the Worlds* (1898), the terrified curate asks 'What are these Martians?', Wells's narrator replies 'What are we?'. This is an illustration of the defamiliarising power of science fiction (and fantasy), a familiar critical trope since Darko Suvin first identified it in the 1960s. Suvin drew on the Russian Formalists and Brecht, while Dentith's conception of hindsight is indebted to Gadamer, Bakhtin and Walter Benjamin amongst others; and Dentith's insistence that defamiliarisation is the province of realist as well as non-realist texts means that his assumptions about 'us' – or, in the words of his title, about 'then and now' – need to be spelt out. In particular, he emphasises the movement from Victorian liberalism through the various forms of twentieth-century statism to contemporary neoliberalism and impending ecological catastrophe; but, though insistent, this book is anything but formula-ridden and dogmatic. Its readings – subtle, complex and always deeply engaged – have an inescapably provisional quality. In an Afterword, Dentith himself applies hindsight with the observation (should it be called an admission?) that '[t]his book has been an exercise in method as much as an effort towards a substantive cultural history' (165). Readers will add their own kinds of hindsight, in a dialogue that Dentith seems positively to welcome. We may, indeed, reflect on the critical paths that he has deliberately not taken.

For example, the connection between hindsight and foresight (a much older term) naturally leads him to a discussion of utopian fiction, since it was in the nineteenth century that most utopias came to be located in the future. Their determination to lay claim to the advantages of hindsight was made explicit in Edward Bellamy's seminal title *Looking Backward*. Dentith looks at various aspects of *News from Nowhere*, which was William Morris's reply to *Looking Backward*; but he offers only a brief and rather dismissive glance at Morris's provocative, much-quoted remark in his original review of Bellamy's work that 'the only safe way of reading a Utopia is to consider it as the expression of the temperament of its author'. It is troubling that Morris of all people should denigrate the political propaganda effect of utopian writing by stressing its origins in personal eccentricity; and troubling, too, that he does so by invoking the idea of 'temperament' which was one of the literary-theoretical clichés of his age. Does this betray the anxiety caused – for Morris and his comrades in the Socialist League – by the extraordinary impact of Bellamy's militaristic state socialism? Perhaps; but Dentith, while conceding that Morris's remark is 'doubtless true' (125), seems determined not to pursue the kinds of truth to which it might lead us. Like other recent critics on the left, he extracts a series of political messages from *News from Nowhere* while largely disregarding the personal and textual idiosyncrasies from which they emerge. A case in point is the episode of the 'Obstinate Refusers', which Dentith discusses in detail as a representation of free, unalienated labour. Yet the main character here – Philippa the master-carver – is an antisocial workaholic who ignores the obligations of fellowship and rudely turns her back on the nineteenth-century visitor. A little like Morris himself perhaps, in some of his moods? The scene suggests that excessive joy in labour – in labour as artistic self-expression – may, as much as the mechanical drudgery which is its opposite, contribute to the denial of full participation in communal living. And this is far from being the only problem of Morris's socialist vision that *News from Nowhere* highlights while not really answering.

Reviews

In his final chapter Dentith looks at the present-day phenomenon of neo-Victorian fiction, contrasting the '"bad" historicism' (63) of a novelist like John Fowles with the effort of disciplined historical recovery that he finds most fully embodied in Peter Carey's *True History of the Kelly Gang*. Once again this is an argument for patient understanding against debunking, for authentic hindsight against facile knowingness. This return to the contested present makes an appropriate conclusion to a book whose wisdom, however hesitant, is satisfyingly hard-earned.

Patrick Parrinder
University of Reading

Rebecca Beasley and Philip Ross Bullock (eds), ***Russia in Britain 1880–1940: From Melodrama to Modernism.*** Oxford: Oxford University Press, 2013. xiii + 309 pp. £55 hb. ISBN 978-0-19-966086-5.

The aim of this book, according to the editors' Introduction, is to examine the presence of Russian culture in Britain in the late nineteenth and early twentieth centuries, using perspectives that go beyond traditional notions of 'influence'. The study of 'institutions, disciplines, and groups' is therefore prioritised over consideration of individuals, and notions of 'circulation, translation, and mediation' replace the idea of 'influence' (1). The 'impact' of Russian culture in Britain is read in terms of transformation and hybridity rather than simple transfer from one supposedly homogeneous nation to another (7). This results in a nuanced approach to the subject and, in addition to the methodological coherence of the whole, the editors deserve much credit for having assembled chapters covering a wide range of textual genres and types of cultural activity.

Although the importance of translation is highlighted in the Introduction (13–4), the book's focus is on contexts and networks of cultural exchange, and the textual study of interlingual translation is largely absent. Whilst I would certainly not advocate a return to source-text/target-text comparison as the best or only means of evaluating the significance of translation, at certain points I was left wondering what the English were consuming when they received Russian works in translation. For example, Charlotte Alston's fascinating account of the international Tolstoyan movement (Chapter 3) does not consider whether readers of Tolstoy in different languages were all reading the same thing: the possibility of domestic ideological manipulation through translation is not explicitly raised. And what were English audiences actually watching when they saw plays by Gorky, Tolstoy and Gogol? The variations in translated titles of Russian plays to which Stuart Young refers in his chapter on 'Non-Chekhov Russian and Soviet Drama' suggest significant adaptation through translation, but the focus remains exclusively on reception. Interlingual translation is explicitly treated in another volume by the same editors, *Translating Russia, 1890–1935*,[1] where, for example, essays by Claire Davison-Pégon on Virginia Woolf and Koteliansky and Philip Ross Bullock on Pushkin combine textual analysis with consideration of historical context and 'the pressures – ideological, critical, personal – that shaped the translation process' (299). *Russia in Britain* nonetheless gives a good sense of the variety of textual practices which come under the broad heading of 'translation', including Katherine Mansfield's pseudo-translations published in *Rhythm* under the pseudonyms Boris Petrovsky and Lili Heron (146, 148), Frank Harris's adaptation of Tolstoy's 'The Three Hermits' as 'The Holy Man' in the same magazine (150), the publication of John Rodker's first novel exclusively in its French translation (191) and the screening of Soviet films with only 'superimposed English titles' to help the non-Russophone audience (253–4).

Translation emerges from this collection as an important and varied practice in the importing of Russian culture into Britain. Travel – a longstanding focus of study for scholars interested in British and European perceptions of the USSR – is also present as a vector of the international circulation of ideas. Pilgrimages to see Tolstoy and visits to other groups were a constituent aspect of the Tolstoyan movement (63); John Rodker's role as the British agent of PresLit, the Moscow Press and Publisher Literary Service, necessitated various trips to the USSR (193, 197), and Ivor Montagu travelled there in order to bring Soviet films to British audiences through The Film Society (228). H.G. Wells's 1934 journey to interview Stalin resulted in the publication of *The Stalin-Wells Talk*, which also comprised the responses of George Bernard Shaw and John Maynard Keynes to the transcript of the interview that had first appeared in the *New Statesman and Nation* (analysed in detail by Matthew Taunton in Chapter 11). The travels of Western intellectuals to the USSR have been widely discussed, notably in the now canonical studies by Paul Hollander and David Caute; this collection suggests some of the ways in which travel interacted with a range of other practices to condition intellectuals' responses to the Soviet experiment.

One of the recurrent themes of the collection is the triangulated nature of cultural relations, France being a significant intermediary in the importing of Russian culture to Britain. Laurence Senelick gives various examples from the theatre, including London productions of Jules Verne's *Michel Strogoff* and Victorien Sardou's *Fédora* (25–8). Young highlights the staging of Gaston Baty's French adaptation of *Crime and Punishment* by the Prague Group of the Moscow Art Theatre at the Garrick in 1931 and Edith Craig's 1929 production

---

1 *Translation and Literature* 20, no. 3 (2011).

of Evreinov's *The Theatre of Life* adapted from a French version (97–8). Studies of Russian music were often translated into English from French (Bullock, 116), as was the most respected Russian reader for Russian language education (Beasley, 182). In literature too, French functioned as a bridge language: Alston notes that Tolstoy was frequently read in French outside of France (55, 60), and Patterson recalls the publication of Zamyatin's *My* in French as *Nous autres*, prior to Rodker's attempt to acquire the English language rights (197). Paris provided a context for the European reception of Sergei Diaghilev's *Ballets russes* (120), including *The Rite of Spring* (129). Triangulation is also evident in the political domain: Robert Henderson describes how the French *Sûreté générale* was collecting information on the English political émigré association known as the 'Whitechapel Group' (80), and Taunton's study of Wells, Shaw and Keynes demonstrates the impossibility of categorising Western intellectuals as simply pro- or anti- USSR (223).

Some of the chapters are in a continuum with recent research based on Soviet archives, such as Michael David Fox's *Showcasing the Great Experiment: Cultural Diplomacy and Western Visitors to the Soviet Union, 1921–1941* (2012) and Ludmila Stern's *Western Intellectuals and the Soviet Union: From Red Square to the Left Bank* (2006), insofar as they examine the mechanisms by means of which the Soviet regime stimulated support, rather than assuming that Western enthusiasm for the Soviet experiment was spontaneous. Examples include PresLit (Chapter 10) and the Moscow Congress of the International Union of Revolutionary Theatres which established film sections in European countries (242). This variegated study of an important aspect of the international character of modernism – which draws on two occasions on Raymond Williams's *The Politics of Modernism* (116; 258–9) – extends the boundaries of existing research and suggests many avenues for future inquiry.

Angela Kershaw
University of Birmingham

Jim McGuigan (ed.), *Raymond Williams on Culture and Society: Essential Writings*. London: Sage Publications, 2014. xxvi + 342 pp. £29.99 pb. ISBN 978-1-8492-0771-3.

Terry Eagleton has observed of Cambridge in the 1960s that most of the English Faculty saw Raymond Williams as 'some kind of sociologist who had strayed through the wrong departmental door and inadvertently got himself caught up with the metaphysical poets'.[1] But Williams defied categorisation

---

1   Terry Eagleton, *Raymond Williams: Critical Perspectives* (Cambridge: Polity Press, 1989), 2.

according to traditional academic boundaries: 'in the end it was impossible to give his project a name' (5).

Jim McGuigan's new and comprehensively edited selection, *Raymond Williams on Culture and Society*, dedicated to representing the 'social-scientific turn in Williams's work' (xv), initially seems to deny that there is any ambiguity in Williams's disciplinary categorisation. Its central claim is for the importance of Williams as sociologist, dismissing the decontextualised theories of 'cultural autonomy' that have dominated sociological studies in recent years, as McGuigan has argued elsewhere.[2] While the implications of Williams's cultural materialism for literary studies are well-established in, for instance, *Culture and Materialism* (1980) and the collection edited by Tony Pinkney, *The Politics of Modernism* (1987), McGuigan focuses on Williams's departure from the 'epiphenomenal' theories of culture current in contemporary sociology (xx). The present collection thus opens up a fresh perspective on Williams's work, renewing and regenerating his ideas for the present generation. Its argument is substantiated through a carefully chosen and representative selection of Williams's texts combined with sage editorial contributions, to provide a comprehensive portrait of Williams as sociologist and cultural critic. In the process, McGuigan leaves space for Williams's own nuanced conception of disciplinary boundaries, his integration of the humanities with the social sciences, as in his 1975 address to the British Sociological Association, 'Developments in the Sociology of Culture'. Here, sociology is perceived as a field of analysis that should include a concern with textual as well as institutional analysis, one in which sociologists should concern themselves with the '*materiality of signs*' (195, emphasis original).

Throughout the volume, Williams's analysis of culture as a socially informed product is stressed, and the collection's chronological structure allows the reader to follow closely the development of Williams's thinking. The widely cited early essay, 'Culture is Ordinary' (1958), sought to relocate the concept of culture in the quotidian: 'culture is ordinary […] every human society has its own shape, its own purposes, its own meanings. Every human society expresses these, in institutions, in arts and learning' (2). 'Structure of Feeling and Selective Tradition' outlines the process by which such 'ordinary' cultures become marginalised. Educational opportunity, Williams suggests in 'Culture is Ordinary' and 'The Idea of a Common Culture', also sharply informs conceptions of culture. John McIlroy and Sallie Westwood have previously anthologised Williams's writings from his years spent in adult education, working for the WEA. McGuigan's editorial introduction to 'The Idea of a Common Culture' usefully dissociates Williams's more 'processual

---

[2] See McGuigan and Marie Moran, 'Raymond Williams and Sociology', *The Sociological Review* 62 (2014), 171.

conception of common culture' (93) from that of the former Vice-President of the WEA, R.H. Tawney, emphasising Williams's concern with the widening of educational opportunity as a means to transform culture, rather than simply increasing access to existing cultural products. At points, however, McGuigan's decision that it would be 'inappropriate to comment' on Williams's imaginative writing (xvi) prompts him to pass over data that might support his case. The autobiographical tenor of 'Culture is Ordinary' seems to prefigure, for example, the depiction of the 'ordinary' *Eistedfodd* in the autobiographical novel *Border Country* (1960).

McGuigan's deft editorial contributions seek to argue for the contemporary relevance of a 'Twenty-first Century Williams' (xxii). 'Means of Communication as a Means of Production' speaks especially to the complexities created by the new electronic media. While Williams saw that new technology overcomes the division between the means of production and the means of communication, this essay questions, nevertheless, the 'real costs of universal-access communication […] much of the advanced technology is being developed within firmly capitalist social relations' (232). This creates a challenge for socialism, as the 'means of communicative production […] have been expropriated by capitalism' (236). Socialism must not only seek to recover 'alienated human capacities', but also to institute 'new and very complex communicative capacities and relationships' (236).

McGuigan depicts Williams's 1983 work, *Towards 2000*, as much more than a *fin-de-siècle* exercise, with relevance far beyond the turn of the present century. His introduction explores particularly the conception of 'mobile privatisation', first adumbrated by Williams in 1964, to suggest that the blending of the public and the private space occasioned by 'all-purpose mobile communication device[s]' has 'normalised' this 'mode of sociality' (xxiii). Further, McGuigan associates 'Plan X', defined by Williams as 'a new politics of strategic advantage' where 'any more general condition is left undefined' (282), with today's neoliberal tendencies. It is in the same marginalised cultures that Williams originally explored in 'Culture is Ordinary' that McGuigan finds an implicit riposte to 'Plan X' and its 'competitive' tendencies (281): despite the 'many dangers in the years towards 2000' there are 'many grounds for hope. There is more eager and constructive work, more active and caring responsibility, than the official forms of the culture permit us to recognise' (303).

The collection's final essay, 'The Future of Cultural Studies', suggests that the responsiveness of adult education to students' own cultural experience formed the basis of Cultural Studies. However, this 'attempt at a majority democratic education […] kept being sidetracked as elements of it got into institutions which then changed it' (318). For Williams, the Open University in particular lacked 'that crucial process of interchange and encounter between the people offering the intellectual disciplines and those using them' (320), because 'technology [is] inserted over and above the social processes of education' (321). Williams sought to alert us to the significance of this 'interchange' as a means to 'revise the syllabus and discipline' of Cultural Studies (326), thus preventing the institutionalisation of cultural norms. For McGuigan, it is in these comments that Williams's ultimate significance lies: he provides a 'humane' voice against 'a commodified and inegalitarian higher educational system' where his democratic values now stand 'seriously beleaguered' (314). Polemical though McGuigan's point may be, this collection amply demonstrates the 'resource of hope' afforded by Williams's work, beyond the qualms of disciplinary categorisation.

Natasha Periyan
Royal Holloway, University of London

Philip Bounds, ***Notes from the End of History: A Memoir of the Left in Wales.*** London: Merlin, 2014. 202 pp. £14.95 pb. ISBN 978-0-85036-611-2.

In 1989, Francis Fukuyama famously framed the collapse of Soviet communism and the increasing hegemony of neoliberal economics and modes of governance as the 'End of History'.[1] Despite a significant critical backlash, the idea that, although domestic and international conflicts may linger, the future was now settled – *there is no alternative* to capitalism – became a dominant, perhaps *the* dominant, Western ideology. It underpinned neoliberal 'common sense' and structured the political imaginary; arguably, it continues to do so. The End of History narrative certainly continues to structure contemporary historical and cultural narratives about the recent past, even in the wake of the 2008 financial crisis that so undermined neoliberal sureties. Sometimes explicitly, more often implicitly, the political conflicts of the 1980s are figured as a quasi-apocalyptic 'Year Zero': a cultural revolution, in which New Times signifies End Times.

Philip Bounds's *Notes from the End of History* is neither a systematic analysis of the 1980s nor an exegesis of Marxist philosophy. Instead, it is a highly personal *Bildungsroman*, retrospectively tracing the ways in which the author's political development was shaped by the historical and cultural forces of the 1980s. Standard ingredients of the eighties coming-of-age memoir – from punk at the beginning of the decade to ecstasy and rave culture at its end – are described with both nostalgic relish and a sharp eye for their political significance. These

---

1 For an in-depth and highly sophisticated analysis of the 'End of History', see Perry Anderson, *A Zone of Engagement* (London and New York: Verso, 1992), 279–375.

cultural experiences are interwoven with Bounds's exploration of political alternatives to Thatcherism. There are youthful epiphanies at SPGB meetings; more sceptical engagements with anarchist groups and Militant Tendency; membership of the CPGB; and periods of disillusionment and wholesale estrangement from organised politics. Bounds is highly critical of his earliest engagements with socialism, presenting them as adolescent self-fashioning driven by a romantic desire for glamorous 'outsider' status in petit-bourgeois South Wales. However, this memoir ultimately presents his relationship with Marxism as 'the most *agonistic* relationship' (117) of his life: punishing but intimately bound up with his subjectivity, attractive and vital because it offers 'personal redemption' as much as 'political progress' (10). For Bounds, one of the reasons that Marxism survived the 'End of History' and the quietism of the 1990s is that, for its believers, 'abandoning socialist politics' would have been 'tantamount to tearing up the sinews of selfhood and starting again from scratch' (10).

Marxism may be presented as a faith in Bounds's narrative of subject-formation, but it never provides uncomplicated solace or straightforward 'personal redemption'. Socialism is discovered, fervently grasped, doubted and agonised over, the 'Marxist passion play' (65) is critically interrogated, reconciled with on different terms, then doubted all over again: the book is less a Gospel and more what Bounds terms a 'chronicle of ambivalence' (181). And he is more than ambivalent about many of the fragmented leftist 'sects' (191) he encountered in the 1980s, mainly because their 'authoritarianism' clashes with his liberal and libertarian beliefs. Identity politics is critiqued in these terms – its authoritarianism is, Bounds argues, 'a symptom of the left's estrangement from universal values' (175). And while he fervently campaigned for the miners in the 1984–85 strike – a struggle that often functions as a metonym for the triumph of Thatcherism in a British variant of the 'End of History' narrative – he criticises what he describes as the 'dreadful mood of illiberality' (82) displayed by some leftist groups and secondary picketers, as well as the NUM leadership's desire to achieve 'unity through nastiness' (86) and exclusion. Indeed, Bounds presents his experiences during the strike as a personal turning-point: 'If previously I'd been a squatter in the House of Marx, Arthur Scargill's intransigence turned me into a liberal irritant in one of its ante-rooms – mouthy, carping wilfully unorthodox. I don't regret it as much as I should' (83). Thirty years on from the strike, opinions like these are rarely voiced in such trenchant terms on the Left, and Bounds's polemical take may not be welcomed by some readers (leftist academia also comes in for criticism). But of course, intellectual debate and contestation are crucial to both historical analysis and political action. And just as importantly, this is a *memoir*, a form that involves an avowedly personal and subjective presentation of the recent past, and which therefore enacts the tensions between social history and biography, and the fraught relationship between history and memory. *Notes from the End of History* is a sustained exploration of Bounds's 'agonised ambivalence' (16) about socialist politics during and since the great reversals of the 1980s; and it is simultaneously a reflexive literary attempt to shape and make sense of a life through the prism of that history. Remembering the 1980s as a period of conflict rather than inevitable triumph is crucial to historicising the End of History and uncovering the ways in which that narrative structures neoliberal common sense. Bounds's memoir is a highly provocative and personal contribution to the historiography of the Left during that decade.

Christopher Vardy
University of Manchester

Liane Tanguay, *Hijacking History: American Culture and the War on Terror*. Montreal and Kingston: McGill-Queens University Press, 2013. xiii + 284 pp. £69 hb; £18.99 pb. ISBN 978-0-7735-4074-3.

Liane Tanguay's *Hijacking History: American Culture and the War on Terror* begins with an apparently straightforward question:

> [H]ow were the 'American people' […] seduced into allowing what transpired in the early years of the War on Terror – the hijacking of power by a unitary executive, the subversion of constitutional and international law in a war that rapidly and increasingly lost any pretence to legitimacy, the demolition of core American values in the pursuit of a new, amorphous enemy, and a rising American death toll in this same pursuit? (3)

While many answers to similar questions have already been proposed, Tanguay's unique angle is to invite us to consider what she terms 'the aesthetics of hegemony'. By this phrase, Tanguay means the way in which popular culture in the form of network television (Fox News, CNN) and blockbuster Hollywood films 'captured the attention of […] the "mainstream" American consumer and held it through the aftermath of 9/11 and the early years of the War on Terror' (5). Among the numerous intriguing cultural artefacts lighted upon by Tanguay are two commemorative DVDs – CNN's *America Remembers: The Events of September 11 and America's Response* and CBS's *What We Saw: The Events of September 11, 2001, in Words, Pictures, and Video* – which at the same time as reasserting the 'traumatic' significance of the attacks on New York and Washington, also indulged the viewer in a kind of 'repetition-compulsion' (147). In this respect, Tanguay argues, trauma took the form of an 'obscene enjoyment' (Lacan's *jouissance*): in the Hollywood-style trailer for the CNN film, 'the overall implication is that the viewer must tune in so as not to "miss out" on the thrill of mass destruction' (151). By sifting through the landscape of popular culture, *Hijacking History* constructs a vivid picture of the US media spectacle in the aftermath of 9/11, demonstrating how it blended an erotics of apocalypse (slow-motion replays of the same spectacular footage, combined with a melodramatic soundtrack), with a mythology of a new beginning or origin for the still-metaphysical 'American people'.

The mediatised event of 9/11 played out, as Tanguay observes, in the context of a new cultural and epistemological framework established at the end of the Cold War: one which she describes as a 'posthistorical structure of feeling' (9ff). Taken in its simplest sense, this concept points to what we might describe as a cognitive trickling down of the claim made by Fukuyama and other liberal supremacists that there is no longer any alternative to the current system, and indeed that liberal-democratic capitalism is the most desirable form of global human governance. Having achieved this liberal utopia in the West, so the argument went, we have now reached the end point of mankind's ideological evolution and thus the end of history. While Tanguay correctly argues that this thesis is itself a 'symptom' of late capitalism, she wishes to assert, drawing on the work of Raymond Williams, that during the 1990s and into the 2000s it nevertheless had a profound impact upon everyday social experience, transforming how certain meanings and values were actively 'lived' and 'felt' (19). It was then, as Tanguay writes, the process by which 'the ostensible superiority of liberal democratic capitalism over its alternatives was translated from the realm of systematic ideology into the cultural structure of feeling' (43) that provided the context within which George Bush Senior could announce a 'new world order' on 11 September 1990 (coinciding with the start of the first Gulf War).

Hijacking History provides a compelling account of the post-9/11 Bush doctrine (an extremist version of a US strategic vision extending back to the end of WWII), its intellectual backstory and the impact which it had upon the American 'cultural imaginary'. The author avoids the obvious pitfalls of ideological determinism (she says at the very start that the aesthetics of hegemony was never 'truly hegemonic to the extent of silencing all dissent' (6)); and what unfolds is an investigation into the modern 'aestheticization of politics' which fully registers the complexity of the process. Tanguay's notion of a 'post-historical structure of feeling' also furnishes us with a useful way of conceptualising the dominant *ideological character* of a relatively short period of US history – one that, I would argue, was more or less extinguished with the 2008 financial crisis. Framing things in economic as well cultural and geopolitical terms allows us to return to the question with which Tanguay's study begins: how were the American people seduced into supporting an illegitimate war? Consent for war, we might suggest, was dependent not simply upon the Bush doctrine (and the Project for the New American Century), but also the continued implementation of the 'Greenspan doctrine': the old mantra that 'spending is patriotic' and that one can always 'buy now and pay later'. Who cares about shock and awe when easy credit has granted one the keys to a new starter home and a gas guzzler in the driveway?

One significant weakness with *Hijacking History* is that while it is able to name the enemy – 'capitalism [and] capitalist ideology itself' (231, 233) – it fails to name a fully coherent strategy for returning to what the book's conclusion calls 'politics proper' (234). What is missing here then, amidst talk of a vague 'hope that […] shifts in the prevailing winds can be harnessed toward genuinely progressive ends' (234), is a politics of class; and indeed we might argue that the 'posthistorical structure of feeling' has as much to do with the systematic destruction of organised labour (both in the USA and Europe) as it does with a complicit media validating and reinforcing certain ideological narratives. This aside, Tanguay's book remains urgent reading for all those concerned with the contemporary geopolitical situation and the role played by culture in propping up an increasingly precarious empire of capital. As the consequences of the (so-called) 'War on Terror' continue to play out both at 'home' and 'abroad', *Hijacking History* is the kind of study that might just enable us to keep our historical bearings.

Ben Ware
Institute of English Studies, SAS

Keith Gildart, *Images of England through Popular Music: Class, Youth and Rock 'n' Roll, 1955–1976*. Basingstoke: Palgrave MacMillan, 2013. ix + 290 pp. £58 hb. ISBN 978-0-230-01969-0.

The impact and importance of popular music and youth culture on post-war society has been marginalised and largely ignored by what Keith Gildart describes as the 'embedded cultural hierarchy' which dominates mainstream conceptions of contemporary English history (5). In this excellent new book, Gildart challenges such omissions by the likes of Dominic Sandbrook and Peter Hennessy by presenting an invigorating and hugely enjoyable account of change and continuity in working-class culture viewed through the lens of rock 'n' roll, Mod, glam and punk. It is these two seemingly contradictory terms, change and continuity, to which Gildart repeatedly returns. His concern is with the 'resilience and complexity of working-class identities and experiences in post-war England' (17), exploring how the youth movements of this period allowed young working-class men and women to 'transcend the boundaries of class, race and sexuality' (104). Gildart's nuanced analysis of how popular music facilitated a transcending of class whilst also reaffirming class identity is the real strength of *Images of England*. His book takes issue with the Hoggartian reading of post-war working-class culture and the perceived erosion of its foundational and ideological base by affluence and the mass arts. '[A]ffluence did not weaken class-consciousness', argues Gildart, 'but merely moved it in different cultural directions' (11). As it is explored in the book, working-class consciousness is located beyond the traditional or institutional frameworks of the labour movement and is expressed in cultural terms, through the everyday lives of the working-class youths who feature so predominantly in Gildart's research.

The book is split into three chronological sections: 'Teddy Boy England', 'Mod England' and 'Glam/Punk England'. The story of these three distinct yet overlapping youth movements are told though key figures who are identified, in the Gramscian sense, as organic intellectuals: primarily Pete Townsend and Ray Davies but also, and to a lesser extent, Georgie Fame, Noddy Holder, David Bowie and the Sex Pistols. The little-known Ronnie Carr opens Gildart's compelling account, however. Carr, known as the 'Lemon Drop Kid', was a coal miner in his hometown of Leigh. By the 1950s he was also a rock 'n' roll convert, performing impromptu sets to his work colleagues deep under the Lancashire coalfield before taking to the concert halls and pubs of Leigh and Wigan as a member of first the Dominoes and then the Beat Boys. What emerges in the telling of such a history from 'below' is the presence of a thriving, alternative class-orientated culture emanating from a rich network of social spaces in which working-class youths could gather, socialise and explore their own changing identities. Rock 'n' roll, as it was experienced and expressed in the coffee bars, pubs, dance halls and social clubs of northwest England, 'reaffirmed and challenged a particular "structure of feeling" that formed part of the shared consciousness of working-class youth', according to Gildart (43). Carr's one-time band mate in the Dominoes, Clive Powell, better known as Georgie Fame, provides a crucial link in the *Images of England*. His merging of northern working-class youth culture with the sounds of black America is described as an 'historic encounter' that 'would influence the development of popular music and youth subculture for the rest of the century' (50). Fame embodied an emerging structure of feeling that allowed for the formation of what Gildart characterises as an 'oppositional Englishness' (12), using Raymond Williams's concept to highlight how 'the working class experienced economic and social life in cultural terms' (3).

The book's reappraisal of Mod culture is particularly fascinating. Rather than an apolitical movement, expressing an emerging consumerist individualism, Mod is figured as a subcultural identity and a way in which working-class youth could challenge and subvert 'social conventions and existing conceptions of masculinity, femininity, and national identity' (109). Importantly, the enabling network of communal spaces upon which the likes of Georgie Fame could call was not restricted to a local or provincial level. Social and cultural networks were made, significantly, with the Mod scene in London's Soho. And working-class youth culture could express itself in increasingly transgressive and challenging ways. The much-mythologised Bank Holiday 'riots' of 1964 are placed in a wider context by Gildart, posited as a form of antisocial behaviour which suggests links between the seaside disturbances and an increasing awareness amongst the young of social inequality coupled with economic and social change. Pete Townsend, in particular, is positioned as a key figure in the construction of an 'oppositional identity' which emerges out of Mod. The Who guitarist and songwriter 'viewed popular music as a transformative aspect of youth culture', according to *Images of England*. By engaging with the frustrations and anxieties of working-class teenagers, Townsend's writing offers an alternative commentary on the perceived affluence and hedonism of 1960s England. He is placed as a central and emblematic figure in a Mod movement summarised by Gildart as a vibrant culture which 'suggested growing affluence' (125) but within which class 'remained fixed' for many (125).

Ray Davies comes in for similar treatment, and the chapter 'Class, Nation, and Social Change in the Kinks' England' is a particular high-point. Like Townsend, Davies is described as an organic intellectual and a significant social historian of working-class culture in both pre- and post-war society. There is a closer and more rigorous engagement with the songs of Davies and the chapter offers a complex reading of his writing. Class is a source of identity and anxiety in the work of the Kinks. And class and locality were key themes for the group throughout the 1960s. Importantly, the lyrics of Davies provide 'an essential source for making sense of the sixties and the experience of the working-class in this much mythologised decade' (147). In albums such as *The Kinks Are The Village Green Preservation Society* (1968) and *Arthur or the Decline and Fall of the British Empire* (1969), a nuanced understanding of the everyday experiences of the working class and a sense of 'the national, the local and the personal' (147) is achieved.

The 1970s see the arrival of glam rock, which Gildart describes as not representing 'a flight from class but […] a restatement of its collective values and hedonistic cultures' (151). The music of Slade, fronted by Noddy Holder, is seen as an affirmation of social class rather than the temporary escape as personified by the appeal of David Bowie. This comparison between the two is particularly illuminating. *Images of England* looks at how Bowie was received by the working class rather than engaging with his music as a working-class artist speaking to distinctly working-class concerns. His songs are explored as being a relief from the failure of the welfare state and the evaporation of post-war hope. Again, the approach to this period, through the way in which these youth cultures were experienced and understood on a personal and local level by the working-class, is one of the book's many strengths. Gildart uses the testimony of young Bowie fans, mainly during his period in the early 1970s as Ziggy Stardust, and concludes that the 'consumption and articulation of Ziggy by working-class consumers represented one strand in an individual and collective contribution to challenging dominant conceptions of masculinity, femininity and sexuality' (168).

A different methodological approach is taken when *Images of England* moves onto its final section with an analysis of punk and the Sex Pistols. The band's infamous 1976 Anarchy Tour is the prime focus, specifically the moral panic surrounding it. Out of twenty-seven planned dates, only six gigs went ahead with just five locations allowing them to play (there were two shows in Plymouth). Gildart follows the events of the tour as the band travel to and are turned away from venue after venue across Britain. By placing an emphasis on the local responses to the Sex Pistols, the final chapter engages with 'the micro-politics of a variety of groups, individuals and localities' (192). This moral panic was not exclusively a media-orientated phenomenon; there was a complex and convoluted response to the group, who were dismissed as immoral yobs by people from across the political spectrum. 'Class was central to the construction of such narratives', according to Gildart (189). There were strong fears of social and moral decline as well as violence in England during this late 1970s period. And *Images of England* suggests that '[w]orking-class youths decoded punk as a genre of music and fashion style to make sense of the difficulties and frustrations that they faced in school, home and workplace' (193). It is the focus on how working-class youth culture was lived and experienced in such social spaces that allows the book to provide a refreshing new approach to what are often simplified and mythologised moments in the history of popular music and post-war English society. As Gildart himself concludes: 'Popular music might not have changed the course of English history, but it reflected its tensions, explored its nuances, and soundtracked the everyday experiences of its working-class' (199).

Phil O'Brien
University of Manchester

Reviews

Robert Appelbaum, *Working the Aisles: A Life in Consumption.* Winchester: Zero Books, 2013. 244 pp. £12.99 pb. ISBN 978-1-78279-357-1.

In this autobiographical history of consumption from the 1960s onwards, Robert Appelbaum teeters on the balancing wire between depression and desire. 'The first thing you have to remember when you walk down the aisles of your local supermarket is that *they do not love you*' (1): that is Appelbaum's mantra to avoid the pitfall of vacuous elation in a consumer-driven society with the supermarket at its centre. It is also the thread on which this engagingly curious tale hangs, about how a New York-born, Chicago-bred, Jewish boy restlessly crisscrosses North America before making a leap for Europe, hopping from professional despair to prosperity. His heart and mind are as complex and multifaceted as the culture around him. A sometime limousine driver-gigolo and second-hand purveyor of semi-sadistic telesex, he is also an unhappily distant father, a love-thirsty boyfriend and, later, a devoted husband, tossed between being a victim of and a hapless semi-agent within neoliberal consumer society. The book successfully entwines personal and cultural history through a dope-fuelled cross-continental car journey, with its only interruption a night spent in jail, a booze-cruise with a twist and a fortnight drenched in a tent in the Loire Valley.

One of Appelbaum's absolute strengths is his flawless sensitivity to the significance to be found in meticulous detail. Casually situating his analysis in the context of Raymond Williams, Appelbaum lifts his gaze to reflect on his own arduously attained maturity in terms of 'the gap between my parents and me [being] representative of the new salience of "culture" as a domain of struggle' (77). To shape his analysis, he compares a good range of national contexts from the 'orderly, mannerly, respectful' aisles of a British Sainsbury's supermarket (8) to the suave casualness of a French youth coming out of his local *supermarché* carrying a baguette. The Swedish state-monopoly alcohol shop, Systembolaget, comes off by far the worst as 'in effect a communist supermarket' with its mission 'to serve the people [and] to give them what they think they want. But not too much: its mission is also to shame the people and suppress the crime of excess' (229). At the other extreme, Applebaum finds the alienating brutality of an American Walmart or Meijer's hypermarket 'where the ketchup bottles are next to the athlete's foot powder and the pantyhose, and the beef steaks are set across from a stack of polyester sweaters' (9).

Appelbaum's everyday paranoia about supermarkets' power to simulate love seems wholly justified. What connects these mercantile ventures globally is how they lure customers by appealing to their supposedly individual tastes, while at the same time enforcing predefined and artificial categories of personal identity. By providing its customers with tailor-made special offers and other forms of targeted advertising, supermarkets use complex algorithms to calculate who we are based only on what we buy, even when the choices we make as customers are at their most erratic.

This is a racy, provocative and largely male-centred story, at times a tad bitter, which embodies its publisher Zero Books' commitment to 'another kind of discourse – intellectual without being academic, popular without being populist' (245). The occasional editorial roughness gives the text authenticity and immediacy, and although there are a few too many typos, the pace of the text makes up for the odd copy-editing slip.

Appelbaum ties the two narrative strands of cultural analysis and cathartic memoir together with physical precision. At one point, he even ends up with a shopping bag round his head in a failed suicide attempt. Tacitly explored throughout is the impact on mental health in general of a neoliberal system living off consumerism, individualism, isolation and humiliation.

But there is hope. What Appelbaum really mourns in the supermarketisation of the West and beyond is heart and connectedness: interhuman contact as well as contact between us and the raw materials of existence. He finds such humanity and warmth in France: in the delicate sensitivity of a provincial restaurateur who has gently boiled and seasoned the *bouillabaisse* he serves to his customers, and who cares with his heart and soul about its delectation. As an upbeat mock-Joycean conclusion to this often rather gloomy cross section of contemporary everyday life comes a handful of semi-orgasmic yeses in the protagonist's sleep (244); though it remains unsaid whether these are spoken in good faith or in bad.

Kristin Ewins
Örebro University

Notes on Contributors

David Alderson is Visiting Professor at Shanghai Jiao Tong University and Senior Lecturer in English Literature at the University of Manchester. In recent years, he has written widely on the relations between neoliberalism, sexuality and gender for journals such as *Camera Obscura*, *new formations* and *Textual Practice*. His forthcoming book, provisionally entitled *Sexuality's Progress: Capitalism, Hegemony, Subculture*, will be published by Zed Books in 2016.

John Connor is an Assistant Professor of English at Colgate University in New York State and presently completing a monograph titled *Modernism, Socialist Culture and the Historical Novel*.

Tony Crowley is the Chair of English Language at the University of Leeds; he has published a number of books on language and politics, including *Scouse: A Social and Cultural History* (2012).

Kristin Ewins lectures at Örebro University, Sweden.

Lisa Henderson is Professor of Communication at the University of Massachusetts, Amherst. Her research interests include cultural production, sexual representation, feminist media studies, cultural studies of social class and critical collaboration between scholars and artists. Her essays appear in a number of collections and such journals as *Signs*, *Journal of Communication*, *GLQ*, *Feminist Media Studies* and *Screen*. Her recent book, *Love and Money: Queers, Class and Cultural Production* (2013), is available from NYU Press.

Angela Kershaw lectures in French at the University of Birmingham.

Claire MacLeod Peters is a Teaching Fellow in the department of Modern Languages at the University of Birmingham. She recently completed a PhD exploring the interconnected dynamics of collective memories of the Holocaust and the Algerian War through contemporary representations of Paris. She continues to be interested in the relationship between different histories of suffering and violence and the ethical dimension to this. Her approach is underpinned by poststructuralist positions and broader theoretical debates about genre and memory.

Stephen Maddison is Head of Humanities and Creative Industries, and Reader in Cultural Theory, in the School of Arts and Digital Industries at the University of East London. He is co-director of the Centre for Cultural Studies Research at UEL (http://culturalstudiesresearch.org/). His research addresses questions of sexuality and gender, cultural politics and popular culture. Stephen's work on pornography, embodiment and cultural politics has appeared in several major collections, including *Mainstreaming Sex* (2009), *Porn.com* (2010), *Hard to Swallow* (2011) and *Transgression 2.0* (2012), as well as in the journals *new formations* (2013, 2004) and *Topia: Canadian Journal of Cultural Studies* (2009). He is also the author of *Fags, Hags and Queer Sisters: Gender Dissent and Heterosocial Bonds in Gay Culture* (Macmillan and St Martin's Presss, 2000) and numerous other articles and chapters on sexuality, gender and popular culture.

Jen Morgan completed her PhD at the University of Salford in collaboration with the Working Class Movement Library, which was a project funded by the Arts and Humanities Research Council.

Phil O'Brien is a PhD candidate at the University of Manchester. His research looks at representations of the working class and neoliberalism in twenty-first century British fiction.

Patrick Parrinder is Emeritus Professor of English at the University of Reading. He has published many books including *Shadows of the Future* (1995) and *Nation and Novel* (2006), and is General Editor of the multi-volume *Oxford History of the Novel in English*.

Natasha Periyan recently completed her PhD in English at Royal Holloway, University of London, where she also teaches undergraduates. Her thesis on *The Decline of the Public School Hero in 1930s Modernism: Education, Social Class and Selfhood* considers Virginia Woolf, W. H. Auden, Stephen Spender, Henry Green and Graham Greene.

Peter Robinson is Professor of English and American Literature at the University of Reading. He is the author of many books of poetry and translation for which he has been awarded the Cheltenham Prize, the John Florio Prize and two Poetry Book Society Recommendations. Among his other publications are volumes of aphorisms, short stories and literary criticism. He is the poetry editor at Two Rivers Press.

Stephen Rogers was Research Assistant and contributor to the *Oxford Critical and Cultural History of Modernist Magazines*. He has a chapter forthcoming in *An Introduction to Ford Madox Ford* (Ashgate, 2015) and is currently working on Ford's journalism and critical writing.

Notes on Contributors

Derek Tatton was a 'mature' student from Coleg Harlech, taught by Raymond Williams at Cambridge. Williams later supervised his Open University PhD, completed whilst working full-time for the WEA as Warden/Principal at the Wedgwood Memorial College where, from 1988, annual weekends on Williams themes led to the start of the Raymond Williams Foundation (RWF; www.raymondwilliamsfoundation.org.uk) for which he is Administrator.

Elinor Taylor is a Postdoctoral Teaching and Research Fellow at the University of Westminster. She is currently completing a monograph entitled *The Popular Front Novel in Britain, 1933–1940*.

Christopher Vardy is completing a PhD at the University of Manchester focusing on twenty-first-century cultural representations of Thatcherism and the End of History. He has upcoming articles on cultural narratives about child sexual abuse and the recent past and on nostalgic materialism in contemporary novels about the 1980s, and is co-editing a collection on the author Rupert Thomson.

Ben Ware is a Visiting Research Fellow at the Institute of English Studies, School of Advanced Study, University of London. He is the author of *Dialectic of the Ladder: Wittgenstein, the 'Tractatus' and Modernism* (Bloomsbury, 2015); his second monograph, *Modernism and the Ethical Turn*, will appear in 2016 in Palgrave's *Language, Discourse, Society* series.

David Wilkinson is Research Assistant on the Leverhulme project 'Punk, Politics and British Youth Culture, 1976–1984'. His monograph *Post-Punk, Politics and Pleasure in Britain* is due for publication by Palgrave Macmillan in 2016.

Raymond Williams Foundation (RWF)

The last year has seen RWF consolidate partnerships and developments, not least with the Raymond Williams Society. The annual Society lecture given by Jim McGuigan at Wortley Hall in November 2013 during the RWF residential weekend was followed by SAGE's publication this year of *Raymond Williams: A Short Counter-Revolution* – Towards 2000 *Revisited*, edited with additional material by McGuigan. His added second chapter makes the case, as in his lecture, that Williams's book is a 'contemporary classic', which illustrates the present in remarkable, decisive ways. McGuigan acknowledges RWS and RWF for the 'excellent discussions ... which helped me sort out my ideas'.

The Society's annual 2015 lecture to be given by Susan Watkins at Ruskin College, Oxford, on 21 November is again being supported by RWF.

The memory of Sheila Jones, our long-time Chair, is being honoured by a Memorial Literature Course Bursary, and the partnerships which Sheila developed (more recently with Shallowford House; the linked literature weekends carrying on the Wedgewood Memorial College, Barlaston, tradition) will be strengthened by the bursary scheme. The Dylan Thomas (RMT Centre, Doncaster) and R.S. Thomas (Wortley Hall) weekends were successful extensions of that tradition too.

The Foundation continues to make small grants to individuals and groups working in spheres linked to our aims: for example, a Grey Power Public Transport Day in Stoke; an Independent Working Class Education network event; Percival Guildhouse, Rugby adult education courses struggling for viability; a Welsh research student's thesis on Raymond Williams and TV 'flow'; an Irish playwright's political drama translated into German; subsidising transport to the annual Philosophy in Pubs (PiPs) conference.

Our Sylvia Pankhurst Library project at Wortley Hall took a big step forward, gaining support from Sheffield University for a librarian intern to create an online catalogue of special collections within the expanding library.

A major development grew from the fully booked November 2014 residential at Wortley Hall on Participation Now with the RWF engaging Nick Mahony, who has worked with the Open University and openDemocracy on that theme, to help take participative democracy forward. This was linked to our ever-widening range of informal local groups and organisations like PiPs, DiPs, Sci-Bars and so on. Contact and networking led to discussions with the Democratic Society and Gladstone's Library to plan, with the RWF, a Democracy Festival in May 2016 at Hawarden – the North Wales border country – using the Gladstone residential library buildings and gardens for a three-day weekend festival embracing lectures; discussions and workshops

Raymond Williams Foundation (RWF)

involving community groups in radical political education; art and music, with cross-generational participation whenever possible. Taking Hay-on-Wye as an example, this could become an annual event.

Derek Tatton
www.raymondwilliamsfoundation.org.uk

Open-Access Policy – Green Route

The Higher Education Funding Council for England (HEFCE) is now committed to supporting open-access publishing, a policy that impacts directly on submissions for the next Research Excellence Framework (REF). (For the most recent HEFCE policy guide, please consult http://www.hefce.ac.uk/whatwedo/rsrch/rinfrastruct/oa/policy/.)

On acceptance for publication in *Key Words: A Journal of Cultural Materialism*, authors may deposit the accepted pre-publication version of their article on a personal or university department website, in a subject repository or in their university's research repository.

As soon as the article is published in *Key Words*, the published version may replace the pre-published version, but only after an embargo period of twenty-four months, during which period the published version may not be made publicly available. Authors may, however, use the published version of the article for teaching purposes or for sharing with research colleagues on an individual, non-commercial basis.

Style Notes for Contributors

Presentation of Copy

Key Words is an internationally refereed academic journal. In the first instance typescripts for prospective publication should be submitted as an email attachment to the Contributions Editor Catherine Clay, Nottingham Trent University, at catherine.clay@ntu.ac.uk. Articles should normally be no longer than 6,000 words; reviews should typically be between 1,500 and 2,000 words. Articles should be double spaced, with generous margins, and pages should be numbered consecutively. For matters of style not addressed below, please refer to *The Chicago Manual of Style*, 16th edn or http://www.chicagomanualofstyle.org/contents.html. Contributors who fail to observe these notes may be asked to revise their submission in accordance with them.

Provision of Text in Electronic Format

Key Words is prepared electronically. Consequently, contributors whose work is accepted for publication will be asked to supply a file copy of their work to the Contributions Editor. The preferred word processing format is Microsoft Word (any version).

References and Bibliographic Conventions

Notes should be kept to a minimum, with all discursive material appearing in the text. Citations in *Key Words* appear as endnotes at the conclusion of each contribution. Essays presented for prospective publication should adopt this style. Endnote markers should be given in Arabic numerals and positioned after, not before, punctuation marks, e.g. '.[1]' rather than '[1].'. With no bibliography, full details must be given in a note at the first mention of any work cited. Subsequent citations should be given in the text. If following straight on a reference to the same work, only the page number should be given within brackets. If cited again later in the article, the author's name should be given with the page number; and if several works by the same author are quoted within the essay, also a short form of the title or a cross-reference needs to be added. Headline-style capitalisation is used. In headline style, the first and last words of title and subtitle and all other major words are capitalised. Titles of books and journals should be formatted in italics (not underlined).

Style Notes for Contributors

Please cite books in the following manner:

> On first citation: Raymond Williams and Michael Orrom, *Preface to Film* (London: Film Drama, 1954).

> On subsequent citations: Williams and Orrom, *Preface to Film*, 12.

Please cite journal articles in the following manner:

> Patrick Parrinder, 'Politics, Letters and the National Curriculum', *Changing English* 2, no. 1 (1994): 29.

Chapters in books should be referenced in the following way:

> Andrew McRae, 'The Peripatetic Muse: Internal Travel and the Cultural Production of Space in Pre-Revolutionary England', in *The Country and the City Revisited: England and the Politics of Culture, 1550–1850*, ed. Gerald MacLean, Donna Landry and Joseph P. Ward (Cambridge: Cambridge University Press, 1999), 41–57.

For internet articles:

> Raymond Williams Society Executive, 'About the Raymond Williams Society', Raymond Williams Society, http://www.raymondwilliams.co.uk/ (accessed 26 March 2012).

Please refer to newspaper articles in the following way:

> John Mullan, 'Rebel in a Tweed Suit', *The Observer*, 28 May 2005, Features and Reviews section, 37.

A thesis should be referenced in the following manner:

> E. Allen, 'The Dislocated Mind: The Fictions of Raymond Williams' (PhD diss., Liverpool John Moores University, 2007), 22–9.

Conference papers should be cited in the following style:

> Dai Smith, 'Translating Raymond Williams' (paper presented at the Raymond Williams's Culture and Society@50 conference, Canolfan Dylan Thomas Centre, Swansea, 7 November 2008).

Quotations

For quotations use single quotation marks, and double quotation marks for quotations within quotations. Punctuation is used outside quotations. Ensure that all spellings, punctuation, abbreviations etc. within a quotation are rendered exactly as in the original, including errors, which should be signalled by the authorial interpolation '(*sic*)'.

Book Reviews

Book reviews should open with full bibliographic details of the text under review. These details should include (in the following order): in bold type, first name(s) and surname(s) of author(s), or first name(s) and surname(s) of editor(s) followed by a parenthetic '(ed.)' or '(eds)'; in italics, the full title of the volume followed by a period and a hard return; then, in regular type, the place of publication, publisher and date of publication; the page extent of the volume, including front papers numbered in Roman numerals; the price (where available) of the supplied copy and an indication of 'pb.' or 'hb.'; and the ISBN of the supplied copy.

For example:

> **Dai Smith,** *Raymond Williams: A Warrior's Tale.* Cardigan: Parthian Books, 2008. xviii + 514 pp. £24.99 hb. ISBN 978-1-905762-56-9.